# THE END OF STABILITY

# THE END OF STABILITY

## Debt, Denial, and the Coming Economic Reckoning

RANGA CHAND

The End of Stability
Debt, Denial, and the Coming Economic Reckoning



This is a work of non-fiction.
The views expressed are those of the author and are based on publicly available information and sources believed to be reliable at the time of writing.
Every reasonable effort has been made to ensure accuracy; however, no responsibility is accepted for errors or omissions.

ISBN 978-1-0668218-0-8
First Edition

Published by Blaines Press
10 9 8 7 6 5 4 3 2 1

# Contents

# INTRODUCTION

The modern economy resembles a vast dam, holding back immense and growing pressure. For years it has appeared solid and well managed, as cracks are repaired, leaks are contained, and confidence in its strength steadily grows. Yet the pressure behind it has continued to build, pushing the structure closer to its limits. What once appeared stable is now under increasing strain, and the question is no longer whether that stability can endure, but how and where it will begin to break.

That strain is no longer confined beneath the surface. Its effects are visible across advanced economies, even as the appearance of stability persists. Wages no longer keep pace with the rising cost of housing, healthcare, and education, and access to asset ownership has become increasingly uneven. Financial markets continue to signal confidence, yet for a growing share of households long-term security is eroding, as saving becomes harder, costs rise faster than incomes, and the expectation of steady progress is beginning to break down across society.

For much of the postwar era, households across the advanced world broadly assumed that economic life would improve steadily over time. Rising wages, expanding homeownership, and growing access to education reinforced the belief that each generation would enjoy greater security and opportunity than the one before. That expectation now feels less certain.

For nearly half a century, the advanced world has lived through an era of remarkable economic stability that began in the early 1980s. Inflation was low, recessions were manageable, and financial markets recovered quickly from shocks. Long-term prosperity appeared broadly secure. Over time, that stability came to feel normal. Policymakers, investors, and households grew accustomed to an environment where inflation remained subdued, financial disruptions were contained, and downturns appeared increasingly more manageable over time.

Falling interest rates played an important role in shaping that environment. Borrowing costs declined across much of the developed world, making mortgages, corporate financing, and government borrowing easier to sustain. Asset prices rose alongside expanding credit, reinforcing confidence that stability had become both more durable and easier to sustain.

Underlying this growing strain is an uncomfortable reality: stability has not been sustained by strength alone, but by rising debt and a persistent reluctance to confront its consequences over many years.

## *The End of Stability*

Yet the conditions that sustained that stability are now shifting, and the economic environment that shaped the modern world is beginning to change. The order that emerged after the early 1980s was not accidental, nor was it entirely self-sustaining. It was built on a particular set of economic forces that reinforced one another over time, shaping how households, governments, and investors understood risk, growth, and stability itself.

At the start of that era, policy interest rates in many major economies exceeded 10 percent. In the United States, the Federal Reserve's policy rate briefly rose above 19 percent in 1981, the highest level in modern monetary history.[1] By the 2010s, those rates had fallen close to zero, and in several developed economies, including parts of Europe and Japan, they even turned negative for a time. Central banks gained credibility as guardians of price stability, while financial markets deepened and expanded across borders and across asset classes.

The effects extended beyond financial markets. Households increasingly based long-term decisions on the assumption that borrowing costs would remain manageable, asset prices would continue to rise over time, and major downturns would eventually be stabilized through policy intervention. Stability became more than an economic condition. It became part of how societies understood the future.

The environment was not only an economic outcome. It also shaped institutions and expectations. Households came to expect modest but consistent growth, low and predictable inflation, and steadily rising asset values. Businesses planned on the assumption that capital would remain available and relatively inexpensive, while governments operated in an environment where deficits could be financed at manageable interest rates.

At the same time, the global trading system expanded, supply chains stretched across continents, and the rules of economic engagement appeared broadly settled. Between 1980 and 2008, global trade rose from roughly 36 percent of world GDP to more than 60 percent, reflecting the rapid integration of the global economy and financial markets.[2]

Compared with the turbulence of the 1970s, marked by oil shocks, runaway inflation, and policy uncertainty, the post-1980 era felt anchored. It also stood in contrast to the upheavals of the interwar period and the stagflationary spiral that followed the collapse of the Bretton Woods system, a period of high inflation combined with weak growth and rising unemployment, appearing orderly and controlled.

Even the crises that did occur, most notably the Global Financial Crisis and the pandemic shock decades later, were met with decisive policy responses that restored calm and reinforced the perception that instability could be managed. Each rescue strengthened confidence in the durability of the system.

## *Stability and Its Hidden Foundations*

Yet this long period of relative calm rested on foundations that were less secure than they appeared, because stability did not mean the absence of risk. Volatility was dampened even as leverage increased. Inflation was contained while asset prices continued to climb. Growth resumed after each downturn, yet it became increasingly dependent on expanding debt and financial support. The surface still appeared calm, even as pressures continued to accumulate beneath it.

In many economies, rising house prices increasingly replaced wage growth as the primary driver of household wealth. Financial markets recovered more rapidly after crises than household balance sheets, while low interest rates encouraged additional borrowing across governments, corporations, and consumers. Stability persisted, but it became progressively more dependent on conditions that required continual support.

The stability that emerged after the early 1980s was not entirely organic. It was increasingly sustained by expanding debt, reinforced by central bank intervention, and protected by a political unwillingness to confront the limits of debt-driven growth. What appears today as a series of isolated economic tensions is better understood as the gradual unravelling of that model. To understand why, it is necessary to examine how that stability was created in the first place.

## *The Paradox of Manufactured Stability*

The framework that advanced economies relied upon for decades was never entirely self-sustaining. Governments borrowed to cushion downturns and maintain spending, central banks intervened repeatedly to prevent financial disruptions from spreading, and financial markets grew accustomed to abundant liquidity and rapid policy support whenever instability threatened.

For a time, the model appeared to work quite well. Each crisis was contained, growth resumed, and confidence returned, but each intervention also left the system more dependent on the same tools that had restored stability. Across the advanced economies, total debt relative to economic output is now far higher than it was at the start of the century. Globally, combined government, corporate, and household debt has risen from roughly 200 percent of world GDP in the late 1990s to around 300 percent today, with profound consequences.[3]

What changed over time was not just the scale of intervention, but the degree of dependence upon it. Financial markets became increasingly sensitive to interest rates and central bank signalling, while governments, corporations, and households adapted to an environment shaped by cheap credit and recurring policy support. Stability no longer rested primarily on underlying resilience. It increasingly depended on the assumption that intervention would continue whenever serious stress emerged.

Debt accumulated across governments, corporations, and households, while the prices of investments such as housing, equities, and other financial assets became increasingly sensitive to interest rates and monetary policy. Economic growth came to rely more heavily on credit expansion than on productivity gains. The implications accumulated gradually.

Over time, this created a paradox in which the policies that preserved stability gradually made the system more fragile. Measures designed to stabilize the economy after crises increased dependence on continued intervention, while rising debt levels heightened the sensitivity of governments and financial markets to changes in interest rates.

Central banks found themselves responsible not only for controlling inflation but also for maintaining financial calm. In doing so, they injected enormous sums into the financial system and accumulated vast holdings of government bonds and mortgage securities. The U.S. Federal Reserve's holdings grew from about $900 billion before the 2008 financial crisis to nearly $9 trillion by 2022.[4] Stability, in effect, became something that had to be continually manufactured. The longer this continued, the less visible those foundations became.

For a time, the approach appeared remarkably successful. Financial crises became less frequent, recoveries seemed more predictable, and confidence in the resilience of the economic system continued to grow.

## *The System Reaches Its Limits*

This dynamic remained largely unnoticed while conditions appeared calm. Global financial markets continued to rise, unemployment remained relatively low, global trade expanded, and technological progress reinforced the sense that advanced economies had entered a new phase of durable prosperity. Yet the foundations of that stability were shifting.

Debt levels climbed to historic highs across much of the developed world, while ageing populations increased fiscal pressures and slowed economic growth. Across advanced economies, the share of the population aged 65 and older has risen from roughly 12 percent in 1980 to more than 19 percent today.[5] Asset prices became increasingly detached from underlying incomes and productivity, and political systems grew more polarized as economic gains became unevenly distributed. At the same time, central banks discovered that reversing extraordinary policies was far more difficult than implementing them.

These pressures did not appear all at once. They accumulated gradually, often beneath periods of apparent calm, yet taken together they point to a deeper shift. The system that once absorbed shocks with relative ease is becoming less flexible, more indebted, and increasingly sensitive to disruption.

This transition does not imply imminent collapse, nor does it suggest that advanced economies are entering permanent decline. These societies retain considerable productive capacity, technological capability, and institutional strength.

The challenge is that strengths developed over decades do not eliminate structural constraints. Productive economies can still struggle under heavy debt burdens, ageing populations, and increasingly polarized political environments. Advanced economies retain enormous resources and capabilities, but they now face limits that were less visible during the long expansion after the inflationary crises of the 1970s. Recognizing those limits is not a prediction of failure, but essential to understanding the pressures shaping the next economic era.

## *A New Era of Economic Uncertainty*

Understanding this transition requires looking beyond the indicators that typically define economic health. Market indices, growth figures, and unemployment rates provide useful information, but they often fail to capture the deeper structural forces shaping economic stability. The questions that matter most concern debt, incentives, and the limits of policy.

Why did advanced economies become so dependent on borrowing to sustain growth? Why did financial markets come to rely so heavily on central bank intervention? Why have political systems struggled to acknowledge the limits of the existing model? The answers lie in the structure of the modern economy itself. Over time, growth became increasingly dependent on rising debt, expanding financial markets, and continued policy intervention. These mechanisms helped sustain stability for a generation, but they also left the system more vulnerable as conditions began to change.

The shift toward instability does not begin with a dramatic collapse. It emerges more quietly, in the widening gap between what economic indicators suggest and what people experience in their daily lives. Markets may continue to rise, unemployment may remain low, and official statistics may still describe expansion, yet beneath these signals many households sense that something has changed. Costs rise faster than incomes, savings feel less secure, and the expectation that each generation will be more prosperous than the last becomes less certain. What matters is the pattern that emerges when they are viewed together.

The challenge is not that these pressures are immediately visible in any single indicator. They emerge gradually across households, businesses, markets, and public finances. Considered individually, each change may appear manageable. Taken together, they point to a system that is less resilient than it once seemed. Recognizing that shift is essential to understanding what comes next.

That growing disconnect is where this story begins. It is not the result of a single crisis or policy mistake, but of a series of changes that accumulated gradually across the economy. Understanding how those changes emerged is essential to understanding the pressures now confronting advanced economies.

## *Mapping the Breakdown*

The chapters that follow examine these dynamics from different perspectives and explore how their combined effects gradually reshape economic stability.

The first section explores the widening gap between the signals of prosperity often presented in financial markets and official statistics and the economic realities experienced by households. The next section examines the mechanisms that sustained stability in recent decades, including easy money, expanding credit, and the financialisation of large parts of the economy. A third section considers the human consequences of this system, including rising inequality, the erosion of traditional forms of economic security, and the growing difficulty of long-term planning.

The book then turns to the forces now intensifying these pressures, including demographic ageing, technological disruption, political fragmentation, and energy constraints. These forces do not operate independently. They increasingly reinforce one another, narrowing the margin for economic and political adjustment. Their combined effect is steadily reducing the range of outcomes available to policymakers while increasing the consequences of delay.

## *Approaching the Turning Point*

These forces are pushing the system toward a turning point. Systems that depend on continually expanding debt and persistent policy intervention eventually encounter limits, and when those limits are reached, stability can give way to fragility with surprising speed. The adjustment is often gradual at first, but rarely remains so for long. Such transitions seldom unfold in a smooth or orderly manner.

The final chapters explore how such transitions unfold. History shows that prolonged periods of economic imbalance rarely resolve quietly. They typically end through some combination of inflation, financial repression, restructuring, or political realignment. These adjustments do not occur in the background. They reshape the economic landscape in ways that are felt directly by households and businesses through higher living costs, weaker growth, financial instability, and rising political tensions.

The precise sequence cannot be predicted with certainty, and different societies will experience these pressures in different ways. Some may adapt gradually through slower growth and periodic instability, while others may encounter sharper financial or political dislocation. Yet across much of the advanced world, the underlying direction of pressure is becoming increasingly difficult to ignore.

The era of stability that defined the late twentieth and early twenty-first centuries was shaped by a particular set of economic conditions, including declining inflation, falling interest rates, expanding globalization, and favourable demographics. Those conditions are now changing. Inflationary pressures are re-emerging, interest rates are no longer on a long downward path, globalization is fragmenting under geopolitical strain, and ageing populations are slowing the growth of the labour force across much of the advanced world. As a result, these developments are reshaping the policy environment.

The advanced world is therefore entering a more demanding phase of economic history, one in which stability can no longer be assumed to operate automatically or indefinitely. Economic systems remain capable of growth and adaptation, but the conditions that once made adjustment relatively manageable are becoming less dependable.

Periods of economic stability often appear permanent while they last, yet history shows that stability built on weak foundations rarely endures indefinitely. When the underlying conditions begin to change, the adjustment can reshape economies, institutions, and societies in ways that are difficult to anticipate. That process has already begun, gradually altering the economic environment that sustained decades of stability.

The long era of stability that shaped the modern advanced economy was real, but it was also contingent. It depended on conditions that gradually reinforced one another over time, and as those conditions weaken, the structure of economic life begins to change with them.

## *The World After Stability*

The decades ahead will not resemble the decades that came before. The stability that defined the advanced world since the 1980s was unusual in both its duration and its underlying conditions. It emerged from a convergence of economic, demographic, geopolitical, and financial forces that reinforced one another over time. As those conditions begin to change, the environment that shaped modern expectations about growth, inflation, markets, and security is also beginning to change.

This shift reflects a reality that earlier generations understood well, particularly those shaped by the disruptions of the 1930s and the inflationary upheavals of the 1970s. Economic systems are never permanently settled. They evolve, they encounter limits, and they periodically pass through periods in which long-standing assumptions no longer hold in the same way they once did. There is growing evidence that another such transition is now well underway.

The advanced world is now entering one of those periods. Debt levels are historically high, demographic trends are weakening growth, globalization is fragmenting, and geopolitical tensions are reshaping economic relationships. The forces that supported decades of relative stability are becoming less dependable, while the policy tools used to manage instability are producing diminishing effects and increasingly difficult trade-offs.

This does not mean that collapse is inevitable or that prosperity disappears entirely. Today, advanced economies remain wealthy, technologically capable, and institutionally resilient. However, the environment in which they operate is becoming more demanding. Stability will likely prove harder to sustain, policy choices more contested, and economic outcomes more uneven than during much of the previous era.

Periods of relative calm have appeared before in modern economic history, but none have lasted indefinitely. Stability is never static. The conditions that sustain it eventually weaken, evolve, or reverse, forcing societies to adapt.

The chapters that follow examine how that earlier period emerged, how debt and intervention became increasingly central to maintaining stability, and why many of the assumptions that governed economic life for decades are beginning to weaken. What is unfolding is not simply a cyclical slowdown or another ordinary downturn. It is a broader transition in the structure of advanced economies themselves, one whose consequences are likely to shape economic and political life for years to come.

# PART I

# THE DISCONNECT

# 1

# THE ILLUSION OF PROSPERITY

Since the early 1980s, advanced economies have grown steadily accustomed to a long period of relative stability that came to be seen as the normal condition of modern economic life. Across the advanced world, the headline indicators appear reassuring. Economic output continues to expand, unemployment in many major economies sits near multi-decade lows, and stock markets in most developed countries have risen sharply over the past two decades. Corporate profits have rebounded from successive shocks, including the global financial crisis, the pandemic, the energy surge, and the recent inflation spike. Judged by the conventional indicators used to assess economic health, the system appears remarkably resilient.

Yet beneath these reassuring indicators a different picture begins to emerge. Household experience told a different story.

In many advanced economies median wages have risen far more slowly than the cost of housing, healthcare, and education. In major cities such as London, Toronto, Sydney, and San Francisco, house prices have increased several times faster than household incomes over the past two decades.[1] In the United States, the ratio of median house prices to median income, which hovered near three to one in the early 1980s, has moved closer to six to one in recent years.[2] Asset markets have surged, yet ownership of those assets has become increasingly concentrated.[3] The benefits of rising asset values have therefore been distributed far less evenly than headline market gains suggest. This divergence extends well beyond financial markets.

The result is a widening gap between official indicators and lived experience. The economy expands and markets rise, yet a growing share of households feel less secure about their financial future. Long-term planning that once seemed routine now feels uncertain, and what appears on paper as stability increasingly masks a deeper sense of vulnerability in everyday economic life.

For many households the economy no longer feels as stable as the headlines suggest. The statistics continue to signal resilience, yet beneath them the experience of everyday economic life has become increasingly strained and uncertain.

This divergence invites two related questions: how can economies appear so strong while so many households feel insecure, and why do financial markets signal confidence even as the foundations of long-term stability grow more fragile? To understand this paradox, it is necessary to look more closely at how modern prosperity is measured. The answer lies partly in what economic statistics capture and what they leave unseen.

## *When Prosperity Stops Feeling Prosperous*

At the centre of this disconnect lies a narrowing definition of economic success. Modern prosperity is measured through familiar indicators such as gross domestic product, employment rates, inflation targets, and financial market performance. These metrics capture activity and scale. They measure motion within the system. They do not necessarily measure durability.

An economy can grow while what the typical household income can actually buy stagnates. Employment can remain high even as job security weakens and income volatility increases. Asset prices can climb while access to ownership narrows. None of these outcomes contradict the data because they remain hidden inside national averages. Headline statistics can obscure important shifts. The underlying picture is often considerably more complex than it first appears to be.

Over the past several decades many advanced economies have experienced steady GDP growth even as improvements in productivity slowed and income distribution became more uneven. Consumption has remained resilient not solely because incomes rose, but because credit expanded, asset values increased, and interest rates fell.

As borrowing became more deeply embedded within the system, debt increasingly filled the gap between what economies produced and what many households could comfortably afford. Debt became less a temporary financial tool and more a permanent support beneath consumption and growth. Household balance sheets stretched to maintain living standards. Governments borrowed to sustain spending. Corporations borrowed to support valuations and financial expansion.

The scale of this transformation is visible in the growth of debt. Across the major advanced economies, total debt, including government, household, and corporate borrowing, now exceeds 330 percent of GDP, reflecting a debt build-up that began in the early 1980s.[4] Growth therefore continued, but the foundation supporting that growth gradually changed.

Prosperity as lived rather than reported rests on different foundations. It depends on the ability to absorb shocks without relying on additional borrowing. It requires savings that retain value, housing that remains attainable, and wages that rise broadly alongside productivity. When those foundations weaken, growth loses its reassuring quality. The statistics remain positive, yet the lived experience of prosperity begins to erode.

What emerges is not simply a cyclical downturn in confidence. It reflects a deeper change in how stability is maintained. The appearance of prosperity increasingly depends on forces less visible in traditional economic measures. Nowhere is that divergence more visible than in financial markets. Their performance has shaped perceptions of economic success, often more than underlying fundamentals.

## *When Markets Rise but Security Falls*

Financial markets play a central role in sustaining the appearance of strength. Rising asset prices are routinely interpreted as evidence that economic conditions are healthy, and market calm is often treated as stability itself. Yet markets primarily reflect financial conditions rather than broader economic wellbeing.

Since the early 1980s, asset prices in advanced economies have become increasingly sensitive to interest rates, the availability of easy money, and signals from central banks.[5] When rates fall and liquidity expands, asset prices tend to rise. When central banks intervene, volatility recedes. Markets respond quickly to these inputs. Households do not.

The gap is amplified by who actually owns financial assets. In most advanced economies financial wealth is heavily concentrated among higher-income households. Stock market gains therefore accrue disproportionately to those already holding financial assets. For households with limited exposure to financial markets, rising valuations do not translate into greater security. They often coincide with rising living costs and higher barriers to entry.

Housing makes the distortion particularly visible. In many major cities, price-to-income ratios now stand two or three times higher than their historical norms.[6] For existing homeowners rising prices represent accumulated wealth, but for younger households and renters they increasingly represent exclusion from one of the primary channels of wealth formation.

For many younger households, the path toward financial security that once defined middle-class stability has become progressively harder to reach. Rising asset prices increasingly separate those who already own wealth from those still trying to build it. For some households this represents wealth; for others, exclusion from ownership. As a result, the same economic outcome can produce very different experiences across society.

From one vantage point rising asset prices symbolize prosperity; from another they reveal growing fragility. Markets increasingly function as instruments of confidence management, projecting calm even as underlying pressures accumulate.

## *Why the System Keeps the Illusion Alive*

The persistence of this divergence raises a natural question: if the imbalance is visible, why does it continue?

Part of the answer lies in incentives. Governments, central banks, and financial markets all benefit from the appearance of stability. Rising asset values support consumption and tax revenues. Calm financial markets reinforce confidence. Intervention often postpones immediate pain.

As a result the necessary adjustments are repeatedly delayed. Borrowing is easier than reform. Keeping money easy and interest rates low is less disruptive than allowing markets to correct. Policies designed as temporary responses to crisis gradually become permanent features of the system.

This persistence is not necessarily the result of deliberate deception. It emerges because the costs of adjustment are immediate and visible, while the costs of postponement are gradual and often hidden. Allowing asset prices to fall, forcing debt restructuring, or reducing public spending can produce economic pain that is felt quickly by voters, businesses, and financial markets. By contrast, maintaining support preserves stability in the short term, even if it increases longer-term vulnerabilities. The incentives therefore favour delay, not because policymakers fail to recognize the risks, but because the alternative often appears more disruptive in the present.

Over time this pattern becomes self-reinforcing. Stability comes to depend on continued support, and each round of support deepens the system's dependence on it. As dependency grows, the room for manoeuvre steadily narrows. The system therefore rarely appears unstable until the moment instability arrives. Apparent stability often masks growing vulnerability beneath the surface. Their origins lie in changes that unfolded gradually over many years.

These patterns did not emerge suddenly. They evolved through decades of crisis management and policy intervention, each period reinforcing the expectation that instability could always be contained. The origins of this dynamic lie in how governments and central banks responded to earlier crises.

## *How Crisis Management Changed the Role of Money*

The modern economic structure was built gradually over decades. It was built through repeated government and central bank actions designed to prevent collapse.

During the Great Depression governments expanded spending and restructured financial systems to halt deflation. After the Second World War many advanced economies carried public debt burdens exceeding 100 percent of national output. Authorities maintained interest rates below inflation for extended periods, restricted capital flows, and steered domestic savings toward government borrowing. Stability was restored through deliberate constraint.

For households and businesses, these policies gradually changed expectations about borrowing, saving, and the role of the state in supporting economic stability. Over time, periods of intervention that were once considered exceptional became increasingly familiar.

The pattern returned on a much larger scale after the financial crisis of 2008. Policy interest rates in major economies fell to near zero and remained there for years. Central bank balance sheets expanded severalfold as authorities purchased government bonds and other assets. When the pandemic struck in 2020, even larger fiscal and monetary measures followed.

These actions were designed to prevent collapse, and in that narrow objective they succeeded. Financial systems stabilized, deflation was avoided, and growth resumed. Yet intervention left a residue. Property and share prices rose faster than wages, and debt accumulated beneath the surface. With each cycle the system became more dependent on continued support.

Money itself began to play a different role in the economy. Instead of disciplining excess, it increasingly buffered it, softening the signals that might once have forced adjustment. Each intervention bought time and reduced the immediate cost of imbalance, yet with every episode the system grew more dependent on continued support. Adjustment was postponed, and that dependence steadily deepened.

What emerged was a form of stability that increasingly depended not on self-sustaining economic strength, but on the continued ability of policymakers to contain stress whenever pressures intensified. Over time, this creates the conditions for a more fragile form of stability, one that can persist for years before breaking under accumulated strain.

## *The Calm That Often Comes Before the Shock*

History shows that prolonged calm often precedes rupture. The United States during the late 1920s provides one example. Credit expanded rapidly. Equity markets surged. Optimism hardened into belief in a permanently higher standard of living. Beneath the surface, leverage and borrowing increased, and the gains were unevenly distributed. When confidence finally broke, markets collapsed, banks failed in large numbers, and economic output contracted sharply.

Periods before major crises often share similar characteristics. Strong markets encourage optimism. Easy credit expands balance sheets. Policymakers attempt to smooth volatility. Stability appears secure until it is not.

The years preceding the global financial crisis followed a similar pattern. Credit expanded rapidly across advanced economies. Housing markets surged. New financial products appeared to spread risk across the system. Stability seemed embedded within the system. The appearance of resilience became widely accepted.

When the correction arrived in 2008 it exposed how much of that stability had depended on rising leverage and sustained confidence. The present moment differs not because the pattern is new, but because the margin for error is smaller.

Debt levels across advanced economies are higher than in previous cycles, while populations are ageing rather than expanding. Interest rates cannot rise indefinitely without putting government finances under strain, political cohesion has weakened in many countries, and central banks now face trade-offs between inflation control and financial stability that did not bind them as tightly in earlier decades.

The institutions and policy tools that once absorbed shocks still exist, but many now operate under tighter constraints and heavier burdens than in earlier periods. The shock absorbers that once stabilized the system have gradually weakened.

## *When Stability Has to Be Engineered*

Stability in the advanced world was once supported by rising productivity, favourable demographics, room in government budgets, and trusted institutions. Today it is maintained increasingly through management.

Systems built on continuous intervention can endure for long periods, but they accumulate pressure. As obligations grow and flexibility narrows, the margin for error shrinks. Each round of intervention may restore calm, yet it also deepens the system's dependence on continued support.

What appears today as prosperity is therefore something more complicated. The advanced economies still function, but the foundations that once sustained their stability have shifted. Growth continues and markets remain elevated, yet the structure beneath them has become increasingly reliant on debt and policy intervention to sustain the appearance of equilibrium.

Behind the appearance of prosperity lies a system sustained by rising debt, defended through repeated intervention, and protected by a reluctance to confront its limits. That stability has not been restored so much as maintained, with each cycle reinforcing the conditions that make the system more dependent on continued support. The vulnerabilities have merely been deferred. Delay reshapes behaviour as well as outcomes.

Over time, this changes not only the structure of the economy, but also the expectations built around it. Stability increasingly comes to depend on the assumption that future intervention will remain both possible and effective.

The illusion of prosperity did not emerge overnight. It developed gradually over several decades as governments, central banks, and financial markets adapted to successive crises, each time choosing stabilization over adjustment.

Understanding how this system evolved is essential to explaining why the gap between economic appearance and economic reality has continued to widen across much of the advanced world. Growth has persisted, markets have remained elevated, and instability has repeatedly been contained, yet beneath that surface the structure of the system has changed in important ways.

# 2

# THE MARKET IS NOT THE ECONOMY

Few beliefs are more deeply embedded in modern economic life than the idea that a rising stock market signals a healthy economy. When major indices climb, reassurance quickly follows. Record highs are treated as confirmation that conditions are sound. Political leaders cite market performance as evidence of successful policy, while commentators interpret volatility as danger and calm as proof of stability. Over time, equity markets came to serve as the public barometer of economic health.

Yet the numbers tell a more complicated story. Beneath the headline gains in equity markets, the underlying pace of income growth and productivity has been far more modest.

Since the 2009 trough following the global financial crisis, the S&P 500 increased by more than 600 percent at its 2021 peak, far outpacing underlying income growth.[1] Over roughly the same period, real median household income in the United States rose by less than 20 percent in cumulative terms.[2] Across advanced economies, productivity growth averaged roughly half the pace recorded in the late twentieth century.[3] Asset prices accelerated, but productive momentum did not keep pace.

The disconnect was no longer confined to financial statistics. Increasingly, it became visible in everyday economic life too. Markets reached repeated highs even as housing affordability deteriorated in major metropolitan areas, where price-to-income ratios climbed beyond levels seen prior to 2008. Equity indices surged during periods when real wage growth struggled to keep up with inflation, and corporate valuations expanded even as long-term investment growth remained modest.

This divergence is no longer cyclical. It has persisted across successive expansions after the dot-com bust, after the financial crisis, and again following the extraordinary stimulus of the pandemic era. The issue is not simply that markets and lived experience differ. The deeper concern is that rising asset prices increasingly came to stand in for economic repair. Gains in valuation were treated as evidence that the system was strengthening even as its foundations were weakening. Stability gradually came to be judged by movements on a screen rather than by improvements in underlying economic conditions.

## *What the Market Actually Measures*

The stock market measures the value of publicly traded companies, not the condition of the economy as a whole. It does not capture housing affordability, healthcare costs, employment stability, or whether wages keep pace with living expenses. Nor does it reveal if households can absorb financial shocks without borrowing. The same limitation applies to businesses.

Publicly listed companies represent only a fraction of total firms and employment in most advanced economies, yet they dominate financial indices and economic commentary. In the United States, small businesses account for roughly half of private-sector employment, but their conditions remain largely invisible in equity benchmarks.[4] Large multinational corporations, diversified across regions and revenue streams, exert disproportionate influence on overall market index performance. Their performance has come to drive headline market returns.

As a result, rising valuations often reflect the profitability of globally integrated corporations more than the financial condition of domestic households. Large firms can continue earning profits through international operations even while local economic conditions weaken for extended periods.

Market prices respond primarily to expected earnings, interest rates, and liquidity. When borrowing costs fall or central banks signal support, valuations adjust quickly, allowing markets to rise even when productivity growth slows and household finances tighten. This is not a malfunction of markets. It reflects how they are structured and what they are designed to measure. The distortion emerges only when this limited signal is treated as a comprehensive assessment of economic health.

## *Who Benefits When Markets Rise*

Ownership concentration magnifies the divide between market performance and the broader economy. In many advanced economies, equity ownership is heavily concentrated among higher-income households, with the wealthiest segments holding the vast majority of directly owned stocks while a large share of households have little or no exposure to equity markets. As a result, gains from rising stock prices accrue disproportionately to those already holding substantial financial assets.

For many others, rising valuations coincide with higher housing prices, elevated financial barriers, and widening wealth gaps. Asset inflation strengthens balance sheets at the top of the distribution while raising entry costs and financial barriers for others. Its effects spread throughout the wider economy.

This dynamic reshapes the structure of demand within the economy. Consumption becomes increasingly tied to asset appreciation and borrowing rather than broad-based income growth. Households borrow against rising home values, rely more heavily on investment gains for retirement security, and become increasingly sensitive to fluctuations in asset prices. When wealth effects dominate wage growth, stability becomes more dependent on continued asset inflation .and rising valuations. What supports stability can also undermine it.

Elevated valuations also create vulnerability. In an environment where wealth is concentrated and leverage widespread, even modest market declines can transmit stress rapidly through confidence, spending, and fiscal conditions. Market strength, presented as resilience, can embed fragility within the system.

## *The Policy Feedback Loop*

This dynamic was reinforced by policy decisions following the global financial crisis. In response to the 2008 collapse, central banks across advanced economies reduced interest rates to near zero and maintained them there for more than a decade, while balance sheets expanded dramatically as part of large-scale asset purchase programs. The Federal Reserve's balance sheet grew from under 1 trillion dollars in 2007 to nearly 9 trillion dollars by 2022, with similar expansions undertaken by the European Central Bank and the Bank of Japan.[5]

These measures achieved their immediate objective of stabilizing financial systems, but they also altered expectations in lasting ways. Markets internalized the assumption that severe declines would likely be met with intervention. Sharp sell-offs increasingly triggered positioning based on anticipated policy responses, and risk came to be evaluated not only on underlying fundamentals but also on the perceived willingness of authorities to provide support.

A reinforcing loop gradually emerged. Elevated asset prices reduced pressure for structural reform, while policymakers became increasingly attentive to market reactions. Sustained declines threatened fiscal positions, financial stability, and political confidence. Over time, financial market stability became an implicit objective of economic management.

What began as emergency stabilization gradually became embedded in the normal functioning of the system. Once that dependence took hold, exit became hazardous. When policy tightening began in 2022, markets reacted sharply. The response revealed how deeply the system had adapted to years of cheap credit and abundant liquidity. Rather than reducing fragility, the process delayed adjustment while increasing the scale of the eventual correction as debt accumulated.

## *Financial Engineering Over Productive Investment*

Corporate incentives adapted to this environment of low interest rates and abundant liquidity. With borrowing costs suppressed and shareholder returns prioritized, firms increased distributions to investors, and in the United States cumulative share buybacks by major corporations exceeded 5 trillion dollars in the decade following the financial crisis.[6] In several years, corporate buybacks rivalled or even surpassed growth in net capital expenditure.

Buybacks raise earnings per share mechanically by reducing the number of shares outstanding. In the short term, they can support valuations even when underlying revenue growth remains moderate. From the perspective of individual firms, this behaviour is rational. From a systemic perspective, however, it shifts emphasis away from expanding productive capacity. When cheap credit finances financial optimization rather than productive investment, future growth capacity weakens. Productivity improvements slow, capital deepening lags, and the expansion of the productive base slows even as market value rises. The incentives behind this shift are straightforward.

Markets reward near-term financial efficiency. The consequences of underinvestment, however, emerge only over longer horizons that lie beyond quarterly reporting cycles. A factory not built, a research programme delayed, or a workforce not expanded rarely affects earnings immediately. The costs appear gradually through weaker productivity growth, slower innovation, and reduced capacity to generate future output.

In the short run, financial markets may reward decisions that enhance shareholder returns. Long-term sustainable economic growth depends on sustained investment in productive assets, skills, technology, and infrastructure. When capital increasingly circulates within financial markets rather than expanding productive capacity, the distinction between rising market value and rising economic strength becomes increasingly important.

## *Markets Price the Future*

Markets price expectations, while households experience current conditions. Stock prices incorporate projections years ahead, and optimism about innovation or efficiency can sustain high valuations long before those gains materialize, while inflation reduces purchasing power immediately and housing costs and employment risk remain immediate pressures for households.

This divergence in time horizons allows markets to remain elevated even as households experience increasing strain. What appears as stability can therefore prolong the build-up of imbalances that make eventual correction more disruptive. That disconnect becomes more dangerous as leverage rises throughout the broader economic system.

Markets can continue to function normally for extended periods even when underlying pressures are building. Investors focus on expected future earnings, while households must contend with current living costs, mortgage payments, and wage growth that may not keep pace with inflation. As a result, rising market values can create an impression of resilience even when financial conditions are becoming more difficult for large parts of the population. The longer these experiences diverge, the easier it becomes to mistake elevated asset prices for broad economic strength. and resilience.

Across sectors, leverage has steadily increased. Global debt reached approximately 350 percent of world GDP in the years following the pandemic response, significantly higher than levels preceding the 2008 crisis.[7] Higher debt increases sensitivity to interest rates and reduces the margin for policy error. The longer repricing is postponed, the more disruptive it ultimately becomes. The adjustment is delayed, but the underlying pressures continue to accumulate.

## *When Price Replaces Repair*

The central risk is a shift: when rising asset prices are accepted as evidence of economic health, the incentive to address underlying economic problems declines. Debt rises faster than the economy's ability to produce, fiscal deficits persist, and raising interest rates becomes politically and financially difficult.

Rising markets reassure policymakers but also hold them back. Policymakers hesitate to risk declines, while investors expect support to continue. The system grows increasingly dependent on low rates and easy credit that inflate asset prices.

Over time, rising asset prices begin to replace real economic progress. Governments delay difficult reforms, businesses focus more on financial returns than real investment, and households come to rely on asset gains to support consumption. Growth appears stable, but it is increasingly driven by price movements rather than real economic strength.

The attraction of rising stock markets and property values is that they appear to solve multiple problems at once. Households feel wealthier, pension funds appear stronger, government revenues improve, and large debt burdens seem easier to manage. Yet these gains are largely financial rather than productive. They create the appearance of greater prosperity without necessarily increasing the economy's ability to produce more goods, services, or future income. As a result, rising market values can gradually become a substitute for reforms that would otherwise be necessary.

This changes how the system behaves. Policymakers respond more quickly to market declines than to long-term problems, and investors take greater risks because they expect support to continue. The longer this dynamic persists, the more difficult it becomes for the system to function without continuously rising asset values and supportive financial conditions. No source of support can expand indefinitely without consequences or growing dependence on its continuation.

## *When the Market Stops Absorbing Shocks*

Markets allocate capital and transmit information. They are indispensable institutions within modern economies. But they are not the economy itself, and they cannot shield a system from structural weakness. Their signals become misleading when rising valuations obscure underlying pressures.

An economy can sustain rising asset prices even as fiscal imbalances widen, productivity slows, and political divisions deepen. Under such conditions, stability is not self-sustaining. It is maintained through policy support and expanding balance sheets. That support cannot expand indefinitely.

When that maintenance can no longer continue, the reversal accelerates. If asset prices have been used as proof of economic strength, their decline exposes vulnerability quickly. Balance sheets weaken, pension funds come under strain, fiscal revenues fall, and political confidence erodes.

Stability in such a system rarely ends through a single external shock alone. It ends when the mechanisms relied upon to offset weakening fundamentals can no longer perform that function. Recognizing that distinction is essential.

The stock market is not the economy. Yet in an era when rising markets increasingly became the primary symbol of economic strength, the distinction gradually became blurred. Financial gains often came to represent national success, even as productivity slowed, living costs rose, and economic insecurity deepened across large parts of society.

Markets still matter. They shape investment, retirement savings, confidence, and the cost of capital across the global economy. But rising equity indices and record asset valuations can coexist with stagnant wages, declining affordability, rising living costs, and growing insecurity across large parts of society.

For decades, rising markets reinforced the belief that economic progress remained broadly intact. Asset prices became shorthand for national strength, political success, and economic resilience. Yet the relationship between financial markets and everyday economic reality has gradually weakened.

Markets can rise even while societies weaken. Financial success and economic health are no longer moving together in the way they once appeared to. The danger is not simply that markets may eventually decline. It is that policymakers, institutions, and the public may increasingly mistake rising asset prices for genuine economic strength, even as deeper structural weaknesses continue to build beneath the surface.

The distinction matters because asset prices can postpone recognition of underlying problems, but they cannot resolve them. Debt, weak productivity growth, declining affordability, and widening financial imbalances remain subject to economic realities that markets alone cannot change. When price becomes the primary measure of success, the need for adjustment often becomes harder to see until it can no longer be avoided

# 3

## STABILITY THAT CANNOT HOLD

At first glance, the modern economic landscape appears calm. Markets rise and fall, but system-wide breakdowns are rare. Banks appear well capitalized, credit continues to flow, and when recessions occur governments and central banks respond quickly with support. By the conventional measures used to judge economic health, the system appears stable. Yet this calm raises a deeper question: what if the appearance of stability is itself a sign that the system has become more fragile than it seems? The evidence appears reassuring at first.

This calm is not accidental. Since the global financial crisis, market volatility has generally remained contained outside brief shock episodes. Banks hold more capital than they did before 2008, and policymakers have become far quicker to intervene when financial stress begins to emerge. The goal is no longer simply to manage recessions after they occur, but increasingly to prevent instability from spreading before it becomes visible.

At the same time, central banks created large amounts of new money to purchase government bonds and other financial assets, dramatically increasing their financial holdings across many advanced economies. In the United States, for example, the Federal Reserve's holdings grew from under $1 trillion before the 2008 crisis to nearly $9 trillion by 2022, while the European Central Bank and the Bank of Japan followed similar paths relative to the size of their economies.[1] By the standards that now dominate public discussion, these interventions appeared successful because financial panic was contained and markets stabilized quickly. The measures that restored stability also altered the foundations on which it depended.

## *Beneath the Surface*

Yet this calm does not reassure. In major cities, home prices relative to income exceed levels seen before 2008, and since the pandemic housing costs have risen faster than wages in several large economies even where unemployment remains low. Across the advanced world, house price-to-income ratios are now typically 30 to 50 percent above their long-term averages, according to data from the OECD.[2]

Government debt in many advanced countries now stands near levels last seen during wartime, while households and companies continue to carry substantial debt after years of exceptionally cheap borrowing. Across advanced economies, public debt now averages roughly 110 percent of GDP, according to International Monetary Fund estimates.[3]

Stability at the system level now coexists with strain at the household level. A modest rise in mortgage rates can double payments for new buyers, and a small increase in the interest governments must pay on their debt can add tens of billions to annual budgets within a few years.

What appears calm on the surface is increasingly sensitive beneath it. Fragility has not disappeared but has instead been redistributed across household balance sheets, public finances, and financial structures that depend heavily on low borrowing costs and stable asset prices.

At the same time, governments have accumulated political commitments that are increasingly difficult to reverse. Delaying adjustment narrows the range of possible outcomes until change can no longer occur gradually. What once appeared manageable begins to require ever larger intervention simply to preserve stability that already exists. This gradual shift altered more than policy. It changed how stability itself was understood. As measures once viewed as exceptional became increasingly normal and widely accepted, the distinction between resilience and intervention began to blur.

## *When Stability Changed Meaning*

Stability once meant durability: the ability of an economic system to absorb shocks without extraordinary support. Today stability increasingly means something narrower, that financial markets continue to function without disruption. If banks remain liquid, credit continues to flow, and asset prices avoid sharp declines, conditions are described as stable.

This shift emerged from trauma. The failures of the 1930s and the financial panic of 2008 demonstrated how financial breakdown can destroy jobs, incomes, and public finances, making the prevention of collapse the overriding objective of economic policy.

Over time, emergency prevention evolved into standard practice. Market corrections that would once have been tolerated began to trigger intervention, and the focus gradually shifted from strengthening the system to preventing visible disruption.

Systems designed to prevent disruption often lose their capacity to adapt. When declines in asset prices are repeatedly softened and heavily indebted firms are repeatedly supported, incentives to reduce leverage or allow inefficient businesses to fail weaken. Risk does not disappear; it accumulates quietly. The longer this process continues, the more stability becomes tied to confidence in continued intervention rather than confidence in the underlying strength of the system itself.

Politics reinforced this change. Rising stock and housing prices became tied to household wealth, pension stability, and public revenues, while governments grew accustomed to low borrowing costs. Under such conditions, returning to more normal interest rates becomes politically risky because allowing markets to reset would impose immediate costs on voters, investors, and public finances. The pressures were no longer purely financial. They became embedded in expectations as well.

Gradually, stability came to depend not only on economic fundamentals but also on the expectation of continued policy support. The more frequently authorities intervened, the more disruptive normal market conditions began to appear. A system can preserve calm for a long time, but preserving calm is not the same as building strength.

## *When the Emergency Became Permanent*

After 2008, interest rates in major advanced economies were pushed to zero or below and remained there for years. Central banks purchased vast quantities of government bonds and other financial assets, expanding their balance sheets to levels unprecedented in peacetime. These measures prevented collapse and restored confidence, yet what began as emergency action gradually became normal practice.

When new stresses appeared, whether during sovereign debt tensions or the pandemic shock, governments and central banks responded even faster and at larger scale. Budget deficits widened, central banks created new emergency lending programs and purchased more assets, and markets absorbed a simple message that instability would be met with force.

This changed behaviour across the system. Investors became more willing to assume risk, governments borrowed more freely, and financial markets increasingly treated intervention as part of the normal economic environment rather than an extraordinary response to crisis.

The deeper shift was that returning to more normal policy settings became increasingly difficult. When central banks attempted to shrink their balance sheets, funding markets became unsettled, and institutions that appeared stable under ultra-low rates struggled once borrowing costs rose.

Governments had amassed debt assuming low interest costs would continue, companies refinanced aggressively during years of cheap credit, and households adjusted to housing and asset prices supported by easy borrowing. Over time the economy reorganized itself around unusually low interest rates, meaning withdrawing support became more disruptive than continuing it. Maintaining calm did not eliminate risk; it stored it.

Policies designed to absorb shocks gradually reduced flexibility, and when returning to normal conditions threatens instability, stability itself becomes conditional.

## *Borrowed Stability*

Debt became the principal mechanism through which instability was postponed. After 2008, advanced economies did not meaningfully reduce debt burdens. Government borrowing rose to levels normally associated with wartime, companies borrowed heavily during years of near-zero interest rates, and in many housing markets household debt expanded again as low rates pushed prices higher.

The scale of debt matters, but dependence on it matters even more. Governments borrowed to avoid deep cuts in spending, companies borrowed to sustain share prices and smooth earnings, and households borrowed to cope with rising living costs. Debt allowed adjustment to be delayed, and over time delay became reliance throughout the economy.

Interest costs that once appeared manageable now rise rapidly when rates increase. Higher borrowing costs strain government budgets, compress corporate profits, and reduce household disposable income, while companies rolling over old debt at higher interest rates face mounting pressure.

High asset prices reinforce this dependence. Stock and housing valuations underpin household wealth, pension stability, and government tax revenues, meaning that a significant decline would ripple through public finances and consumer confidence with surprising speed.

Debt now anchors the system. Continued growth depends on continued credit, government finances depend on contained interest costs, and financial stability depends on asset prices shaped by supportive policy. The system remains functional so long as financial conditions remain unusually favourable, yet the economy becomes increasingly rigid because reversing those conditions threatens disruption across multiple sectors at the same time. Debt that began as a bridge over crisis has gradually become the structure itself.

## *Security Becomes Conditional*

For households, this loss of flexibility does not appear as collapse but as persistent insecurity. Income has become less predictable for many workers, and a large share of households report that they would struggle to cover an unexpected expense without borrowing or selling assets. Surveys across advanced economies consistently show that roughly one-third to one-half of households lack sufficient liquid savings to cover an unexpected expense without borrowing or drawing down assets.[4] Younger generations face housing costs that absorb a far larger share of income than previous generations experienced at the same age, while retirees rely heavily on financial markets to preserve savings in a low-yield environment.

Low unemployment does not guarantee security, moderate inflation does not ensure affordability, and economic growth does not necessarily provide resilience. Headline indicators suggest that the system is functioning, but they do not reveal whether it is providing durable stability.

Over time expectations adjust as risk-taking declines, long-term commitments are postponed, and political attitudes harden when confidence in upward mobility weakens. Insecurity becomes normalized. It is not dramatic enough to trigger panic, but it is persistent enough to erode trust.

As households become more financially exposed, tolerance for recession declines and political pressure to avoid economic pain intensifies. When wealth depends heavily on asset prices, even moderate corrections begin to carry wider social and political consequences. The result is a system that becomes progressively less tolerant of adjustment over time. The conditions for self-correction gradually begin to disappear.

## *Why This Structure Cannot Self-Correct*

Under normal conditions, excessive debt is reduced through slower growth, tighter credit, and falling asset prices. Weak firms fail, prices adjust, and balance is gradually restored.

In the current structure, those mechanisms are constrained. Large declines in asset prices would weaken government revenues and strain credit markets. Meaningful interest rate increases would sharply raise government interest bills and corporate refinancing costs. Sustained inflation would erode purchasing power and strain social cohesion. Severe spending cuts or large tax increases would risk recession and instability.

Even faster growth is unlikely to provide an easy escape. Ageing populations, weaker productivity gains, and slower labour-force expansion limit the pace at which advanced economies can outgrow their debt burdens. Productivity growth across advanced economies has slowed to roughly 1 percent per year since the global financial crisis, far below the pace seen in the late twentieth century.[5] The margin for growing out of debt has narrowed considerably.

Each apparent solution runs into limits built into the system itself. Stability depends on continued low interest rates and policy support, yet continued support sustains high debt and elevated asset prices. High debt makes adjustment more painful and the range of workable outcomes steadily narrows.

What appears as resilience is accumulated brittleness. Systems that cannot tolerate small corrections rarely fail in small ways. They remain outwardly calm while pressure builds beneath the surface until fiscal strain, financial shock, or political rupture crosses a threshold and adjustment occurs more abruptly than gradual reform would have required.

Gradual repair requires tolerance for short-term pain, and in a system designed increasingly to avoid visible pain that tolerance steadily weakens. Stability therefore becomes less a sign of strength than a sign of how dependent the system has become on preventing disruption.

## *When Stability Reaches Its Limits*

Since the early 1980s, when inflation was contained and interest rates began a long decline, advanced economies have preserved stability by expanding debt, suppressing financial disruptions, and postponing difficult political trade-offs. Each intervention prevented an immediate crisis, each round of borrowing absorbed strain, and each episode of monetary support restored confidence. Yet these actions did not reduce dependence on debt and low borrowing costs. They increased it.

Government debt has grown faster than the productive capacity needed to sustain it, and interest payments are beginning to claim larger shares of public budgets across the advanced world. In the United States alone, federal interest payments are projected to exceed $1 trillion annually within the next decade[6], making them one of the largest components of the federal budget. Similar pressures are emerging elsewhere as ageing populations, rising borrowing costs, and years of accumulated debt place increasing strain on public finances in Europe, Japan, and other major economies.

Households rely increasingly on housing and financial markets to preserve wealth. Pension systems rely on elevated asset prices, governments on low borrowing costs, and companies on continued access to affordable refinancing. Stability persists so long as financial conditions remain unusually favourable, yet those conditions cannot be guaranteed indefinitely. The apparent stability is therefore more fragile than it appears.

The deeper problem is that these vulnerabilities are increasingly synchronized. Governments, households, pension systems, and financial markets have all become dependent on the same conditions: low borrowing costs, stable asset prices, and continued confidence that instability will remain contained.

If borrowing costs rise meaningfully, fiscal pressure intensifies. If inflation persists, political tolerance erodes. If asset prices fall sharply, financial balance sheets weaken simultaneously across governments, firms, and households, and mechanisms that once absorbed shocks begin to transmit them.

## *When the System Can No Longer Adjust Gradually*

At some point the constraints will bind. Debt cannot expand faster than income indefinitely, interest rates cannot remain suppressed without consequence, and political systems cannot promise protection while avoiding adjustment. The structure now rests on conditions that must eventually change, and when they do the adjustment will not reflect a sudden error or a single failed policy but limits that were reached gradually and then enforced abruptly.

What appears today as durable stability is a structure resting on conditions that cannot indefinitely hold. It remains intact not because the underlying system has become more resilient, but because the policies and financial conditions supporting it are still in place and broadly accepted.

When those limits are reached, the shift will not resemble an ordinary recession. It will mark the moment when the mechanisms that once preserved stability begin to amplify instability instead. The calm that defined the advanced world for decades will give way to a far more uncertain period in which economic, financial, and political systems are forced to adjust at the same time and often under pressure.

Long periods of stability rarely end through a single dramatic event. More often, underlying conditions weaken gradually while the appearance of normality remains intact. Dependence deepens, flexibility narrows further, and intervention becomes increasingly necessary simply to preserve stability.

This is why periods of apparent stability deserve closer examination than periods of obvious crisis. Crises reveal weaknesses that already exist; long periods of stability often conceal the conditions that allow those weaknesses to accumulate. Understanding how that process unfolds is essential to understanding why today's economic system has become progressively less resilient.

The danger is not merely that the system carries more debt or requires more support than before. The deeper danger is that the capacity to absorb shocks weakens even as dependence on continued stability grows. What once appeared durable increasingly depends on conditions that cannot endure indefinitely without growing consequences.

# PART II

# THE MACHINERY

# 4

## THE AGE OF EASY MONEY

To understand the stability that defined the advanced world for decades, it is necessary to understand how money itself changed. Not money as it appears in everyday transactions, but money as it is created, priced, and sustained through policy. Over the past several decades, and decisively since the global financial crisis, money has taken on a different character. A stabilizing tool once reserved for emergencies gradually became a permanent feature of economic management.

The effects eventually reached far beyond central banks and financial markets. Mortgage rates fell to historic lows, governments borrowed on an enormous scale at unusually low cost, investors moved steadily into riskier assets searching for returns, and traditional savings increasingly failed to keep pace with inflation. Conditions that initially appeared temporary gradually became embedded within everyday economic life.

The shift was gradual, rarely acknowledged as a structural change, and justified at each stage as temporary. Yet repetition transformed exception into baseline. Over time, policies introduced to stabilize crises incrementally reshaped the financial system, making economic stability increasingly dependent on their continued presence. What began as adaptation gradually evolved into a new operating model.

The period since 2008 marks a decisive turning point in the architecture of the advanced world's stability. In earlier crises emergency conditions were temporary. Interest rates were cut, liquidity was supplied, and once recovery took hold, policy gradually returned to normal. After 2008, normalization never truly arrived. Near-zero interest rates, large-scale asset purchases, and sustained intervention persisted for more than a decade, far longer than in any comparable episode in modern economic history.[1]

In the United States, policy rates remained near zero for roughly seven years following the crisis, compared with much shorter easing cycles in earlier recessions.[2] The Federal Reserve's balance sheet expanded from under $1 trillion before 2008 to more than $4 trillion within a decade and would later rise even further.[3] The change reflected something more fundamental.

This was not merely an extension of policy. It marked a deeper transformation in how stability itself was maintained. Markets increasingly depended less on their ability to absorb shocks independently and more on continued intervention from central banks and governments. Support was no longer reserved for moments of panic but became embedded in the system's normal functioning. Markets adjusted to it, governments relied upon it, and asset prices incorporated it.

This transformation was not accidental. It was the logical outcome of an economy that had grown increasingly leveraged and increasingly sensitive to disruption. When debt levels are high, even modest shocks can trigger outsized consequences. Policymakers responded rationally to prevent collapse, yet each successful intervention also reduced the system's tolerance for future stress.

The result was a gradual but important shift in the character of stability itself. Stability was preserved, but resilience quietly weakened beneath the surface. Emergency measures gradually became permanent features of the system. Once that happened, removing support became increasingly difficult without creating instability across financial markets.

## *The Permanent Emergency*

Crisis has always been a catalyst for monetary change. When financial systems seize up, the consequences are immediate and severe. Credit dries up. Businesses fail. Unemployment rises sharply. In such moments, hesitation is costly, and policymakers intervene not to fine-tune outcomes but to prevent collapse.

During the global financial crisis, interbank lending froze, major institutions required emergency support, and global trade contracted at a pace not seen since the early 1930s.[4] Liquidity vanished across markets, exposing how dependent the global economy had become on continuous access to credit.

In September 2008, the strain became visible to the public. Lehman Brothers collapsed, money market funds briefly "broke the buck," and companies across the United States and Europe struggled to roll over even short-term borrowing. Firms that had always assumed credit would be available suddenly discovered that it was not. The modern financial system had come within days of seizing entirely.

Global trade volumes fell by more than 10 percent within a single year.[5] Major banking systems required trillions in emergency liquidity support. Central banks lowered interest rates to near zero and supplied emergency funding and cash to financial markets on a scale without modern precedent.

These actions succeeded in stabilizing markets, but what followed proved historically unusual. In earlier crises, emergency measures were eventually withdrawn once conditions normalized. After 2008, however, support remained in place long after the immediate panic faded.

When new stress emerged, whether during the euro-area debt crisis, the pandemic, or episodes of regional banking strain, the response followed a familiar pattern. The policy playbook became familiar. Rates were cut rapidly, balance sheets expanded, and liquidity was supplied in abundance. Emergency measures gradually became normal policy.

Each episode reinforced a new expectation: when instability appeared, intervention would arrive quickly, forcefully, and for as long as necessary. Over time that expectation became structural. Emergency measures were no longer deviations from normal policy but increasingly came to define it. Markets adjusted to the assumption of support, governments calibrated fiscal decisions around it, and investors priced assets on the belief that severe downside would be contained.

Crisis therefore ceased to function solely as disruption. It increasingly reinforced the structure that had emerged after 2008. Each intervention stabilized the system in the short term while also deepening reliance on future intervention.

A financial system that requires emergency tools to function under ordinary conditions is no longer fully resilient. It becomes conditioned to support, and conditioning, once deeply embedded, is difficult to reverse without causing disruption.

## *How Easy Money Changed Behaviour*

By the middle of the 2010s, the consequences of easy money had begun to appear in everyday financial decisions. Mortgage rates in several advanced economies fell to levels unseen in modern history. Corporations issued record amounts of cheap debt, sometimes borrowing simply because markets rewarded it. Investors searching for returns moved steadily into stocks, property, and riskier assets as traditional savings accounts yielded almost nothing.

Cheap money reshapes incentives across the economy. Debt feels less dangerous, leverage appears manageable, and risk seems containable. These perceptions are reinforced by experience. When downturns occur, intervention follows. Losses are contained and markets recover. Each cycle strengthens the belief that severe consequences will be limited.

Household borrowing expands even when real wage growth remains modest. Consumption is sustained not primarily by rising incomes but by access to credit. Across many advanced economies, household debt grew faster than disposable income during the post-crisis recovery, reflecting spending increasingly supported by borrowing rather than wage growth.[6]

Corporations raise leverage not only to invest in productive capacity but also to refinance liabilities, acquire competitors, and return capital to shareholders. Complex financial strategies designed to boost profits often deliver quicker rewards than long-term expansion.

Saving, meanwhile, loses its anchor. When safe assets offer little or no real return, the incentive to defer consumption weakens. Capital does not disappear. It migrates toward assets that promise appreciation or protection from erosion, and the search for yield becomes a defining feature of the system.

Over time, behaviour adapts to these conditions. Corporate planning, pension assumptions, housing decisions, and government budgets increasingly come to rely on the expectation that low interest rates and abundant liquidity will persist. Policies originally introduced as temporary stabilization gradually become embedded within long-term decision making.

This shift alters more than balance sheets. It alters expectations. When stability rests on the belief that support will arrive quickly and consistently, that belief itself becomes part of the system's structure. The longer it endures, the more disruptive its eventual reversal becomes.

Withdrawal is no longer merely a technical policy adjustment. It becomes a shock to behaviour, valuations, and political tolerance. A system conditioned to expect rescue remains stable only while rescue remains credible.

The deeper that dependence became, the more difficult it was to allow market signals to operate freely. Among the most important of those signals was the price of money itself. Over time, that signal began to lose much of its traditional function. The price of money no longer conveyed the same information.

## *When the Price of Money Stopped Working*

Over time the function of interest rates changed. Traditionally, interest rates coordinate an economy. They balance saving and borrowing, risk and reward, and signal scarcity. They help determine whether capital flows toward productive investment or speculative activity. In the age of easy money that coordinating role weakened. Rates increasingly reflected policy decisions rather than underlying economic conditions.

In many advanced economies, inflation-adjusted interest rates remained negative for extended periods. Borrowing was effectively subsidized, while saving guaranteed a gradual loss of purchasing power.[7] This was not accidental. It was a conscious trade-off. Low rates reduced the cost of servicing debt, supported asset prices, and cushioned fragile recoveries, but they also shifted costs quietly from borrowers to savers.

For households that relied on traditional savings, the change was profound. Deposits that once generated modest but dependable income increasingly failed to keep pace with rising prices. Retirees, pension funds, and conservative investors were pushed steadily toward greater risk simply to preserve purchasing power. The adjustment was not confined to investors.

When borrowing is kept artificially cheap for long enough, behaviour adjusts. The adjustment is rational. Households borrow because debt appears manageable and persistent. Firms increase leverage because capital is inexpensive and markets reward financial efficiency. Governments expand deficits because low rates make the burden appear sustainable.

The problem is not irresponsible behaviour but that the signal itself has changed. When the price of money no longer reflects risk or scarcity, financial decisions are guided less by productive opportunity and more by policy assurance. Debt expands not only because it is useful but because the system increasingly encourages and normalizes it. The longer this process continues, the more deeply debt becomes woven into economic decision-making. The shift gradually becomes self-reinforcing.

Over time this creates a trap. As debt accumulated under years of artificially low rates, the system itself became increasingly sensitive to higher borrowing costs. Asset prices, government finances, housing markets, and corporate balance sheets all adapted to conditions that depended on unusually cheap money. The longer this persisted, the harder reversal became. The adjustment became progressively more difficult.

Returning interest rates toward historically normal levels therefore became increasingly difficult. What once functioned as stimulus gradually became constraint. The larger the stock of debt, the narrower the exit. A system built around subsidized borrowing cannot easily tolerate the removal of subsidy itself.

## *Rising Asset Prices and the Illusion of Stability*

Financial assets became the primary destination for surplus capital. Equities, bonds, and real estate absorbed sustained inflows, and prices often rose far faster than underlying economic output or income growth. With savings generating little return, investors increasingly turned to stocks, property, and other assets in search of growth. The resulting inflows helped push valuations higher, often faster than the underlying economy was expanding.

In the decade following the global financial crisis, major equity indices in advanced economies more than doubled, significantly outpacing GDP growth and median income expansion.[8] These gains were widely interpreted as evidence of renewed strength, yet a substantial portion of the rise reflected monetary conditions rather than a comparable surge in productivity or long-term earnings power.

Equity valuations expanded despite modest structural growth. Housing prices climbed far faster than median incomes, pushing affordability toward historic extremes. In several major cities, price-to-income ratios surpassed their pre-2008 peaks.[9]

What appeared as wealth accumulation for existing asset holders increasingly translated into exclusion and higher leverage for those attempting to enter the market for the first time.

Market calm reinforced the illusion. Volatility declined relative to prior crisis periods. Corrections were brief and frequently followed by renewed rallies, while the expectation that policy support would arrive during periods of stress became increasingly embedded in market behaviour. Risk did not disappear. It was deferred. The vulnerabilities continued to accumulate beneath the surface year after year.

Over time markets ceased functioning as reliable early warning systems. Elevated valuations no longer signalled caution but confidence that intervention and liquidity would continue. Higher prices reinforced optimism, and optimism in turn justified even higher prices.

This dynamic increasingly blurred the distinction between rising asset prices and genuine economic strength. Financial markets appeared healthy even while many households experienced stagnant purchasing power, rising living costs, and weakening affordability.

Asset values climbed while real wage growth remained subdued and household purchasing power eroded under rising costs. Calm increasingly became a substitute for resilience. The longer markets depend on policy support rather than durable income growth, the more fragile that calm ultimately becomes. When confidence in intervention weakens, adjustment rarely unfolds gradually because valuations have drifted too far from their foundations.

## *The Debt Trap*

As debt accumulates across households, firms, and governments, sensitivity to interest rates increases. Before the global financial crisis, global debt stood at roughly three times world output. In the years that followed it climbed to well over three and a half times global GDP, reflecting expansion across both public and private sectors.[10] In several advanced economies government debt alone rose above levels previously associated with wartime.[11] What once appeared to provide flexibility now increasingly imposes constraint.

Higher rates no longer affect only marginal borrowers. They reverberate through entire balance sheets. Asset valuations compress, mortgage payments rise, corporate refinancing costs increase, and government interest expenses expand rapidly. In highly indebted systems even modest rate increases translate into significant fiscal and financial consequences.

This creates a reinforcing loop. High debt makes normalization painful, and the anticipation of that pain discourages normalization. Policy remains accommodative not only to encourage growth but increasingly to prevent destabilization of the structures built under low rates.

Eventually easy money ceases to function as temporary stimulus and instead becomes foundation. Pension funds project returns based on elevated asset prices, governments draft budgets assuming manageable debt-servicing costs, and corporations structure themselves around the expectation that refinancing will remain inexpensive and continuously available.

This marks an important threshold in the evolution of the system. Stability becomes increasingly dependent on suppressing the price of money, yet suppressing that price encourages even more borrowing and greater sensitivity to future shocks. In such a system, raising rates risks financial strain while not raising them risks inflation and currency erosion. What once appeared as flexibility gradually reveals itself as entrapment.

The dependence develops slowly and is therefore easy to underestimate. Yet over time the system ceases merely to benefit from easy money and instead reorganizes itself around it. Investment decisions, asset valuations, borrowing patterns, and public finances gradually adjust to assumptions that no longer feel temporary. What begins as support increasingly becomes a foundation of the system.

## *The Limits of Easy Money*

Easy money does not eliminate economic constraints. It relocates them. Financial claims expand faster than the economy's ability to produce goods and services. For a time this imbalance can persist without visible strain. Asset prices rise, credit flows, and markets appear orderly on the surface.

History is consistent on this point. When financial claims grow materially faster than real output, adjustment eventually follows. The late 1920s and the years preceding 2008 both exhibited this pattern with remarkable clarity.

The constraint re-emerges most visibly through inflation. When prices begin to rise persistently, the trade-offs that once appeared manageable become acute. Supporting asset valuations conflicts with protecting purchasing power, and maintaining low borrowing costs conflicts with restoring price stability. The same policies that once preserved calm begin to amplify tension.

At that stage the options narrow. Raising rates exposes the debt accumulated under years of cheap financing, while keeping rates low risks currency erosion and entrenched inflation. Either path carries destabilizing consequences, and monetary comfort reveals itself as monetary dependence.

Yet the deeper consequences of easy money extended beyond interest rates themselves. Over time, governments, financial markets, corporations, and households increasingly adapted to conditions that were never intended to become permanent. Governments became more reliant on cheap borrowing to sustain spending and manage rising obligations.

Corporations operated in an environment where capital remained unusually inexpensive for prolonged periods, encouraging refinancing, leverage, and financial engineering. Investors moved further into riskier assets in search of returns,

while rising asset prices increasingly came to be treated as evidence of economic health itself and continued stability.
Financial markets adapted over time. Investors increasingly assumed that central banks would intervene forcefully during periods of instability. Even modest increases in interest rates began triggering sharper market reactions because asset prices, borrowing structures, and expectations had all become conditioned to prolonged monetary support.

What once appeared as control gradually revealed itself as constraint. What appeared as durable stability increasingly proved conditional. The system had been stabilized repeatedly, but each round of intervention required greater scale while producing diminishing resilience.

The age of easy money therefore became more than a temporary policy response. It evolved into the defining architecture of modern stability. It helps explain why debt levels reached historic highs, why asset prices detached from underlying income growth, and why financial calm persisted even as structural fragility quietly deepened beneath the surface.

Its effects extended far beyond monetary policy. It reshaped incentives, risk-taking, and economic behaviour across the broader system. Stability increasingly depended not only on growth and productivity, but also on the continuation of the financial conditions that had sustained expansion for more than a decade across the advanced world.

Intervention could delay adjustment, but it could not remove the underlying constraints building beneath the surface. The longer imbalances accumulated under conditions of cheap money, the more disruptive eventual adjustment became likely to be once it arrived.

The era of easy money ultimately succeeded in preserving stability for far longer than many expected. Yet the stability it produced came at a cost. Debt expanded, asset prices drifted further from underlying income growth, and economies became increasingly dependent on conditions that could not continue indefinitely. The pressures continued to build beneath the surface. Their origins stretch back decades.

The present strains within the advanced world are therefore not a sudden break from the past. They are the delayed consequences of a monetary order that gradually transformed emergency policy into permanent structure.

What began as a response to crisis ultimately reshaped the foundations of the financial system itself. Borrowing became easier, asset prices rose, and stability appeared to strengthen. Yet beneath that stability, dependence deepened. Markets adapted to continuous support, governments adapted to permanently lower borrowing costs, and households adapted to an environment in which financial assets increasingly determined economic security.

The result was not the elimination of economic constraints, but their postponement. Over time, the pressures that once would have forced adjustment accumulated beneath the surface. The era of easy money succeeded in delaying many consequences. It could not remove them entirely.

# 5

# WHERE THE MONEY ACTUALLY GOES

A simple question sits beneath much of today's economic unease: if the world has experienced an extraordinary surge in borrowing and money creation in recent decades, why has economic growth remained relatively modest? Across advanced economies, growth has averaged around 1.5 to 2 percent in recent years, down from roughly 3 to 4 percent in the preceding generation.[1] The two trends moved in opposite directions.

Yet over the same period, financial markets have surged, with major stock indices rising several hundred percent since the global financial crisis and property prices in many countries far outpacing incomes. Wages feel constrained, everyday costs continue to rise, and yet vast amounts of money have been created. Where does it all go? The question is not rhetorical. It reflects a growing sense that something fundamental no longer aligns between rising financial wealth and the economic experience of ordinary households. It points to a deeper shift in how modern economies function beneath the surface.

In the past quarter century, the scale of borrowing and money creation has been extraordinary. Total global debt has risen from roughly $80 to $90 trillion at the turn of the century to about $350 trillion by 2025.[2] Today, global debt stands at well over three times the size of the world economy.[3] The increase has been broad-based, extending across governments, businesses, and households alike creating an economy in which borrowing has become integral to growth, spending, and financial stability.

Since the global financial crisis, major central banks have expanded their holdings by more than $20 trillion at their peak, an increase without precedent in peacetime.[4] The Federal Reserve alone grew from under $900 billion in 2007 to nearly $9 trillion by 2022.[5] Money has been created, borrowed, and circulated on a scale once associated with major wars or systemic collapse. Yet for many households, daily life has not reflected a comparable expansion in security or opportunity. The contrast is difficult to ignore. Financial wealth has expanded dramatically, yet the broader sense of economic stability has become more fragile rather than less.

Money does not disappear. It follows incentives. And over time, the incentives within the modern economy have changed profoundly. The result is not simply more debt or larger financial markets, but a system in which newly created money increasingly flows toward financial assets rather than broad-based productive expansion. Understanding that shift is essential to understanding why modern economies can appear financially strong while feeling economically insecure at the same time.

## *Where the Money Really Flows*

The modern stability model depends on low borrowing costs, abundant liquidity, and rising financial markets. When growth weakens, policymakers rarely step back. Instead, they intervene by lowering interest rates, injecting liquidity into financial markets, or expanding central bank asset purchases so that credit continues to flow and a broader downturn can be avoided. When markets falter, borrowing conditions are eased to prevent financial stress from spreading through the economy.

Each intervention stabilizes the moment. Over time, however, these responses also influence where money ultimately flows. Increasingly, money creation sustains the prices of stocks, property, and other financial investments rather than expanding productive capacity or strengthening household finances. The shift is gradual and often difficult to see in real time because rising asset prices can create the appearance of prosperity even when underlying growth remains weak for extended periods.

This shift is not accidental, nor is it primarily a moral question. It reflects the mechanics of how the system now operates. When the cost of borrowing is held below the level the market would normally set for extended periods, money naturally flows toward whatever benefits most from cheap financing, particularly investments that can be leveraged, traded, and repriced quickly. Financial assets respond far more quickly to cheap money than factories, infrastructure, or long-term productivity improvements. Gradually, the stability of the system comes to rely more heavily on rising stock markets and property values.

Stability no longer rests primarily on productivity growth, broad wage gains, or expanding output. Instead, it depends increasingly on the continued support of financial markets. Market performance begins to shape confidence itself. Rising portfolios and rising property values create the impression that the broader economy remains healthy, even when wage growth, productivity, and investment remain comparatively subdued.

That redirection does more than distort how prosperity appears. It also makes the system more fragile. When rising markets become the primary means through which policy supports the economy, resilience weakens. Stability begins to depend on conditions that cannot last indefinitely.

The longer this continues, the harder the system becomes to normalize. Financial markets adjust to the expectation of low borrowing costs, governments become accustomed to financing deficits cheaply, and households increasingly organize long-term decisions around elevated asset values. What began as temporary support gradually becomes embedded in the structure of the economy itself.

When those conditions eventually change, whether through higher inflation, growing fiscal pressure, or a loss of confidence, the consequences are no longer gradual. Financial markets come under pressure, borrowing becomes more expensive, and economic growth slows. What once appeared to stabilize the system begins to expose how dependent the system had become on permanently favourable financial conditions.

## *When the Price of Money Stops Working*

Interest rates are not a technical detail. They are the economy's central coordinating signal. They influence whether saving is rewarded, whether borrowing is restrained, and whether money flows toward long-term investment or short-term gain. When they function properly, they balance patience and risk, impose discipline on excess, and reward deferred consumption. In effect, interest rates help determine what kinds of economic behaviour are encouraged and what kinds are discouraged.

For much of the post-war era, real interest rates remained positive on average. Saving offered modest but reliable returns above inflation, and borrowing carried a visible cost. Risk and reward were linked in ways that households and businesses could understand. Money was not free, and that imposed a natural discipline on financial behaviour.

That relationship began to change after the global financial crisis. Policy rates in the United States, the Eurozone, the United Kingdom, and Japan were reduced to near zero and remained there for more than a decade.[6] In several economies, inflation-adjusted interest rates fell below zero for extended periods. At various points in the 2010s, more than $15 trillion in global government debt carried negative nominal yields.[7]

This represented a profound shift in how modern financial systems operated. Interest rates were no longer simply encouraging or restraining borrowing over the normal course of the business cycle. Instead, exceptionally low borrowing costs became a semi-permanent feature of the economic environment. Price increasingly reflected policy rather than scarcity.

When the price of money remains unusually low for years rather than months, its signalling role begins to weaken. Interest rates stop clearly directing businesses, investors, and governments toward what is economically sustainable over the long term. Investment decisions become less driven by productivity and more influenced by the availability of cheap financing. Projects that would not survive under normal borrowing costs begin to appear viable, while investments that can be leveraged and traded quickly become more attractive than those requiring time, patience, and uncertain effort.

Lower interest rates also change how investors think about future profits. When borrowing becomes cheaper and safe investments offer little return, profits expected years from now begin to look more attractive. Investors become willing to pay higher prices today for those future earnings, allowing stock and property prices to rise even if the underlying pace of economic growth does not accelerate. Financial valuations begin drifting further away from the slower-moving reality of wages, productivity, and underlying economic output.

The effects unfold gradually. Saving becomes less attractive because safe instruments struggle to preserve purchasing power. Pension funds, insurers, and long-term savers are pushed toward riskier markets in search of acceptable returns. Borrowing costs fall across governments, corporations, and households, encouraging larger debts and greater sensitivity to future rate changes.

As these conditions persist, the system adapts. Debt rises because borrowing is inexpensive. Financial markets adjust upward because financing remains abundant. Investment strategies evolve around the assumption that easy money will continue. Over time, behaviour that initially appeared temporary becomes embedded in the structure of the financial system itself.

This marks a turning point. When interest rates no longer discipline economic behaviour, they begin to protect it. Markets rise not only because earnings grow, but because borrowing remains inexpensive. Governments finance deficits at low cost and postpone difficult choices. Corporations refinance rather than restructure. Households stretch their borrowing because payments appear manageable. The broader economy adjusts in similar ways.

At first, this environment feels stabilizing. Volatility declines, asset prices rise, and financial stress appears easier to contain. Yet beneath the surface, dependence steadily deepens. As debts grow larger and valuations rise further, the system becomes increasingly sensitive to even modest changes in borrowing costs. Flexibility gives way to dependence.

Once that dependence takes hold, returning interest rates to more normal levels becomes destabilizing. Even relatively small increases begin exposing how heavily market prices, debt burdens, and government finances rely on cheap borrowing. What once appeared to strengthen stability gradually reveals how much of that stability depended on conditions that could not realistically continue forever.

At this stage, interest rates no longer function simply as a tool for managing growth and inflation. They become a source of systemic tension themselves. The price of money, which once anchored the economy, increasingly becomes one of its greatest sources of instability.

## *When Money Has Nowhere Safe to Go*

When safety no longer preserves wealth, money does not remain still; it moves. This shift is driven less by speculation than by necessity. It is a rational response to an environment in which holding money can mean losing purchasing power. If cash produces little return and government bonds fail to keep pace with inflation, investors are pushed outward along the risk spectrum simply to maintain the value of their savings.

Over time, this changes the behaviour of the entire financial system. Investors who might once have accepted modest but stable returns begin taking greater risks simply to preserve long-term purchasing power. Pension funds, insurers, and households gradually adapt to an environment in which caution itself becomes financially costly over time.

Financial markets become the natural destination. Since 2009, major stock indices in advanced economies have risen several hundred percent, far outpacing wage growth and the pace of economic expansion.[8] The divergence is striking. The prices of financial investments have risen far more rapidly than the incomes that ultimately support them. The gap between financial markets and the lived economy steadily widens.

Rising prices attract additional money. Higher market values strengthen corporate finances, enabling more borrowing, which in turn supports further investment in financial markets. The cycle reinforces itself. Prices rise not only because businesses become more productive, but because alternatives offer little return. The system increasingly rewards ownership of assets rather than the slower process of building productive capacity.

Real estate follows the same logic. Cheap borrowing amplifies demand, pushing prices well ahead of incomes. In many advanced economies, house prices have risen two to three times faster than median incomes.[9] Housing increasingly functions as an investment as much as a place to live. For many households, owning property becomes less connected to shelter or stability and more connected to financial survival itself.

This is asset inflation. Unlike consumer price inflation, which raises the cost of everyday goods, asset inflation raises the price of investments already owned. Rising asset prices increase wealth on paper without necessarily improving household incomes. The gains flow primarily to existing asset owners, while those seeking to enter the market face barriers that rise year after year.

Gradually, stability becomes tied to rising financial markets. Households feel secure as home values rise, pension systems appear well funded as markets perform, and governments benefit from stronger financial activity. Market performance becomes a proxy for economic health and future prosperity.

This alters behaviour in subtle but important ways. Consumers spend more confidently when asset prices rise, governments become increasingly sensitive to market declines, and policymakers grow more reluctant to tolerate falling valuations that could weaken confidence and slow activity.

The system begins to depend on these conditions. If stock markets or property prices stall or decline, the effects spread quickly through household confidence, government finances, and financial institutions. What once appeared to support economic stability becomes one of its central pillars.

Money does not disappear. It accumulates where returns appear strongest and risks seem contained. In an environment defined by cheap borrowing and abundant liquidity, that often means financial markets rather than productive investment.

The shift is gradual but profound. As more money flows into existing assets, the economy's centre of gravity moves away from production and toward valuation. Stability becomes less about creating new capacity and more about sustaining elevated prices. Financial markets continue to prosper, even as improvements in productivity, affordability, and economic security become harder to achieve for many.

What begins as a subtle change eventually becomes a structural feature of the system.

## *From Investment to Financial Engineering*

Corporations respond to incentives just as investors do. When borrowing is cheap and markets reward rising share prices, behaviour changes.

In the years following the global financial crisis, many firms devoted substantial resources to share buybacks and dividends. In the United States alone, companies spent trillions repurchasing shares, often exceeding investment in new productive capacity.[10]

Returning cash to shareholders frequently provided a faster and more predictable boost to share prices than expanding operations.

This shift did not necessarily reflect corporate short-termism in the conventional sense. It reflected a financial environment in which markets increasingly rewarded immediate financial performance over slower and less certain long-term expansion. When borrowing costs remain exceptionally low and investors focus heavily on quarterly results, financial strategies often appear safer and more rewarding than large productive investments whose returns may take years to materialize.

This behaviour reflects the incentives of the system. When borrowing is inexpensive and markets respond quickly to financial metrics, financial strategies become more attractive than long-term investment. Under these conditions, the financial side of the corporation gradually begins to dominate the productive side.

The consequences accumulate. Resources that might have expanded production are redirected toward financial support. Corporate finances grow larger, but not necessarily in ways that strengthen long-term output. Balance sheets expand, yet the economy's productive capacity often grows far more slowly.

Gradually, the nature of growth changes. Productivity growth remains subdued despite technological progress, while wages lag behind rising stock and property prices. The financial sphere accelerates while the real economy moves more slowly.

Over time, this changes how success itself is measured within the economy. Rising valuations, financial efficiency, and shareholder returns increasingly take precedence over expanding productive capacity, raising wages, or strengthening long-term resilience. Financial performance becomes easier to achieve than broad-based economic renewal.

This shift is subtle at first. Companies remain profitable, markets continue rising, and economic activity appears stable on the surface. Yet beneath that stability, the relationship between finance and production gradually changes. More resources flow toward sustaining financial performance, while the work of expanding productive capacity gradually loses priority.

The result is not the disappearance of productive investment, but a growing imbalance between financial expansion and productive renewal. The economy continues to generate wealth, but an increasing share of that wealth is linked to financial valuation rather than the expansion of underlying productive capacity itself, with growing consequences.

## *When Support Becomes Dependence*

Policy reinforces these dynamics. Central banks act to stabilize markets and support activity, easing borrowing conditions when stress emerges. Over time, markets begin to expect these interventions, and prices increasingly reflect not only fundamentals but also the likelihood of policy support.

This expectation changes behaviour. Borrowers assume refinancing will remain available, investors assume sharp declines will be contained, and governments assume financing will remain affordable. What begins as an emergency response gradually becomes an expectation that serious financial disruption will be contained before it threatens the wider system. Stability becomes self-reinforcing, but only as long as support remains credible.

As the cycle continues, the system adapts. Debt expands, markets rise, and deficits widen. The entire system becomes calibrated around low borrowing costs and continued intervention. Behaviour that once appeared temporary slowly becomes normal. Financial markets price assets around the expectation of support, governments structure spending around inexpensive borrowing, and households increasingly organize financial decisions around elevated asset values.

The dependence deepens quietly because the system often appears stable while it is building vulnerability beneath the surface. Rising markets reinforce confidence, low volatility encourages greater risk-taking, and years of intervention create the impression that instability itself has become manageable.

The difficulty emerges when conditions change. If inflation rises and forces tightening, higher borrowing costs expose underlying vulnerabilities. Policymakers face a dilemma between controlling inflation and preserving stability. Measures designed to restore discipline begin threatening systems that have adapted to the absence of discipline for many years.

Under these conditions, even modest increases in interest rates can have outsized effects. Governments face rising debt-servicing costs, corporations confront more expensive refinancing, and households experience growing pressure on mortgages, credit, and living costs simultaneously. What once appeared manageable under conditions of cheap money suddenly becomes far more fragile when borrowing costs normalize. The underlying weakness is finally exposed.

At this point, dependence becomes fragility. Systems built on continuous support can function for long periods, but they are inherently vulnerable. The longer intervention suppresses adjustment, the more difficult eventual adjustment becomes. What once appeared to strengthen stability gradually increases the system's sensitivity to change.

## *Stability That No Longer Feels Secure*

The effects of rising financial markets do not remain confined to investors. They reshape how people experience opportunity and security. When stock and property prices rise much faster than incomes, the link between effort and advancement begins to weaken, and ownership comes to matter more than participation

Over time, this changes how economic life is perceived across society. Wealth increasingly flows toward those who already own assets, while those relying primarily on wages find it harder to build financial security through work and saving alone. The economy may continue expanding on paper, yet access to that expansion becomes increasingly uneven.

Those who hold assets see their wealth expand, while others face rising barriers to entry. For younger generations, this shift is especially visible, as homeownership is delayed not by preference but by affordability, and debt increasingly becomes a prerequisite for participating in markets that earlier generations could enter through saving alone.

This alters expectations in subtle but important ways. Long-term planning becomes more cautious, financial risk feels more dangerous, and economic advancement increasingly appears tied to existing wealth rather than future opportunity. The perception that the system rewards participation fairly begins to weaken. People adapt to the incentives they face.

As these patterns take hold, expectations begin to adjust. Risk-taking declines because failure carries greater consequences, savings feel inadequate because safe returns remain low, and long-term planning becomes more cautious. These changes rarely appear dramatic in any single year, but they accumulate steadily as the system evolves.

Asset inflation thrives in this environment of relative calm. It expands under conditions of steady policy support and low volatility, allowing the system to drift rather than break. Yet this drift carries its own consequences. With each year of rising market prices, reliance on fragile conditions deepens, as debts grow larger, pension systems become more dependent on financial market performance, and governments rely increasingly on strong markets to support tax revenues.

The appearance of stability gradually masks a growing dependence on conditions that are becoming harder to sustain. Pension systems depend on strong market returns. Households rely on rising property values to maintain financial security. Governments become increasingly vulnerable to market weakness that can erode growth and public revenues.

As this process continues, adjustment becomes more costly. Falling stock markets or property prices no longer represent routine corrections; they begin to threaten household wealth, government finances, and financial institutions simultaneously.

What appears stable on the surface becomes increasingly sensitive beneath it, as resilience gives way to dependence through the steady accumulation of pressures that make the system more vulnerable to change. The economy continues functioning, but confidence in its long-term fairness, resilience, and accessibility begins to erode more quietly underneath.

Taken together, these developments point to a deeper structural problem. The pressures are no longer isolated; they have become embedded in the way the system functions.

## *A System That Can No Longer Correct Itself*

None of this depends on conspiracy or recklessness. Markets perform essential functions, investors respond to incentives, policymakers act to prevent immediate collapse, and corporations adapt to the environment in which they operate. The difficulty lies in the structure of the system itself, which has evolved in ways that reinforce the very imbalances it was meant to contain over many decades.

When borrowing costs remain unusually low, debt expands faster than economic output and policy repeatedly supports financial markets, money flows toward what benefits most from cheap financing. Financial markets rise, debt accumulates, and the value of financial investments increases, reinforcing the same pattern again and again.

Over time, the effects become increasingly difficult to reverse. Liquidity flows more easily into financial assets, property markets, and debt-supported consumption than into the slower and more uncertain work of expanding productive capacity. The financial system becomes highly effective at supporting valuations, yet far less effective at generating broad-based economic renewal. The incentives created by low rates increasingly reshape where capital flows.

Money that might once have supported long-term productivity, infrastructure, or wage growth is increasingly redirected toward sustaining financial markets, while debt that once served as a temporary bridge through downturns gradually becomes a permanent support mechanism. As a result, the economy becomes progressively more dependent on financial expansion simply to maintain stability. The distinction between financial strength and economic strength begins to blur.

As financial expansion increasingly detaches from broad productive renewal, rising asset prices create the appearance of prosperity even as much of the expansion remains concentrated within the financial system itself. Financial markets grow larger relative to the productive economy, and asset ownership becomes increasingly important to household security.

This changes the character of economic stability itself. Market calm increasingly depends on continued intervention, elevated valuations, and confidence that borrowing conditions will remain manageable. Governments function more easily because financing costs remain low, financial institutions appear secure because asset prices remain elevated, and households feel more stable because rising property and financial values support balance sheets.

Yet beneath that stability, resilience steadily weakens. The system becomes less capable of absorbing higher borrowing costs, falling asset prices, or slower growth without broader disruption spreading through the economy.

If borrowing costs rise meaningfully, debt sustainability comes into question. Even modest increases in interest rates can translate into hundreds of billions of dollars in additional borrowing costs across major economies, placing pressure on governments, corporations, and households at the same time.

This is the deeper problem created by prolonged financial dependence. The system can continue operating for extended periods, but correcting the imbalances that accumulate within it becomes increasingly destabilizing. Measures that would once have represented normal economic adjustment begin threatening financial stability itself.

The system of rising financial markets and debt-supported stability can persist for long periods and can create the impression of resilience. But it does not resolve the imbalances it generates. Money increasingly circulates within financial systems rather than generating broad productive renewal across the wider economy. It postpones adjustment while increasing the scale of the underlying distortions throughout the system.

When stability depends on permanently low borrowing costs, continuously rising financial markets, and repeated intervention, the margin for error narrows to almost nothing.

At that stage, correction no longer feels cyclical or temporary. It begins to resemble a broader transition away from the conditions that defined the previous generation. What once functioned as a framework for stabilization gradually evolves into a structure that depends on continued financial expansion simply to preserve equilibrium.

The transition away from the conditions that defined the past generation is no longer theoretical. It has already begun. The defining question is no longer whether the old framework can be preserved, but how economies, institutions, and societies adapt as it gives way to something fundamentally different.

# 6

# LIVING ON BORROWED TIME

For most of modern history, societies borrowed in moments of crisis. Today, the advanced world borrows simply to keep the system running. What was once an exceptional tool, used during wars or recessions, has become permanent.

Since the early 1980s, total debt in advanced economies has risen far faster than output. It has not merely increased. It has undergone a structural transformation, rising to levels that are now roughly double those observed relative to economic output in earlier decades.

Before 2000, borrowing still retained a largely cyclical character, expanding during periods of stress and receding, at least in part, during recoveries. After 2000, that pattern shifted. Debt no longer declined meaningfully in periods of growth. It accumulated across cycles, becoming progressively embedded in the system over time.

In many of these economies, combined public and private debt now exceeds several multiples of national income, often ranging between 200 and 300 percent of GDP across most advanced economies, with some exceeding that level.[1] That is roughly double the levels common in the early 1980s. Each cycle has ended with more borrowing than the last. Public liabilities have expanded. Corporate balance sheets have grown heavier. Households carry larger mortgage and consumer obligations. Growth has continued, but so has reliance on credit.

At first, this shift appeared manageable. It did not arise from recklessness. It emerged because borrowing delivered results. It softened downturns, supported asset prices, and reduced the immediate cost of adjustment. Governments met obligations without cutting spending. Companies sustained earnings and valuations through borrowed capital. Households maintained living standards even as income growth slowed, with real wage growth in several advanced economies stagnating or weakening notably after the early 2000s.[2] Credit absorbed pressures that might otherwise have forced structural reform.

Over time, borrowing moved from being a stabilizing tool to a structural requirement. That change is easy to miss because it does not initially appear as crisis. The system continues functioning. Governments refinance existing obligations. Companies roll over debt. Households extend repayment horizons. Markets remain calm. Yet beneath that appearance of continuity, the economy becomes progressively more dependent on credit simply to preserve stability.

That transition altered the character of stability itself. When borrowing rises during stress and falls during recovery, it functions as a buffer. When it rises in both phases, it becomes load-bearing. Stability then depends not on balance, but on the continued expansion of credit. At that point, the system begins to lose its ability to correct without disruption. Adjustment becomes harder with each cycle rather than easier. The question is no longer simply whether debt is elevated. It is whether an economy organised around continuous refinancing can withstand a world in which refinancing is no longer cheap, easy, and widely available.

This chapter does not argue that debt alone causes collapse. It argues something more structural. Once borrowing becomes the operating principle of the economy, stability rests on confidence that credit will remain available and affordable.

When that confidence eventually weakens, the fragility that has accumulated over decades does not unwind gradually. Asset prices reprice suddenly. Credit conditions tighten. Governments face growing fiscal strain. Political tensions intensify as economic strain spreads through households and financial markets alike.

## *From Cycles to Dependence*

For much of the twentieth century, debt followed a recognisable pattern. It expanded during extraordinary periods and receded when growth returned. War debts were worked down over time. Post-crisis borrowing was absorbed through expansion, moderate inflation, or fiscal restraint. Adjustments were often painful, but they occurred. Balance sheets did not expand without limit, as seen in the decades after the Second World War when strong growth and moderate inflation helped reduce public debt ratios across many advanced economies.

That pattern began to shift in the late twentieth century. From the early 1980s onward, debt in advanced economies rose not only during recessions but also during expansions. Public debt did not meaningfully decline in good times. Corporate borrowing continued even as profits recovered. Household mortgage balances expanded alongside rising property prices rather than stabilising after each cycle.

The numbers reflect this change clearly. In the United States, federal debt stood at roughly 30 percent of GDP in 1980.[3] It did not return to that level after subsequent expansions. Instead, it climbed across cycles and surged after 2008 and again after 2020, now standing several times higher as a share of national income, reaching around 120 percent of GDP in recent years.

A similar pattern emerged across much of the advanced world. After the global financial crisis, total debt did not contract in aggregate. Private retrenchment was offset by public borrowing. Each recovery began with a heavier burden than the one before it, with government debt in the Eurozone, for example, rising from roughly 70 percent of GDP before 2008 to around 90 percent afterward.[4] The pattern became increasingly difficult to ignore. The significance lay less in the quantity than in the consequences.

This shift mattered more than the absolute level of debt. When borrowing rises during stress and falls during recovery, it functions as a counterweight. When it rises in both phases, it becomes structural. Instead of absorbing shocks and then receding, debt remained permanently embedded in the system. Each cycle carried unresolved obligations of the previous one. What had once functioned as temporary support gradually became part of the economy's underlying operating structure.

Once debt ceases to fall during good times, the system loses its self-correcting capacity. Expansion no longer repairs prior excesses. It builds on them. Recessions no longer cleanse balance sheets. They justify additional borrowing. What had once been cyclical became cumulative.

At that point, stability no longer rests on resilience. Instead, it depends on continuation. The economy must grow enough to service expanding obligations, and financial conditions must remain favourable enough to refinance them.

Even relatively modest changes in borrowing costs or growth conditions can then create stress simultaneously across governments, corporations, and households. The scope for policy error narrows as heavily indebted systems become more vulnerable to disruption.

This is the transition from an economy that uses debt to manage shocks to one that depends on debt to function. That distinction is critical. A system that uses debt episodically can still adjust and recover. By contrast, a system that depends on debt continuously becomes vulnerable to any interruption in the flow of credit on which its stability rests.

Once dependence replaces discipline, adjustment ceases to be gradual. It becomes a test of confidence in a structure that requires ever-expanding credit simply to avoid contraction. As dependence deepens, it becomes harder to distinguish genuine economic expansion from growth sustained primarily by borrowing. That distinction becomes increasingly important as economic growth slows and credit expands.

## *Debt as a Substitute for Growth*

The rise of structural borrowing coincided with a slowdown in underlying growth across the advanced world. From the postwar period through the early 1970s, productivity growth in many advanced economies averaged around 3 to 4 percent annually. In the decades after 2008, that pace fell closer to 1 percent or below, with productivity growth in economies such as the United States, the United Kingdom, and the Eurozone often averaging near or below 1 percent in the post-crisis period.[5]

At the same time, demographic tailwinds began to fade. Populations aged. Labour force participation plateaued. Working-age populations began to contract in countries such as Japan and parts of Europe. The economic conditions that had supported decades of rapid expansion gradually became less favourable. The environment had changed.

Yet expectations did not adjust. Living standards were still expected to rise, and asset values to appreciate. Pension promises, healthcare commitments, and public spending trajectories remained anchored to an earlier era of faster expansion. Political systems continued to operate as if those earlier growth rates would persist indefinitely.

Debt increasingly filled the widening gap between slower economic capacity and expectations formed during a period of stronger growth. Where organic growth slowed, credit expansion sustained demand. Household consumption continued even when real income growth weakened, with real wages stagnating across large segments of the population in several advanced economies after the early 2000s. Governments financed spending without matching increases in revenue, with fiscal deficits persisting even during periods of economic expansion. The same incentives shaped business decisions.

Corporations adapted to the same environment. Borrowing financed not only investment, but also share buybacks, mergers, and financial restructuring. In the United States alone, corporate share buybacks reached hundreds of billions of dollars annually in the years preceding the pandemic.[6] Rising asset prices sustained the appearance of prosperity even as productivity growth weakened beneath the surface.

In this environment, borrowing did not merely supplement growth. It replaced it. Expansion increasingly depended on financial conditions rather than underlying output. Asset prices rose faster than wages, with property and equity markets in many advanced economies significantly outpacing income growth over the past two decades. Debt grew faster than income. Economic momentum became increasingly tied to cheap credit, rising valuations, and the ability to refinance existing obligations rather than to broad-based gains in productivity and output.

This substitution altered incentives. When rising credit can preserve stability, the pressure to undertake structural reform diminishes. Difficult adjustments are postponed. Political systems avoid confronting limits. Markets reward continuation over correction until pressures accumulate.

The central issue was not merely that credit expanded. It was that borrowing allowed advanced economies to preserve promises, expectations, and financial valuations built for a faster-growth world that no longer existed .

Similar dynamics have appeared before. In the late 1920s, credit expansion sustained consumption and asset valuations even as income growth slowed. Prosperity persisted until refinancing faltered. In the 1970s, governments relied on borrowing and monetary expansion to maintain growth expectations despite weakening productivity and demographic headwinds. The result was not durable expansion, but stagflation that exposed the limits of debt as a substitute for real growth. These episodes differed in form, but all revealed the limits of relying on borrowing to compensate for slower growth.

The difference today lies in scale and duration. The substitution of borrowing for organic expansion has persisted across multiple cycles and across all major sectors. What began as temporary support has become embedded practice. Debt assumed a different role across society.

Advanced economies no longer simply use debt during periods of weakness. In many cases, they now rely on continued credit expansion to sustain growth, asset prices, fiscal stability, and household consumption simultaneously.

Once growth becomes dependent on expanding credit, the direction of causality reverses. The economy no longer uses borrowing to accelerate expansion; it requires expansion to justify accumulated debt.

When growth weakens under those conditions, the pressure does not remain confined to financial markets. It spreads through public finances, corporate balance sheets, household confidence, and political stability alike.

## *An Economy Locked Together*

Dependence on borrowing did not remain confined to one sector. It spread across governments, corporations, and households, binding them together in ways that reduced flexibility and increased shared vulnerability throughout the system. Each sector responded in its own way.

Governments borrowed to meet rising obligations tied to healthcare, pensions, and social stability. In many advanced economies, public spending commitments expanded even as growth slowed, with age-related spending projected to rise by several percentage points of GDP over the coming decades.[7] Low interest rates made borrowing appear manageable. Political constraints made tax increases and spending cuts difficult. Budget deficits persisted across expansions. Public debt ratios rose steadily rather than falling during good years. The shift was not confined to governments.

Corporations quickly adapted to the same environment. Cheap financing rewarded balance sheet expansion. Borrowed capital funded share buybacks, mergers, and financial restructuring, often supporting valuations more than productive capacity. In several advanced economies, corporate debt as a share of output climbed to record levels even in periods of steady growth, with non-financial corporate debt in the United States rising from roughly 40 percent of GDP in the 1980s to around 70 percent in recent years. Companies became more sensitive to interest rate changes, not less.

Households absorbed the consequences. Housing costs, education expenses, and healthcare spending rose faster than median wages in many countries. Mortgages extended further into the future. Consumer credit shifted from discretionary borrowing to essential bridging.

For a growing share of households, debt ceased to function primarily as a tool for advancement and became part of the cost of remaining economically secure. The mortgage, the student loan, the car payment, and the credit card balance increasingly became permanent features of everyday financial life rather than temporary obligations that could realistically be worked down over time. In countries such as the United Kingdom and Canada, household debt exceeded 100 percent of disposable income.[8]

Once embedded across all sectors, borrowing ceased to be sectoral and became systemic. Governments rely on stable bond markets to finance deficits. Corporations rely on accessible credit to roll over obligations and sustain valuations. Households rely on income stability and affordable interest rates to service mortgages and consumer loans.

Each sector's stability increasingly became dependent on the stability of the others. Governments depend on functioning financial markets. Financial markets depend on central bank credibility. Households depend on stable employment and asset prices. The system became progressively more interconnected and less capable of absorbing disruption in isolation.

This interdependence alters the nature of adjustment. In earlier periods, stress could be absorbed sequentially. Today, high debt levels across all sectors reduce that sequencing. Tightening in one area transmits quickly to the others.

The clearest warning comes from economies where private-sector debt problems were not resolved but instead transferred to the public sector. Japan's experience after 1990 illustrates the consequences. When private-sector borrowing collapsed after the asset bubble burst, public borrowing expanded to offset the contraction. This prevented an immediate collapse but shifted the strain onto the government. More than three decades later, Japan still carries one of the highest public debt burdens in the developed world, with government debt exceeding 230 percent of GDP and a continuing dependence on ultra-low interest rates. The problem was redistributed, not resolved.

The broader economic risk in the current environment is synchronization. When governments, large corporations, and households all carry elevated obligations, a rise in borrowing costs or a fall in asset values affects them simultaneously. What might once have emerged as a contained correction within a single sector increasingly carries the potential to become system-wide strain. Stress no longer remains compartmentalised. It moves rapidly through interconnected balance sheets, financial markets, and public finances.

An economy locked together through shared dependence on credit does not adjust in stages. It adjusts all at once, as pressures that were previously contained emerge together.

## *Stability Through Postponement*

Debt reshaped the meaning of stability. Borrowing smoothed consumption, supported asset prices, and reduced the visible impact of downturns. Shocks that might once have forced rapid adjustment were absorbed, refinanced, or transferred across balance sheets. Markets calmed. Output stabilised. The system appeared resilient. The pressures, however, did not disappear.

But this resilience was conditional. Borrowing did not remove imbalances. It deferred them. Each additional layer of debt reduced short-term volatility while increasing long-term sensitivity. Governments could continue spending without immediate contraction. Corporations could refinance rather than restructure. Households could extend repayment horizons rather than reduce liabilities already accumulated over time.

What appeared stable on the surface increasingly depended on pushing financial pressure further into the future. Problems were not resolved so much as rolled forward.

The global financial crisis marked a decisive expansion of this approach.[9] Central banks lowered policy rates to near zero and expanded balance sheets to unprecedented levels, with the U.S. Federal Reserve's balance sheet growing from under $1 trillion before 2008 to over $4 trillion in the following years, and later approaching $9 trillion after the pandemic.[10] Sovereign borrowing rose sharply as public finances absorbed private-sector losses.

The response prevented a deeper collapse, but it also changed expectations. Financial markets came to assume that severe disruptions would be met with intervention, liquidity support, and lower borrowing costs whenever necessary.

Total debt did not contract in aggregate. It shifted and continued rising. These measures prevented immediate collapse. They also reinforced the principle that financial stress would be countered with accommodation. Markets adapted quickly. Risk premiums compressed. Asset prices recovered and surpassed prior peaks, often within months.

Over time, investors, governments, corporations, and households adjusted their behaviour to the assumption that borrowing would remain cheap and widely available. Financial markets no longer treated ultra-low interest rates as temporary emergency measures. They increasingly treated them as part of the normal structure of the system itself.

Borrowing costs remained historically low for more than a decade, with policy interest rates near zero across much of the advanced world during this period. In this environment, low interest rates ceased to be supportive and became necessary. Financial systems adjusted to the assumption that credit would remain abundant and affordable. What began as temporary support became expected.

Delay gradually became embedded in policy itself. The objective increasingly shifted from resolving imbalances to preventing disruption. Stability came to depend less on underlying resilience and more on the continued ability to refinance obligations at manageable cost.

Over time, it transformed risk rather than eliminating it. The system grew calmer on the surface and more fragile underneath. Periods of calm therefore became increasingly deceptive. The absence of crisis no longer necessarily reflected underlying strength. In many cases, it reflected the continued success of policies designed to postpone adjustment.

History suggests that such arrangements do not unwind gradually. The longer imbalances are deferred, the greater the risk that adjustment arrives more abruptly when confidence, growth, or financial conditions begin to deteriorate. When postponement reaches its limits, adjustment emerges through abrupt repricing of risk, tightening financial conditions, and pressure on political systems that relied on continued calm.

As debt spreads across the entire economy, the options for resolving it become progressively more constrained. Each remaining path carries higher costs than before.

## *The Disappearance of Exit Paths*

At sufficient scale, debt changes the range of possible outcomes. When obligations are modest relative to income, growth, inflation, or fiscal adjustment can gradually reduce burdens. When obligations become large across all sectors simultaneously, those traditional exit paths narrow.

Growth remains the least disruptive solution, but sustained acceleration is difficult in ageing societies with slower productivity gains, particularly in advanced economies where trend growth has often fallen to around 1 to 2 percent in recent decades.[11] The underlying arithmetic has changed.

The conditions that once allowed economies to outgrow debt burdens have weakened considerably. Demographic growth has slowed, productivity gains have weakened, and already elevated debt levels make rapid acceleration far harder to sustain than in earlier decades.

Inflation can erode liabilities, but it carries visible costs and destabilises expectations. Fiscal restraint is politically difficult and often contractionary in the short term. Monetary tightening restores discipline but raises refinancing costs across the entire system, as seen when interest rate increases after 2021 sharply raised debt-servicing pressures across governments, firms, and households. No option remains without significant cost.

Each traditional path now imposes immediate strain. Continued borrowing, by contrast, offers temporary calm. That is what makes the current environment so difficult to escape. The policies that might gradually reduce debt burdens often produce immediate economic and political pain, while continued borrowing postpones pressure and preserves short-term stability. Delay merely changes the timing of adjustment.

This is the defining trap. Debt postpones reckoning, but in doing so narrows the range of viable resolutions. The longer dependence persists, the more abrupt adjustment becomes when refinancing conditions change.

History offers consistent patterns. In the 1930s, excessive leverage resolved through contraction. The inflationary shocks of the 1970s unwound imbalances through rising prices and stagnating growth. After 1990, Japan experienced a prolonged period of economic stagnation instead. Although the form of adjustment differed in each case, the underlying pattern remained similar. High debt progressively reduced economic flexibility until gradual correction became increasingly difficult to sustain. The consequences now extend across the entire system.

Today, elevated debt is broad, persistent, and interconnected across the advanced world, with total economy-wide debt across many advanced economies now representing a historically high share of GDP. That breadth matters. Earlier crises could sometimes be isolated within specific sectors or regions. The current environment is now more synchronised. Governments, corporations, households, and financial markets are now tied together through overlapping dependence on refinancing and easy credit throughout the economy.

That breadth reduces the possibility of isolated adjustment. When stress emerges, it spreads. Debt had become more than a financial tool.

## *Debt as a Governing Principle*

Debt is no longer merely a financial instrument used to manage fluctuations. It has become a governing principle of the modern economic order. Policy is designed around its sustainability. Markets are calibrated to its continuation. Households organise decisions around the assumption that credit will remain accessible and affordable for the foreseeable future.

In practice, stability has increasingly come to mean the uninterrupted servicing and refinancing of accumulated obligations. The system functions smoothly so long as credit remains available, borrowing costs stay manageable, and confidence in refinancing endures throughout the economy.

This dependence reshapes behaviour. Governments avoid actions that could disrupt bond markets. Central banks respond quickly to financial stress. Corporations prioritise liquidity. Households monitor interest rates as closely as wages.

Over time, entire economies adapt psychologically as well as financially to these conditions. Rising asset prices, low borrowing costs, and central bank intervention gradually become embedded assumptions rather than temporary supports.

Financial markets come to depend on sustained liquidity, while public finances increasingly rely on borrowing costs remaining manageable. The system adjusts not to reduce debt, but to preserve its serviceability.

That distinction matters enormously. A system attempting to reduce debt behaves very differently from one trying to sustain it indefinitely. Over time, policy shifts increasingly toward preserving continuation rather than restoring balance. The danger does not lie in borrowing alone. It lies in the confidence that sustains it. Debt remains manageable only while lenders believe it will be repaid and borrowers believe it can be refinanced. Its durability has clear limits.

Once that shared confidence weakens, borrowing no longer stabilises the system in the same way. Instead, it begins to amplify stress. Rising borrowing costs, falling asset values, or tightening credit conditions start transmitting pressure across governments, corporations, households, and financial markets simultaneously. That does not make debt inherently harmful.

Debt has supported genuine progress. It has prevented deeper recessions and preserved social cohesion. It has bought time.[12] But borrowed time is not costless. It postpones adjustment while allowing obligations to continue accumulating beneath the surface.

As obligations accumulate, the scope for painless adjustment diminishes. What began as a temporary response to crisis gradually became embedded in the structure of the system itself. Debt no longer functions primarily as a bridge through periods of stress. In many advanced economies, it has become part of the foundation supporting growth, asset prices, public finances, and household stability.

An economy organised around continuous borrowing can endure for extended periods. But stability built on perpetual refinancing is conditional rather than self-sustaining. The central danger is not simply that debt levels are high. It is that institutions, financial markets, governments, and households have gradually reorganised themselves around the assumption that credit will remain cheap, abundant, and continuously available. The deeper issue lies elsewhere.

The question is no longer how much debt exists. It is whether advanced economies can continue functioning normally without the conditions that allowed debt to expand so easily for so long. The answer depends on how the system responds when those conditions begin to change. The real test begins when long-standing assumptions come under pressure.

History shows that debt-driven systems rarely fail because growth suddenly disappears altogether. More often, they weaken when the mechanisms used to postpone adjustment lose effectiveness or credibility. At that point, even relatively modest disruptions begin carrying wider consequences.

The breaking does not necessarily arrive as a dramatic external shock. It can emerge from within the structure itself, as systems built around continuous refinancing discover that stability was more conditional than permanent all along.

The greatest danger in highly indebted systems is not that fragility suddenly appears. It is that dependence becomes so familiar it no longer feels exceptional. Borrowing, refinancing, and intervention gradually become part of normal economic life. Stability then rests less on resilience than on the continued ability to delay pressures building beneath the surface.

# 7

# THE HIDDEN COST OF STABILITY

Few mechanisms have shaped the stability of advanced economies more decisively than financial repression. It does not announce itself, nor does it require dramatic legislation or visible coercion. Yet for more than a decade, it has influenced how wealth accumulates, how debt is sustained, and how economic calm is preserved. Its apparent success was widely accepted.

For years, this system worked. It allowed heavily indebted governments to refinance at low cost. Asset prices remained supported and volatility subdued. It helped prevent immediate crisis after 2008 and again during the pandemic, creating the impression that stability had been restored when, in reality, it had been carefully maintained rather than restored.

But stability maintained through suppression is not the same as stability built on balance. When borrowing costs are held below inflation for extended periods, debt burdens are reduced not through repayment, but through erosion, as purchasing power declines gradually, savers lose ground over time, and asset owners adapt and often benefit. The structure of the economy shifts in response as financial pressures accumulate.

Most households experience the consequences without ever encountering the term. Savings fail to keep pace with prices, housing rises faster than wages, and debt remains manageable for institutions yet restrictive for families. These outcomes are often described as disconnected symptoms of a complex global economy, yet in practice they are linked by design, forming part of a system that redistributes value quietly but persistently.

## *The Quiet Engine of Modern Economic Stability*

In many advanced economies, cumulative consumer price inflation since 2020 has exceeded cumulative real wage growth, while housing price-to-income ratios in major cities now stand well above their pre-2008 peaks.[1]In the United Kingdom, cumulative inflation between 2020 and 2023 exceeded 20 percent, while real wages remained broadly flat over the same period.[2] At the same time, average house prices have risen to more than eight times median earnings, compared with closer to five times in the early 2000s, the widening gap between income and asset values.[3] The system was about to be tested.

The post-2020 inflation surge did more than strain household budgets. It revealed how dependent the system had become on keeping real borrowing costs suppressed.

Financial repression is not an aberration or policy accident. It is a way of managing a heavily indebted system. It preserves the present by drawing steadily on the future, turning what begins as temporary crisis management into a long-term condition of economic life.

The longer this framework persists, the more stability depends on its continuation. Over time, the system adapts to conditions that were initially presented as temporary. Governments refinance cheaply, markets price assets around low borrowing costs, and households reorganize financial decisions around rising asset values and weaker returns on savings.

Financial repression is therefore not just a technical instrument of monetary policy. It is one of the central mechanisms through which advanced economies have postponed structural adjustment for decades. Its importance lies not only in how it stabilizes debt, but in how it quietly redistributes pressure across the economy. Savers lose purchasing power gradually, younger households face rising barriers to ownership, and institutions become increasingly dependent on conditions that cannot easily be reversed without significant disruption or economic strain.

## *The Mechanics of Financial Repression*

At its simplest, financial repression occurs when governments and central banks keep interest rates below the rate of inflation for extended periods. The result is straightforward. Money held in cash or low-risk assets retains its nominal value but loses purchasing power in real terms. Debt, by contrast, becomes easier to carry because it is repaid in money worth less than when it was borrowed in real terms over time.

The transfer does not require legislation or explicit taxation. It happens through arithmetic. If inflation runs at four percent while government bonds yield two percent, two percent of purchasing power shifts each year from those holding savings to those carrying debt. Over a decade, the cumulative effect is substantial. What appears stable on a statement reflects steady erosion beneath the surface over long periods. The change is gradual enough that many barely notice it.

For households, the process often feels confusing rather than dramatic. A savings account may still show the same nominal balance, yet the purchasing power behind that balance declines steadily over time. The number remains intact while the value quietly erodes. The source of that erosion is often overlooked.

Following the global financial crisis, real yields on government bonds across much of the developed world remained negative for years.[4] At various points during the 2010s, trillions of dollars of sovereign debt offered returns below inflation.[5] The distortion became even more pronounced.

At its peak in 2020, more than 15 trillion dollars of global bonds traded at negative nominal yields, meaning investors were effectively paying governments for the privilege of lending to them.[6] Savers accepted these conditions not because they were attractive, but because alternatives were limited and volatility elsewhere appeared risky for prolonged periods.

In the United States, real yields on 10-year Treasury securities remained negative for much of the period between 2011 and 2021,reinforcing the steady transfer from savers to borrowers.[7] Over time, this reduced the incentive to save and pushed households toward riskier assets in search of returns. It also contributed to rising asset prices, further entrenching the financial system on continued asset appreciation.

The consequences extend beyond individual portfolios. Each period in which inflation exceeds safe returns reduces the real value of accumulated savings while easing the pressure on heavily indebted governments and institutions. Over time, this reshapes incentives. Saving becomes less rewarding. Borrowing becomes less burdensome. Capital flows toward assets that promise protection rather than toward projects that promise productivity. The consequences are unevenly distributed.

Debtors benefit without explicit forgiveness. Savers bear costs without explicit taxation. Adjustment occurs through gradual dilution rather than confrontation, allowing the system to evolve without triggering immediate resistance.

Because the losses are dispersed and incremental, resistance is muted. Because the relief to debtors is indirect, the policy rarely appears controversial. By the time distortions become widely recognized, they are already embedded in household finances, pension systems, and public finances. Reversal then becomes risky, not because repression was harmless, but because the system has reorganized itself around it.

## *Why Governments Turn to Financial Repression*

Financial repression does not begin with ideology. It begins with arithmetic. When public and private debt levels are high, policy options narrow quickly, and governments are forced to choose between alternatives that all carry visible economic and political costs. The problem is that every available path carries costs that policymakers would prefer to avoid.

Default threatens the banking system and risks financial contagion. Sharp austerity can trigger recession, weaken growth, and provoke political backlash. Rapid growth, often presented as the ideal solution, is difficult to engineer in mature, ageing economies where productivity gains tend to be slower and demographic support weaker than in earlier decades.

Each conventional path therefore carries risks that are immediate and visible. In contrast, holding interest rates below inflation offers a quieter alternative. Debt burdens shrink in real terms without formal restructuring. Governments refinance at manageable cost. Financial institutions avoid large write-downs. The appearance of continuity is preserved while the adjustment takes place gradually through erosion rather than confrontation.

This approach is not new. After the Second World War, public debt in several advanced economies exceeded 100 percent of GDP. Rather than pursue destabilizing fiscal contraction or risk default, authorities maintained borrowing costs below inflation for much of the late 1940s and 1950s.

In both the United States and the United Kingdom, real government borrowing costs were negative for extended periods. Debt ratios declined over time, supported by strong growth, expanding industrial capacity, and favourable demographics. Younger populations entered the workforce. Productivity rose steadily. Industrial output expanded. Inflation reduced debt burdens while growth absorbed them. The strategy succeeded because the broader economy was expanding rapidly. Debt was gradually reduced within a context of rising incomes, increasing productivity, and favourable demographics.

Today the backdrop is far less supportive. Debt levels are high not only in governments but across corporations and households. Populations are ageing rather than expanding. Productivity growth has slowed across much of the developed world. Entitlement commitments are rising as demographic support ratios weaken and growth becomes harder to sustain.

In many advanced economies, public debt ratios now exceed levels once associated with wartime mobilization, but without the same growth tailwinds that followed. Across advanced economies, total debt, combining government, corporate, and household liabilities, now exceeds 250 to 300 percent of GDP in several cases.[8] These levels reflect systemic leverage far beyond post-war norms.

Under these conditions, financial repression stabilizes debt more than it reduces it. It prevents immediate crisis, but it does not restore balance. The longer rates remain suppressed, the more fiscal planning, asset pricing, and private borrowing assume their continuation as the norm.

What was once a bridge back to sustainability risks becoming a permanent fixture. Governments rely on repression because the alternatives are disruptive, but reliance changes the structure of the system itself. When stability depends on keeping borrowing costs below their natural level, policy ceases to manage the economy and begins to shield it. Shielding, extended for too long, weakens the capacity to absorb shocks. The same calculations that once bought time begin to constrain it.

## *From Emergency Tool to Permanent Framework*

In the modern era, financial repression returned in subtler form. Explicit capital controls and formal interest rate ceilings largely disappeared. In their place emerged a combination of ultra-low policy rates, large-scale asset purchases, regulatory incentives, and institutional dependence. The objective, however, remained largely unchanged: to keep borrowing costs low enough for highly indebted economies to remain stable.

Following the global financial crisis, central banks reduced policy rates to near zero and kept them there for more than a decade in several major economies.[9] Balance sheets expanded dramatically. In the United States, the Federal Reserve's assets rose from under 1 trillion dollars before 2008 to nearly 9 trillion dollars at their peak, reflecting an unprecedented monetary support.[10] Other major central banks followed suit on a comparable scale, though with variations.

The European Central Bank and the Bank of Japan followed similar paths relative to the size of their economies. At the same time, regulatory frameworks encouraged banks, insurers, and pension funds to hold government debt regardless of yield, helping sustain demand for low-yield assets while embedding suppression more deeply within the financial system.

Each measure could be defended as a response to crisis. Together, they created an environment in which borrowing costs were persistently suppressed and safe returns persistently diminished. Global debt levels rose even as interest rates fell to historic lows. Cheap refinancing became an assumption rather than an opportunity. Global debt rose from approximately 200 trillion dollars in 2008 to more than 300 trillion dollars by the early 2020s.[11] Debt expanded even as borrowing costs declined, reinforcing the dependence on continued suppression.

Markets adapted quickly. Governments extended maturities and locked in low rates. Corporations increased leverage to fund buybacks, acquisitions, and refinancing. Pension funds adjusted return assumptions and increased exposure to riskier assets. Asset prices rose, not only because fundamentals improved, but because borrowing costs remained unusually low for years. What began as emergency intervention gradually became a permanent feature of economic policy.

Over time, economic behaviour adjusted to that environment. Investment models, fiscal projections, and household expectations increasingly assumed that low borrowing costs would continue indefinitely. The longer suppression persisted, the more debt structures, asset valuations, and financial planning depended on it. Reversal therefore ceased to mean a return to normal and increasingly came to signify strain. The system had become increasingly sensitive to change.

The rise in interest rates during the early 2020s quickly exposed underlying vulnerabilities. Debt servicing costs increased. Asset valuations adjusted. Financial institutions exposed to long-term interest-rate risk experienced losses. Public budgets absorbed higher interest expenditure. The speed of the adjustment revealed how deeply the system had reorganized around prior conditions. An economy conditioned on suppressed borrowing costs is not easily weaned from them.

What was designed to stabilize the system became the condition under which the system could function. Stability increasingly relied on continued intervention rather than organic balance. Those policies reshaped economic behaviour.

## *How Financial Repression Shapes Behaviour*

When saving no longer preserves value, behaviour changes. For decades, saving was viewed as deferred consumption rewarded over time. Interest compensated patience. It provided security and optionality. Under prolonged financial repression, that relationship weakens. When inflation outpaces safe returns, discipline is no longer rewarded. Money held conservatively loses ground.

Capital does not remain idle in that environment. It searches for protection. Real estate, equities, and alternative assets become substitutes for traditional saving. Prices rise not only because underlying prospects improve, but because avoiding erosion becomes the primary objective. This shift is often defensive rather than optimistic. Assets are purchased not because returns appear exceptional, but because holding cash or low-yield instruments guarantees loss in real terms.

Over time, the line between investment and preservation blurs. The distributional effects are significant. In the United States and other advanced economies, equity ownership is concentrated among wealthier households. In the United States, the top 10 percent of households own roughly 85 to 90 percent of equities.[12] Gains from rising asset prices therefore accrue disproportionately to those already invested. The effects are not limited to equities.

At the same time, housing price growth in many advanced economies has exceeded income growth for more than two decades. In cities such as London, New York, and Sydney, house price-to-income ratios have doubled or more since the early 2000s.[13] The result is a widening gap between those who benefit from asset inflation and those who are priced out of it. Debt expands alongside this shift. Governments refinance at suppressed rates. Corporations borrow cheaply. Households rely increasingly on leverage to access housing.

Borrowing becomes not only attractive, but increasingly necessary to participate. Housing markets, fiscal planning, asset pricing, and household financial decisions all begin to assume that low borrowing costs will continue. Over time, behaviour reorganizes around that assumption. The economy becomes less driven by productive expansion and more dependent on maintaining the financial conditions that support asset values and debt sustainability

## *The Redistribution of Risk*

Financial repression does not eliminate risk. It shifts it. When safe assets fail to preserve purchasing power, investors move outward along the risk spectrum. Pension funds increase exposure to equities, private credit, and alternative assets.[14] Insurance companies extend duration or accept lower credit quality. Banks hold sovereign debt at low yields while operating with compressed margins. In several advanced economies, pension funds now allocate more than 60 percent of their portfolios to equities and alternative assets. These shifts reflect the structural pressure created by suppressed real returns.

Households face a different version of the same pressure. Savings accounts offer little protection against inflation. Bonds provide limited real income. Participation in financial markets becomes necessary to preserve wealth. The distinction between prudent investing and forced risk-taking begins to narrow. At the aggregate level, markets may appear stable. Volatility can remain subdued for extended periods. Markets may appear calm even as risk continues to migrate beneath the surface. The appearance can be misleading.

Yet beneath that surface, financial cushions erode. Pension systems rely on optimistic return assumptions. Households depend on rising asset values to offset stagnant income growth.

Risk that once sat more visibly with governments and central banks gradually disperses across institutions, pension systems, and households. Stability at the top is increasingly preserved through vulnerability below. When shocks arrive, they meet institutions and households operating with reduced margins of safety. The very policies designed to prevent abrupt adjustment gradually weaken the safeguards that once contained it.

In this way, repression alters not only who bears risk, but how the system responds to stress.

## *The Addiction Problem*

The longer financial repression persists, the more difficult it becomes to reverse. Low interest rates reshape balance sheets over time, and economic actors adjust gradually to conditions that appear temporary but become structural. The danger is not simply that financial repression distorts markets. It is that, over time, the system becomes unable to function comfortably without it, even in expansion.

Governments issue debt that looks affordable under suppressed borrowing costs. Corporations build capital structures dependent on regular refinancing at low rates. Asset valuations incorporate assumptions about ongoing monetary accommodation. Pension systems project returns that require sustained exposure to increasingly volatile financial markets.

Each year that rates remain compressed, these assumptions harden. What begins as temporary support becomes embedded in fiscal planning, corporate financing, and household expectations throughout the economy.

When interest rates rise, even modestly, the effects multiply. Public debt servicing costs increase. Corporate refinancing becomes more expensive. Asset prices adjust as future earnings are valued more conservatively. Institutions holding long-duration assets experience losses. Fiscal space narrows as interest expenditure absorbs a larger share of budgets. In highly indebted advanced economies, even small changes in borrowing costs translate into significant shifts in public finances.

In the United States, for example, a one percentage point increase in interest rates can add hundreds of billions of dollars to annual government interest costs over time.[15] This sensitivity illustrates how deeply the system has become conditioned on low borrowing costs. What once would have been considered a return to normal becomes a source of strain.

Policymakers therefore face a narrowing set of choices. Raising rates to restore price stability risks destabilizing public finances, asset markets, and heavily indebted institutions. Keeping rates low may preserve short-term calm, but it allows inflationary pressure and financial distortions to persist. By the early 2020s, interest payments had become one of the fastest-growing areas of public spending in many advanced economies.

Over time, dependence replaces flexibility. Stability relies less on the economy's capacity to absorb shocks and more on the expectation that intervention will continue. Markets begin to price not just economic fundamentals, but expected policy support. An economy structured around sustained suppression is not easily recalibrated. Adjustment that might once have unfolded gradually now compresses into shorter, sharper episodes. Delay makes the eventual adjustment larger.

The longer normalization is delayed, the greater the eventual repricing of debt, assets, and expectations. What stabilizes the system in the short term reduces **room** to manoeuvre in the long term. Each intervention narrows the scope for the next, and repression that begins as a bridge becomes a constraint.

## *Stability Without Resolution*

Financial repression suppresses visible stress. Low borrowing costs support asset prices, liquidity dampens volatility, and financial markets can remain steady even when underlying imbalances persist. Calm therefore becomes evidence of success. Yet calm achieved through sustained distortion differs fundamentally from stability grounded in balance.

When price signals are muted for long periods, capital does not necessarily flow to its most productive uses. Instead, it flows to what can be financed most easily, allowing debt to accumulate faster than productive capacity while asset values expand more quickly than incomes. Growth continues, but it increasingly depends on financial conditions rather than broad improvements in productivity, wages, or investment efficiency.

Since the global financial crisis, productivity growth across much of the developed world has been weaker than in previous decades, even as public and private debt levels continued to rise. Across advanced economies, productivity growth has slowed to around 1 percent or less in recent years, compared with closer to 2 to 3 percent in earlier decades.[16]

Economic expansion has persisted, but it has relied more heavily on credit conditions and asset appreciation than on broad gains in output per worker. Over the same period, debt has continued to expand at a significantly faster pace than output. This widening gap reflects an imbalance between financial claims and real economic activity, leaving economies more financially sensitive even while appearing outwardly stable. The damage is often cumulative.

The result is not collapse, but gradual erosion. Flexibility declines, fiscal space narrows, and monetary policy becomes increasingly constrained by the side effects of its own past actions. Each intervention reduces the margin for the next. The system appears stable, yet its capacity to absorb disruption weakens. The absence of crisis is often mistaken for proof that the system remains sustainable, even though stability built on suppressed borrowing costs remains conditional and fragile.

Remove the support, and strain surfaces quickly. Maintain the support, and the distortions deepen further. In this environment, the line between management and maintenance begins to blur. Policymakers no longer guide the economy back toward balance, but instead work to prevent visible fracture as imbalances accumulate beneath the surface. Stability without resolution therefore does not eliminate adjustment. Instead, it postpones it, concentrates it, and ultimately makes the eventual correction more difficult to manage when it comes.

## *When Financial Repression Reaches Its Limits*

Financial repression is often presented as the least disruptive option. Compared to default, austerity, or systemic crisis, gradual erosion appears manageable. During periods of acute stress, suppressing borrowing costs can prevent disorder and buy time. Yet the limits to repression are not ideological or moral. They are structural, and they follow a recognizable pattern.

Repression relies on three conditions. Inflation must remain contained, investor confidence in sovereign debt must persist, and political tolerance for declining purchasing power must endure. When any of these conditions weaken, the strategy becomes harder to sustain. If inflation accelerates beyond comfort, central banks face pressure to raise rates, and higher rates increase public debt servicing costs while exposing leverage across corporate and household balance sheets.

Between 2021 and 2023, central banks raised policy rates at the fastest pace in four decades, and this tightening exposed how sensitive financial systems had become to higher borrowing costs after years of suppression.[17] Government interest expenditure rose sharply, bond prices declined, equity markets corrected, and portfolios built on years of low-rate assumptions came under pressure. Financial institutions exposed to long-duration assets experienced stress, demonstrating both the scale of dependency and the difficulty of recalibration.

Investor confidence introduces another limit. Advanced economies have long benefited from deep capital markets and reserve currency status, allowing governments to refinance large debts cheaply. But confidence rests on belief. It depends on the belief that institutions remain capable of managing both inflation and fiscal sustainability. If that belief weakens, investors demand higher compensation for risk, and borrowing costs rise not because policymakers choose them, but because markets impose them. Markets are not the only constraint.

Political tolerance is equally finite. Gradual erosion is sustainable only while households perceive stability as broadly shared. When asset inflation benefits a minority and real incomes stagnate for many, trust in the system declines. At that point, repression no longer appears as quiet stabilization. It begins to resemble a system that protects financial structures while shifting the burden outward toward households and savers. Each intervention leaves a legacy.

The deeper issue is cumulative. Each cycle of suppression followed by tightening leaves the system more leveraged and more sensitive than before. Debt ratios remain elevated, asset valuations embed expectations of continued support, and fiscal commitments expand as the room for manoeuvre narrows. Financial repression can delay adjustment for years, even decades, but it cannot eliminate arithmetic. Debt must either be serviced, inflated away, restructured, or grown out of. When growth is modest and demographics are unfavourable, the remaining options carry increasing strain, and the machinery that once absorbed shocks begins to transmit them. The economy becomes more vulnerable to shocks it once absorbed.

What matters most is not any single crisis, but the gradual weakening of resilience beneath the appearance of calm. Stability preserved through sustained distortion eventually confronts its boundary, not because policymakers intend failure, but because constraints tighten and accumulated imbalances surface together. Change often arrives by degrees.

The consequences unfold gradually enough that they begin to feel normal. Saving no longer builds security as reliably as it once did. Housing increasingly separates ownership from income. Younger households delay milestones that earlier generations often took for granted, while older households become more dependent on rising asset values to preserve financial stability. The system continues to function, but the character of stability begins to change. Economic calm is maintained, yet resilience weakens beneath the surface as households adapt to slower progress, higher costs, and growing financial insecurity.

When stability rests on suppression rather than balance, its end is rarely sudden, but it is rarely gentle. The constraints tighten gradually, the margins narrow, and the mechanisms that once sustained calm begin to lose their effectiveness. What once absorbed shocks begins to amplify them, and what once appeared stable begins to reveal its underlying fragility.

What appears stable at the national level increasingly feels fragile at the personal level. And as that gap widens, the foundations of long-term social and economic stability begin to erode from within.

# 8

# PROFITS WITHOUT PRODUCTION

For much of the past four decades, rising corporate profits have been treated as proof that advanced economies remain fundamentally sound. When growth appeared uneven, profits reassured. When wages stalled, profits suggested efficiency. When debt climbed, profits implied that businesses were strong enough to manage it. Corporate earnings became one of the central indicators used to defend the idea that the system still worked. The message spread quickly through financial markets.

Markets reinforced that belief. Strong quarterly results lifted equity prices. Expanding valuations signalled confidence. Political leaders cited record profits as evidence of national competitiveness. Even during periods of weak investment and modest wage growth, profitability offered reassurance. As long as corporate earnings remained strong, many assumed the broader economy remained healthy beneath the surface.

In the decades after the Second World War, rising earnings were closely tied to production. Firms invested in machinery, infrastructure, research, and labour to expand capacity. Higher profits typically reflected stronger demand, greater efficiency, or genuine innovation. Productivity gains translated into wage growth, and wage growth sustained consumption. Corporate success and economic strength moved broadly together, reinforcing a cycle in which investment, wages, and growth supported one another.

Over time, however, that relationship began to change. Corporate profits continued to rise, but they became increasingly disconnected from the expansion of productive capacity. Earnings remained strong even as investment weakened, productivity slowed, and wage growth lost momentum across many advanced economies. What profits appeared to signal and what was actually happening beneath the surface gradually moved further apart in important economic ways.

## *The Great Divergence: Profits and Production*

In the United States, corporate profits as a share of GDP rose from roughly 7 percent in the early postwar period to peaks exceeding 11 percent in the decade after the 2008 financial crisis.[1] At the same time, labour's share of national income moved in the opposite direction, falling from around 65 percent in the 1970s to closer to 57 percent in recent years.[2]

The divergence extended beyond income distribution. Productivity growth, which averaged roughly 2 to 3 percent annually in the postwar decades, slowed markedly after the mid-2000s, while median real wages advanced far more slowly than headline earnings.[3] Corporate profitability remained strong, but the broader economic gains that once accompanied rising profits became weaker and more uneven.

The divergence is not limited to the United States. Across advanced economies, profits recovered rapidly after 2008, while investment, productivity, and wage growth recovered far more gradually. Corporate margins expanded even as business investment remained comparatively weak, suggesting that profitability was increasingly being sustained through financial efficiency rather than productive expansion. The historical relationship between rising profits and broad-based economic improvement gradually began to loosen across many advanced economies. The meaning of strong profits also changed. Profits came to reflect financial conditions more than economic strength..

This shift matters because profits have served as one of the final signals of resilience. If governments run persistent deficits and households borrow more to sustain living standards, rising corporate earnings can still be cited as evidence that the underlying economy remains healthy. As long as profits continue rising, deeper structural weaknesses are easier to dismiss or postpone.

But when profits grow independently of production and capacity, they no longer confirm strength in the way they once did. Instead, profitability can begin to reflect a different set of forces: financial strategy, pricing power, cost compression, and access to inexpensive funding rather than expanding output or rising productivity, or long-term investment.

For years, record profits were used institutionally and politically to argue that structural reform was unnecessary. Strong earnings were treated as evidence that globalisation, financialisation, and monetary accommodation were working as intended. High margins helped sustain confidence even as debt levels rose, investment weakened, and inequality widened. Profitability dulled urgency. Imbalances in debt, investment, and income distribution were acknowledged but not seriously confronted. The adjustment was merely postponed.

An economy can sustain this arrangement for a time. Earnings can remain elevated. Markets can remain confident. But when profitability becomes detached from the expansion of real capacity, profits stop functioning as reliable indicators of underlying resilience. Instead, they become increasingly dependent on favourable financing conditions and investor optimism. That dependence matters because it reduces flexibility. When borrowing costs rise or confidence weakens, adjustment moves more quickly through balance sheets, investment decisions, and employment.

If corporate profits have been one of the pillars supporting the perception of stability, then understanding what now drives those profits becomes essential. The issue is no longer simply whether firms remain profitable. The deeper question is whether those profits still reflect durable economic strength, or whether they rest on foundations that are less secure than they appear. That distinction becomes increasingly important as financial conditions grow less supportive and growth becomes harder to sustain.

If profits remain strong while growth weakens, debt rises, and investment disappoints, then profitability alone can no longer be taken as proof of economic health. Understanding how those profits are generated becomes increasingly important to understanding the stability of the system itself.

## *From Production to Financial Engineering*

If profits have detached from production, the next question is why. The answer lies in how the financial environment changed after the late 1990s and especially after 2008. For more than a decade after the global financial crisis, interest rates across advanced economies were pushed toward zero while central bank balance sheets expanded rapidly. Large firms could borrow at exceptionally low rates, changing the incentives that shaped corporate behaviour.

This altered corporate behaviour in ways that were entirely rational under the circumstances. When capital is inexpensive and abundant, borrowing becomes attractive not only for expansion but also for restructuring balance sheets and supporting shareholder returns. Companies discovered that issuing debt to repurchase their own shares could lift earnings per share even if total profits did not grow. By reducing the number of shares outstanding, reported profitability improved mechanically, and markets rewarded the result because higher earnings per share often translated into stronger valuations.

Between 2010 and 2022, companies in the S&P 500 returned more than six trillion dollars to shareholders through buybacks.[4] In several years, repurchases exceeded spending on new plants, equipment, and research. The emphasis gradually shifted from expanding productive capacity toward supporting valuations and sustaining shareholder returns.

None of this required fraud or recklessness. It required only a financial environment that rewarded immediate returns more consistently than uncertain long-term investment. Executive compensation structures reinforced the shift. Pay packages tied closely to share price performance encouraged strategies that boosted earnings per share quickly and predictably, making debt-financed buybacks particularly attractive compared with capital projects carrying longer time horizons and greater uncertainty. When borrowing costs rise, however, the picture changes quickly, exposing how dependent corporate earnings had become on cheap and abundant credit.

Corporate debt reflected this transition. In the United States, non-financial corporate debt rose from roughly 40 percent of GDP before the 2008 crisis to over 50 percent in the years that followed.[5] Similar patterns appeared across several advanced economies, indicating that the shift toward financial engineering was not confined to a single market but reflected a broader structural trend.

At the level of individual firms, the strategy made sense. Cheap debt supported valuations, strengthened earnings metrics, and rewarded shareholders. At the level of the system, however, the consequences became more complicated.

Capital was increasingly circulated within financial markets rather than extended into productive expansion. Balance sheets grew heavier. Equity bases narrowed through repurchases. Firms became more exposed to changes in interest rates and credit conditions. Corporate resilience became more dependent on continued access to inexpensive funding and stable investor confidence during this period.

In earlier postwar decades, investment recoveries were rapid and sustained, reinforcing productivity growth that averaged above 2 percent annually. By contrast, the recovery in non-residential investment after 2008 was among the slowest in modern economic history.[6] Profits rebounded quickly, but productive expansion lagged behind, widening the gap between financial performance and underlying productive capacity across much of the broader economy.

That distinction matters during periods of stress. When profits are anchored in expanding capacity, downturns can often be absorbed through retained earnings, accumulated capital, and stronger balance sheets. When profits depend more heavily on financial strategy and favourable credit conditions, downturns spread more quickly into valuations, borrowing costs, and employment decisions. The effects become more widespread.

What had once strengthened resilience gradually evolved into a source of sensitivity. The corporate sector still appeared profitable, but its stability became increasingly tied to financial conditions that could not remain permanently supportive.

## *Buybacks and the Shift in Corporate Finance*

Share buybacks became one of the clearest expressions of the shift in corporate finance. They reshaped how companies allocated capital and how profitability was interpreted by markets. Rather than expanding productive capacity, firms increasingly directed cash toward supporting earnings per share, valuations, and shareholder returns.

A share buyback occurs when a company uses cash, or borrowed funds, to repurchase its own shares from investors. By reducing the number of shares outstanding, earnings per share rise even if total profits remain unchanged. This mechanical effect can lift valuations and improve performance metrics without requiring additional production, investment, or hiring.

In earlier decades, corporate profits were more closely tied to expanding capacity. Firms invested in factories, equipment, research, and workforce growth to increase output. A growing share of corporate capital, however, gradually shifted toward financial management rather than productive expansion and long-term investment. Instead of building new assets, companies increasingly used excess cash or borrowed funds to return capital to shareholders and support share prices.

This shift also changed corporate balance sheets. Traditionally, firms strengthened their financial position by accumulating assets and retained earnings. Share buybacks reversed part of that process. Equity was reduced as shares were retired, while debt often increased when buybacks were financed through borrowing. The result was a corporate structure that appeared efficient during periods of stability but became more sensitive to changes in borrowing costs and market conditions.

Between 2010 and 2022, companies in the S&P 500 repurchased more than six trillion dollars of their own shares.[7] In multiple years, total buybacks exceeded capital expenditures. Cash that might once have funded additional factories, long-term research, or workforce expansion was increasingly directed toward supporting share prices and shareholder returns.

This shift coincided with a steady rise in corporate borrowing. Low interest rates made debt inexpensive. Bond markets remained highly receptive. Firms could issue long-term debt at historically low yields and use the proceeds to boost reported earnings, increasing the emphasis on supporting valuations rather than expanding productive capacity.

When shares are repurchased, the equity base contracts and earnings per share increase even if total net income remains unchanged. Valuations often rise as a result, especially when executive pay is tied closely to share prices. Investors benefit from appreciation and reduced share supply, reinforcing incentives across management and financial markets to continue buybacks. The pattern became deeply embedded

Over time, these incentives reshaped corporate balance sheets. Debt levels climbed while equity bases narrowed. The ratio of debt to earnings increased across many sectors. In favourable conditions, this configuration appeared highly efficient. When revenues remained stable and borrowing costs low, higher indebtedness magnified returns, strengthening the appeal of financial engineering relative to long-term investment. The strategy appeared efficient because easy credit concealed many of the risks until conditions changed.

The vulnerability becomes visible when financial conditions begin to tighten. As interest rates rise, refinancing becomes more expensive. Firms carrying large debt burdens face higher servicing costs. If earnings weaken simultaneously, pressure compounds quickly. Because equity buffers have been reduced, there is less internal capacity to absorb shocks.

Hiring slows. Investment plans are postponed. Cost-cutting accelerates. What initially appeared to be disciplined balance-sheet management can then become a mechanism through which tightening spreads more rapidly across the broader economy. The same practices take on a different meaning.

What appears during expansion as financial efficiency can become, during tightening, a source of fragility. The issue is not that buybacks are inherently reckless. The issue is that prolonged periods of inexpensive credit encouraged corporate structures that became increasingly dependent on stable financing conditions, rising valuations, and continued market confidence.

## *The Breaking Mechanism*

For more than a decade, corporate profitability depended heavily on favourable financing conditions. Low borrowing costs allowed firms to refinance existing debt easily, issue new bonds, and sustain buybacks without placing immediate strain on cash flow. As long as credit remained inexpensive and widely available, the system appeared stable.

The arrangement worked while interest rates remained low, credit stayed widely available, and demand did not weaken sharply. But systems built around cheap financing become more vulnerable once those conditions begin to reverse.

If borrowing costs rise, debt service expenses increase. Firms that rolled over obligations at extremely low rates face materially higher refinancing costs. Margins compress even if revenues remain stable, as strategies that once supported earnings begin to weaken them, reinforcing the effects.

Pressure intensifies if revenues soften at the same time. Companies must then choose between reducing investment, slowing hiring, cutting employment, or suspending shareholder returns. Falling valuations tighten financial conditions further by increasing the effective cost of capital across the economy.

The adjustment does not remain confined to financial markets. As earnings weaken and equity prices decline, balance sheets deteriorate. Credit spreads widen. Investment plans are delayed. Hiring slows. Layoffs follow. Financial stress begins moving outward into the broader economy.

Reduced hiring and weaker wage growth place pressure on household income. Consumption softens. Lower consumption feeds back into corporate revenues, reinforcing the slowdown. Tax receipts decline as profits and employment weaken, placing further strain on public finances. What began as pressure within the corporate sector spreads through the broader economy.

In previous downturns, central banks could cut interest rates aggressively and expand balance sheets without generating major inflationary pressures. Today, however, higher public debt levels and periods of persistent inflation constrain that response. Fiscal authorities face heavier interest burdens, while political tolerance for large-scale rescues has weakened. The capacity to stabilise another broad shock through policy alone is now more limited than it was in 2008.

The corporate sector was once viewed as a source of economic resilience. Increasingly, however, it has become a channel through which financial tightening spreads more quickly. Balance sheets built around inexpensive funding and stable valuations become more exposed when financial conditions change abruptly.

Because adjustment becomes compressed, deterioration can accelerate quickly. What once appeared stable begins to reveal how dependent corporate profitability had become on easy credit, market confidence, and continued monetary support. That is when stability begins to weaken.

## *When Corporate Profits Weaken Economic Resilience*

When profitability depends less on expanding output and more on financial strategy, the effects extend well beyond corporate balance sheets. Investment supports productivity. Productivity supports wages. Wages support consumption. When investment weakens over long periods, that chain gradually begins to weaken as well, slowly eroding one of the central mechanisms that sustains economic resilience.

Across several advanced economies, labour's share of national income has declined since the late twentieth century even as corporate margins expanded.[8] Corporate profitability recovered strongly after 2008, while wage growth recovered far more slowly, widening the gap between corporate performance and household income growth. The gains were not shared equally. The difference reflects more than income.

The distribution of financial assets magnifies the divide. In many advanced economies, the majority of equities are held by the top decile of households.[9] When financial markets rise, the gains accrue disproportionately to those who already own most financial assets, concentrating wealth and reinforcing inequality.

As wages advance more slowly than housing, healthcare, education, and other essential costs, households adapt. Borrowing fills part of the gap. Household debt as a share of disposable income increased significantly in the decades leading up to and following the 2008 crisis across a number of advanced economies, reflecting a growing reliance on credit to maintain living standards for many households.[10]

The pattern increasingly mirrored developments within the corporate sector. Firms relied more heavily on debt to sustain earnings and valuations. Households relied more heavily on debt to sustain living standards and consumption. In both cases, borrowing increasingly substituted for organic income growth.

That parallel matters because it creates vulnerability across multiple parts of the economy at the same time. When both corporations and households become more sensitive to credit conditions, tightening reverberates more broadly through the system and the wider economy.

Corporate retrenchment weakens employment and wage growth. Weaker household income slows consumption. Slower consumption feeds back into corporate revenues and profitability. The adjustment reinforces itself, creating a feedback loop that amplifies economic slowdowns and weakens resilience across the broader economy.

What may appear efficient at the level of individual firms can produce very different outcomes at the level of the system. Strategies that support profitability during long periods of inexpensive credit can also reduce the economy's ability to absorb shocks once financial conditions tighten.

The issue is not simply that corporate profits remain high while wages lag behind. The deeper concern is that weak investment, slower productivity growth, heavier debt burdens, and rising inequality gradually erode the foundations that once allowed advanced economies to absorb pressure more effectively during downturns. The appearance of resilience can persist for long periods under these conditions. The challenge is that stability becomes increasingly dependent on factors that may prove less durable than they first appear.

## *Stability Without Strength*

For years, rising corporate profits reassured investors and policymakers that advanced economies remained durable. Markets could remain calm even when underlying growth weakened, because as long as financing conditions stayed supportive, asset prices continued rising and confidence held.

Yet the ability of an economy to withstand shocks depends on more than elevated valuations and strong quarterly earnings. It depends on productive depth, balanced balance sheets, rising incomes, and the capacity to absorb periods of stress without requiring continuous intervention.

Each round of monetary support stabilised markets. Each period of low interest rates encouraged additional borrowing. Corporate strategies adapted accordingly, gradually reinforcing dependence on inexpensive credit, supportive liquidity conditions, and stable investor sentiment.

Over time, that adaptation reduced flexibility. Even moderate increases in borrowing costs began producing outsized effects once debt levels became elevated and balance sheets were increasingly structured around inexpensive funding.

The appearance of stability could therefore persist for long periods. But beneath that stability, sensitivity continued building. When financial conditions eventually changed, adjustment accelerated across firms simultaneously. Strategies that appeared efficient during expansion became more difficult to sustain during periods of tightening. Firms that had adapted to inexpensive credit suddenly faced a financial environment that was far less forgiving.

This is one of the central vulnerabilities of debt-dependent systems. Stability becomes increasingly conditional on maintaining the financial environment that supports it. The longer supportive conditions persist, the more behaviour adapts around them and the harder adjustment becomes once those conditions reverse.

What once appeared as resilience can gradually reveal itself as dependency. Profits remain strong, markets remain elevated, and confidence remains intact, yet the underlying capacity to absorb disruption quietly weakens beneath the surface.

# PART III

# THE HUMAN COST

# 9

# WHEN SAVING NO LONGER WORKS

For much of the postwar era, saving was not merely a personal habit. It was one of the quiet stabilizers of advanced economies. Households set money aside, earned modest returns, and built resilience over time. That resilience mattered not only for families but for the broader economy. When shocks arrived, accumulated savings absorbed part of the impact. The system relied on this reservoir of caution.

For ordinary households, the arrangement felt dependable. Saving was grounded in a simple logic. Income earned through work could be preserved without speculation. Bank deposits and government bonds generated returns above inflation in most years from the 1950s through the early 1980s.[1] Real interest rates in the United States, the United Kingdom, and other advanced economies were generally positive. A saver who avoided risk could still maintain purchasing power. Compounding worked in their favour. The reward was not dramatic wealth, but steady security. The effects extended beyond individual households.

This arrangement reinforced social stability. Prudence was credible because it delivered predictable outcomes. Effort translated into accumulation. Time strengthened balance sheets. Financial planning did not require sophisticated strategies or exposure to volatile markets. Risk-taking was available, but it was not required for financial security.

That relationship has weakened profoundly. Saving remains responsible behaviour, yet its outcomes feel far less certain. Money set aside no longer carries the same promise of preservation. The connection between restraint and protection has loosened. Caution no longer guarantees reassurance.

This shift is not cultural or psychological. It is structural. The economic environment that once rewarded preservation has slowly changed. The shift did not arrive all at once. It emerged through years of policy decisions aimed at stabilizing financial markets and sustaining growth. Over time, those decisions altered the meaning of safety itself.

The consequences extend beyond bank accounts and retirement balances. When the foundation that once protected savers begins to erode, the effects spread into pensions, public finances, and economic confidence. The weakening of safe saving is more than a financial shift. It signals a deeper change in the relationship between caution, security, and economic stability. The meaning of financial security also changed.

## *When Safety Stopped Compounding*

At the centre of this transformation lies the prolonged suppression of interest rates following successive crises. In earlier decades, saving generated visible and dependable returns. A household that placed money in bank deposits or government bonds could expect income that generally exceeded inflation. The reward was not dramatic, but it was reliable.

That relationship shifted decisively after the global financial crisis. Policy rates in the United States fell to near zero in 2008 and remained exceptionally low for more than seven years.[2] The United Kingdom followed a similar path. The European Central Bank pushed rates below zero, and Japan continued a policy of near-zero rates that had already persisted for years. From 2009 to 2021, ten-year government bond yields in many advanced economies rarely rose above two percent and often remained close to zero.[3] In several cases, deposit rates fell to zero or below. Inflation did not disappear during this period. Even modest annual price increases of two to three percent were enough to outpace returns on conservative savings. The result was sustained negative real returns for households that avoided risk.[4] Money that appeared safe gradually lost purchasing power year after year. Preservation became erosion.

The arithmetic is straightforward. If savings earn one percent while prices rise at three percent, purchasing power declines by roughly two percent each year. Over a decade, that gap compounds into a loss approaching twenty percent. No speculation is required. No mistakes are necessary. The loss is embedded directly in the structure of returns.

For many households, the shift was subtle at first. Each year's difference appears manageable. The effect accumulates gradually, reducing the real value of deposits and fixed-income holdings without visible crisis. A saver who behaves cautiously finds that time no longer works in their favour. The same patience that once built resilience now weakens it.

This is the deeper break. The consequence is not simply lower income from savings. It is the reversal of the underlying contract. The financial system once treated safety as a virtue. In the low-rate era, safety became a liability. Money held conservatively did not merely stand still. It lost ground.

When the safest assets no longer preserve value, the meaning of saving changes. It ceases to be a stabilizing force and becomes a source of anxiety. Households are left with a difficult choice: accept steady erosion or seek exposure to markets they may not fully understand. The system no longer rewards caution in neutral terms. It pressures savers to adapt or fall behind.

This shift was not simply the result of changing market conditions. It reflected deeper pressures within an economic system increasingly dependent on low borrowing costs and rising debt. Someone ultimately had to bear the cost of preserving cheap credit.

## *Why Savers Had to Lose*

The extended period of suppressed returns was not a technical miscalculation. It was the price of sustaining a debt-saturated system that could no longer function normally under higher interest rates.

Over the four decades since the early 1980s, advanced economies accumulated public and private debt on a scale rarely seen in modern times.[5] Government debt rose steadily. Corporate borrowing expanded. Households relied increasingly on mortgages, consumer credit, and student loans. By the time of the global financial crisis, debt levels in many advanced economies had climbed so high that even modest increases in interest rates risked severe disruption across the economy.

As debt expanded, the financial system became increasingly sensitive to borrowing costs. When debt levels are modest, interest rates can rise without threatening the broader economy. When debt is large, even small increases in rates translate into substantial increases in interest costs. Governments face higher refinancing burdens. Corporations confront thinner profit margins. Households encounter larger monthly payments. What appears to be a minor adjustment in monetary policy can ripple through balance sheets with force. Small changes can produce outsized effects.

In such an environment, maintaining stability requires keeping borrowing costs contained. The alternative is rapid deleveraging, asset price declines, and recession. Policymakers chose the path of rate suppression because it minimized immediate damage. That choice preserved calm in financial markets and supported asset valuations. It also quietly changed who benefited from the system and who absorbed the cost of maintaining it.

The benefits of that approach were visible and immediate. The costs were less obvious, accumulating gradually over time and falling unevenly across different groups within the economy.

## *The Quiet Transfer from Savers to Borrowers*

The redistribution that followed was gradual but significant. Low rates benefit borrowers. They reduce the cost of rolling over existing debt and encourage new issuance. Asset prices such as equities, housing, and other financial assets tend to rise as discount rates fall, lifting valuations across the broader economy. Those who already owned property and equities saw their wealth increase. At the same time, the income earned on deposits and bonds declined. Conservative savers found themselves moving backward even as asset markets moved higher.

This is not an accidental outcome. It is arithmetic. A system carrying very high levels of debt cannot simultaneously offer strong real returns to savers without imposing heavy interest burdens on borrowers. Something must give. In the post-crisis era, it was the saver. Prudence no longer produced the same protection it once had in earlier decades.

The transfer does not occur through an explicit tax. It operates through policy settings. When rates are held below inflation, the real value of outstanding debt falls gradually. That decline eases pressure on borrowers, including governments. The cost is borne by those holding cash or fixed income. Purchasing power shifts away from preservation and toward indebtedness.

For a time, the arrangement appears workable. Borrowing remains affordable. Asset prices rise. Defaults are contained. Yet the underlying tension intensifies. If rates remain low, savers continue absorbing losses and money increasingly flows toward assets inflated by cheap borrowing. If rates rise meaningfully, debt-servicing costs increase and asset prices face downward pressure. Stability becomes conditional on continued central bank support.

To prevent the visible disruption of deleveraging, policymakers accepted the gradual weakening of conservative saving. The choice postponed adjustment, but it did not eliminate it. When a system depends on discouraging saving in order to sustain borrowing, it undermines one of its own foundations. Saving is not merely a private act. It supports long-term investment, pension funding, and financial resilience. Weakening that base may delay crisis, but it also reduces the capacity to absorb the next shock.

The erosion of saving is therefore not a side effect. It is evidence that the system has become increasingly dependent on debt, low rates, and rising asset values to preserve stability. What once functioned as a source of resilience has gradually been repurposed to support the debt structure itself.

## *The Forced Migration into Risk*

When conservative saving no longer preserves value, behaviour adjusts. The adjustment is not driven by speculation or exuberance. It is driven by necessity.

Households that once relied on deposits, government bonds, or traditional retirement products increasingly found that these instruments failed to keep pace with rising prices. A savings account, a conservative pension fund, or a government bond no longer offered the same sense of protection it once had. Faced with steady erosion, many moved toward equities, property, high-yield credit, and other investments. Participation in equity markets broadened after the financial crisis, not only because optimism surged, but because alternatives weakened.

This shift altered the social distribution of risk. In earlier decades, exposure to market volatility was largely a choice. Conservative households could accept lower but stable returns. In the low-rate era, the distinction blurred. Avoiding risk increasingly meant accepting loss. Seeking preservation meant embracing fluctuation. The result was that more households became exposed to market movements.

The consequences reach beyond individual portfolios. As more households depend on rising asset prices to maintain purchasing power, the stability of the system becomes increasingly tied to market valuations. A downturn no longer affects only investors. It affects retirement timelines, housing equity, and perceived financial security across a wider segment of society over time.

The psychological shift is significant. Time, which once worked quietly in favour of savers, now feels uncertain. Years of disciplined saving no longer guarantee improved affordability or security. Delayed consumption no longer produces reliable reward. The relationship between patience and protection begins to weaken. When prudent behaviour yields unstable outcomes, confidence gradually erodes among ordinary households.

This broadening exposure also narrows the system's margin for error. If stability depends on elevated asset prices, and households rely on those prices to offset weak returns elsewhere, then corrections carry greater consequences. Market volatility translates more directly into social strain.

The result is a feedback loop. Low rates encourage borrowing and push investors toward financial assets. Rising asset prices draw in more participation. As participation expands, dependence on continued central bank support deepens. The economy becomes even more sensitive to changes in interest rates, liquidity, and broader market confidence.

In effect, households increasingly function as informal shock absorbers for the financial system. Their retirement accounts, housing equity, and market holdings bear pressures that earlier systems might have absorbed through higher real returns, lower debt levels, or slower credit expansion. The protection once offered by safe saving has gradually been replaced by exposure to valuation cycles and market volatility.

This is not a temporary adjustment. It is a structural realignment. When preservation requires risk, the line between stability and speculation begins to blur. The system grows more interconnected, more reactive, and more dependent on confidence remaining intact. The implications reach far beyond investment returns. Retirement systems could not remain insulated. Few institutions illustrate that transformation more clearly than pension systems.

## *Pensions and the Breakdown of the Saving Contract*

The pressure on savers does not stop at individual households. It extends into the architecture of retirement systems across the advanced world.

Many public and private pension plans were designed in an era when steady, positive real returns could be expected from conservative portfolios. Long-term actuarial assumptions often relied on annual returns of six to eight percent.[6] When government bonds yielded five or six percent, these targets were demanding but plausible. Time and compounding did much of the work. The old arithmetic no longer held.

In the low-rate era, those assumptions became increasingly difficult to sustain. When ten-year government bond yields fell toward one or two percent, and in some cases below zero, fixed income no longer generated sufficient income to meet long-term liabilities.[7] Pension funds faced an uncomfortable choice. Either reduce expected returns and acknowledge funding gaps, or increase exposure to equities, private credit, real estate, and alternative assets.

Many chose the latter. Exposure to market risk expanded not out of preference, but out of necessity. Stability in retirement outcomes became tied more closely to asset valuations and favourable market conditions. When markets performed well, funding pressures eased. When markets corrected, deficits widened quickly.

This changed the character of retirement security itself. Pension systems once depended primarily on steady compounding and conservative long-term returns. Increasingly, they became dependent on elevated asset prices and continued financial stability. Retirement outcomes grew more sensitive to market cycles, valuation levels, and central bank policy. The obligations did not disappear. in the background but still had to be met.

The consequences extend beyond pension funds themselves. Funding shortfalls do not disappear. They must eventually be addressed through higher contributions, reduced benefits, or public support. In systems where governments backstop retirement promises, deficits translate into fiscal strain. In private systems, they translate into delayed retirements, reduced income, or greater insecurity for older households.

The broader social contract also begins to weaken. The original saving framework assumed that discipline, patience, and time would provide reasonably predictable security. In the new environment, outcomes depend more heavily on timing, market exposure, and continued policy support. The connection between effort and certainty weakens.

This transformation also deepens generational tension. Younger workers contribute to systems whose long-term returns appear less assured, while older cohorts depend increasingly on asset markets remaining elevated. The stability of retirement income becomes intertwined with the continuation of the same asset inflation that prolonged low rates helped sustain.

The strain rarely appears dramatic in any single year. It accumulates gradually as funding ratios fluctuate, assumptions are revised, and liabilities expand faster than safe returns. Yet the underlying vulnerability becomes harder to ignore. Retirement systems built on stable compounding now operate in an environment defined by suppressed yields and elevated dependence on financial markets.

When long-term saving vehicles can no longer rely on preservation and steady growth, the social foundation they were designed to support becomes less certain. The consequences extend beyond finance. They influence labour markets, intergenerational expectations, political pressure, and long-term confidence in economic security. These changes extend well beyond financial markets into everyday economic life.

The effects are not distributed evenly. Some households possess the assets and flexibility to adapt, while others remain far more exposed to financial strain. The gap lies not only in wealth, but in the ability to withstand economic shocks. Access to financial buffers determines who can absorb disruption, reinforcing inequality during periods of economic stress.

## *Unequal Exposure and Diminishing Resilience*

The erosion of safe saving does not affect all households equally. Its impact follows existing lines of wealth and access. Households with significant exposure to property and equities have largely offset weak deposit returns through rising asset values. Those who already owned appreciating assets benefited from falling discount rates and expanding valuations. For them, suppressed yields were inconvenient but manageable.

Others faced a different reality. Households whose wealth remained concentrated in cash, basic savings accounts, or fixed-income instruments absorbed the full effect of negative real returns. Without meaningful exposure to rising markets, their purchasing power declined steadily. Entry into asset ownership became more difficult as property prices and equity valuations moved further beyond income growth.

The divide widened between those who could rely on asset appreciation and those who depended primarily on earned income and cautious saving. The system increasingly rewarded participation in markets rather than preservation of capital. Access to that participation remained uneven.

Once saving no longer provides equal protection, the financial system begins to feel less neutral. As this gap expands, the economy's ability to absorb shocks weakens. Financial resilience depends on households maintaining adequate savings relative to expenses. When real returns are persistently suppressed and living costs continue rising, precautionary savings struggle to keep pace. Many households operate with only limited capacity to withstand unexpected income loss or sudden expense increases.

This reduction in resilience carries broader consequences. In earlier decades, accumulated savings allowed households to smooth consumption during downturns. Today, when savings erode and exposure to markets is higher, downturns transmit more quickly into reduced spending, delayed purchases, and rising financial stress. The system becomes more reactive.

The psychological effects are significant as well. When disciplined saving fails to protect purchasing power while asset owners prosper, confidence in the economic framework begins to weaken. Frustration builds not because prosperity has disappeared entirely, but because its distribution increasingly appears detached from effort and restraint.

Over time, the strain spreads beyond household finances. It shapes political attitudes, voting patterns, and trust in institutions. It influences debates over fiscal policy, housing affordability, retirement security, and inequality. What begins as financial pressure gradually evolves into broader social tension.

The erosion of safe saving therefore narrows more than household margins. It reduces the system's collective capacity to absorb volatility. An economy that depends increasingly on asset inflation while offering limited preservation to cautious households becomes more exposed to correction. The tolerance for downturns declines sharply as dependence deepens.

When resilience fades and exposure rises, stability becomes more brittle. The system may appear calm, but it rests on narrower support. In such conditions, shocks that once would have been absorbed can trigger sharper reactions.

## *Why This Cannot Last*

Saving has not disappeared. It remains necessary for households and institutions alike. What has changed is the environment in which it operates. That distinction matters.

An economy can sustain high debt and low interest rates for a period of time. It can support elevated asset prices and rely on central bank intervention to contain volatility. It can manage appearances through liquidity and policy coordination. What becomes increasingly difficult is preserving the foundations that allow societies to absorb shocks without constant intervention.

Stable systems require preservation as well as growth. They require a base of accumulated savings that can absorb disruption without immediate recourse to borrowing or public support. When real returns remain persistently below inflation, that foundation gradually weakens. Households then assume greater exposure to financial markets to preserve purchasing power, allowing vulnerability to spread through the system.

The pressures that emerge are difficult to reconcile. Borrowing must remain affordable. Asset prices must avoid sustained decline. Inflation cannot rise high enough to force prolonged tightening. Yet each condition increasingly conflicts with the others.

If interest rates rise materially, debt-servicing burdens increase across governments, corporations, and households. If asset prices fall sharply, retirement systems and household balance sheets come under strain. If inflation remains elevated, purchasing power continues to erode. The system becomes progressively more dependent on careful management to prevent instability from surfacing openly.

The suppression of returns was intended to reduce immediate risk. It succeeded in preventing abrupt collapse after successive crises. Yet it introduced a deeper contradiction. A financial system that depends on discouraging conservative saving in order to sustain borrowing weakens one of its own stabilizing mechanisms. The longer the arrangement persists, the more stability relies on continued support from policymakers and financial markets.

This is the deeper distinction now emerging. Organic stability absorbs disruption because resilience already exists within households, savings, and institutions Maintained stability requires increasingly active support from monetary policy, asset markets, and government balance sheets. The difference matters because maintained stability becomes progressively harder to sustain as debt accumulates and flexibility narrows. The capacity to absorb shocks weakens at the same time.

As these constraints tighten, the pressures intensify as debt continues to expand, political tolerance for inflation or austerity weakens, and asset valuations become harder to support without renewed intervention. The margin for policy error narrows.

The erosion of safe saving is therefore not an isolated financial concern. It changes behaviour as households save, invest, borrow, and plan differently. Risk increasingly becomes a requirement rather than a choice, and what was once considered prudent begins to feel insufficient. The adjustment is gradual, but over time it reshapes how societies think about security, retirement, and long-term stability.

For savers, this marks a profound reversal. Beginning in the early 1980s and extending into the early 2020s, the advanced world built decades of relative calm on expanding debt, falling interest rates, and rising asset values. That arrangement rewarded borrowers and asset holders. It asked cautious savers to accept weaker returns in exchange for financial stability. As debt levels increased and rates approached their lower bound, the trade-off became harder to sustain.

There comes a point when postponed adjustment begins to reassert itself. Either returns normalize and higher borrowing costs strain heavily indebted economies, or rates remain suppressed and purchasing power continues to erode. Neither outcome restores the earlier link between prudence and financial security. The problem is therefore systemic.

An economy that cannot reward saving without destabilizing its debt structure stands at a turning point. Stability in such a system depends on conditions that cannot be extended indefinitely. The consequences are no longer abstract.

That is why saving no longer feels fully safe. The framework that once protected preservation has increasingly been repurposed to support debt, asset prices, and financial stability. The shift helped prevent immediate crisis. It also reduced the system's ability to absorb future shocks without renewed intervention. The behavioural effects often prove surprisingly durable and difficult to reverse once established.

Over time, societies adapt as preservation becomes harder to achieve. Households save differently, invest differently, borrow differently, and plan differently. Risk increasingly becomes a requirement rather than a choice. What once appeared prudent begins to feel inadequate for many savers. The change is ultimately one of confidence.

The unease surrounding saving is therefore rational. It reflects recognition that the link between effort, restraint, and security has fundamentally changed. The erosion is not temporary. It is structural. And structural changes, once deeply embedded, rarely reverse quickly or easily. The consequences extend far beyond financial markets. Over time, they alter expectations, behaviour, and trust in the institutions that once promised long-term stability. What once felt dependable increasingly begins to feel conditional and uncertain for many households and long-term savers.

# 10

## THE HOUSING DIVIDE

Few institutions reveal the foundations of modern economic stability more clearly than housing. Housing sits at the point where finance, politics, debt, and everyday life intersect. It exposes the dividing line between what appears stable and what is genuinely secure, and nowhere is it more evident how advanced economies have come to depend on rising asset values to preserve confidence. Housing provides the clearest example.

For millions of households, the cost of shelter now shapes not only living standards, but perceptions of opportunity, security, and fairness itself. What was once a foundation of personal stability has gradually been transformed into a financial asset whose appreciation is treated as essential to economic order.

This shift has done more than widen inequality. It has bound social calm to property inflation. Economic stability itself has become increasingly dependent on rising housing values, leaving economies more exposed when prices falter. The result is a system in which ownership moves further out of reach for growing numbers of people.

In the advanced world, housing is no longer simply shelter. It is collateral for banks, retirement security for households, a revenue base for governments, and a political constituency that resists falling prices. For many existing owners, rising property values came to feel less like speculation and more like financial survival. The effects reached far beyond the housing market.

When property values rise, household finances improve and consumption expands. Policymakers face less immediate pressure. Households feel wealthier, banks lend more confidently, and governments collect more revenue from housing activity.

When prices stall or decline, the consequences extend far beyond individual owners. Banking systems feel strain, fiscal positions weaken, and political tensions intensify. In such a system, housing is no longer peripheral, but central to the preservation of stability itself.

This is what makes the housing divide so consequential. Stability has come to rely on conditions that exclude a growing share of the population. Rising prices reward those already inside the system while raising barriers for those attempting to enter.

Access to ownership increasingly depends on timing, inheritance, or family assistance rather than income alone. In many cities across the advanced world, even middle-income households with stable employment now struggle to purchase homes that earlier generations could afford on ordinary salaries. The result is not merely a gap in wealth, but a structural divide in opportunity in which stability becomes unevenly distributed.

Residential property now represents the largest component of household wealth in most advanced economies.[1] For middle-income households, owner-occupied housing commonly accounts for more than half of total net worth, making economic policy highly sensitive to property values, interest rate decisions inseparable from their impact on housing markets, and meaningful correction politically hazardous. .

Governments, central banks, and financial institutions become increasingly cautious about any adjustment that could seriously weaken prices. A system built on rising valuations cannot adjust easily without unsettling the very order it seeks to protect.

Housing therefore lies at the heart of this book's broader argument. The stability of the past four decades since the early 1980s was sustained in part by expanding credit, declining interest rates, and steady asset appreciation, conditions that helped drive property prices steadily higher across advanced economies.

Years of cheap money and expanding credit steadily pushed housing away from its traditional role as shelter and toward its newer role as a financial asset expected to rise continuously in value. What once functioned as a stabilizing anchor has become a structural fault line. The more housing functions as capital, the more the system depends on rising prices. As stability comes to depend on prices that cannot be allowed to fall, the system moves closer to a breaking point.

## *When Housing Was a Foundation, Not a Strategy*

For much of the postwar period, housing reinforced economic stability rather than distorting it. Prices tended to move broadly in line with household incomes and demographic demand. In many advanced economies during the 1950s, 1960s, and 1970s, house price-to-income ratios commonly clustered around three to four times median annual earnings.[2] Ownership required discipline and saving, but it was not structurally prohibitive. For many households, purchasing a home was difficult but realistic. A single middle-income salary could often support ownership within a reasonable period of saving. The pathway was demanding yet attainable within a single working lifetime.

Mortgage structures reflected this alignment. Terms were shorter, down payments were substantial, and borrowing was constrained by stricter lending standards. Interest rates were often high in nominal terms, particularly during the inflationary 1970s and early 1980s, but debt burdens remained limited because prices themselves had not detached from incomes. Housing functioned primarily as shelter and long-term security rather than an engine of wealth accumulation. Homes were expected to provide stability first and financial gain second. The connection between effort and reward seemed relatively clear.

This alignment anchored expectations. Work, saving, and gradual accumulation formed a coherent sequence in which rising incomes supported higher property prices and ownership signalled stability rather than speculation. The connection between effort and security still appeared broadly intact. Younger households could reasonably expect that steady work and disciplined saving would eventually allow them to buy a home.

That relationship began to change in the 1980s and accelerated after the 1990s. As inflation declined and central banks gained credibility, interest rates fell across the advanced world. In several major economies, mortgage rates that had exceeded 12 to 15 percent in the early 1980s declined steadily over the following decades, eventually approaching 2 to 3 percent in the years after the global financial crisis.[3]

Each reduction in rates altered the mathematics of borrowing. Buyers could service larger loans for the same monthly payment, and credit expanded in step. What initially appeared to improve affordability gradually pushed prices higher instead. Prices responded accordingly. Since the 1990s, and especially after the early 2000s, house price-to-income ratios doubled in a number of advanced economies.[4] In major metropolitan areas, property values rose to six, eight, or even ten times median income. In many cities, ownership increasingly depended less on income and more on how early buyers entered the market.

The shift was not confined to one country or one regulatory model. It appeared across North America, Europe, Australia, and parts of Asia. Different political systems, tax policies, and housing rules shaped the process differently, but the broader direction remained remarkably similar. Over time, the pattern became too widespread and too persistent to dismiss as a local imbalance or temporary cycle.

The change was structural. When borrowing costs fall for decades, the present value of land rises. What households can pay each month becomes the binding constraint rather than the underlying relationship between income and price. Lower rates do not restore affordability in aggregate; they permit higher valuations that eventually become embedded in balance sheets, bank collateral, and government tax bases. Cheap credit does not eliminate the affordability problem. It delays it by allowing households to take on larger debts in order to meet rising prices.

Housing ceased to be merely a foundation of stability and instead became an instrument through which monetary conditions were transmitted into asset inflation. The transition was gradual, but its consequences were cumulative. Ownership shifted from a life milestone to a financial position that conferred advantage, and entry became increasingly dependent on timing and access to credit rather than income and effort. Over time, the housing market stopped rewarding primarily those who worked and saved consistently and increasingly rewarded those who already owned assets. What had once reinforced social cohesion began to divide it.

## *Why Familiar Explanations Fall Short*

The transformation of housing is often attributed to familiar forces such as population growth, urbanization, planning restrictions, and limited construction. Each of these factors influences prices at the margin, yet none adequately explains the scale, duration, or cross-country pattern of housing inflation in the advanced world.[5] These explanations contain elements of truth, but they do not fully explain why housing costs accelerated so sharply across so many different economies at roughly the same time.

Population growth has been modest or even stagnant in several economies where prices have surged. Japan provides a useful contrast, where demographic contraction limited price appreciation for extended periods despite low interest rates. In contrast, countries with sharply different demographic profiles such as Canada, the United Kingdom, Australia, and parts of Western Europe experienced sustained price acceleration over the same decades. Urbanization explains local pressure but does not explain synchronized national price booms. Cities naturally become more expensive as populations concentrate in them, but urban growth alone cannot explain why housing inflation became so widespread across the advanced world.

Supply constraints are also uneven. Some countries maintain restrictive zoning regimes, while others possess abundant land and comparatively flexible construction sectors. Yet housing valuations rose across both types of systems. This does not mean supply is irrelevant. It means supply alone cannot explain the breadth and persistence of the increase. Even markets with fewer land constraints experienced substantial price inflation once cheap credit became widely available.

More importantly, prices continued to climb even as affordability deteriorated. If scarcity alone were the driver, declining purchasing power would eventually restrain demand. Instead, higher prices were accommodated through expanded borrowing as households stretched repayment horizons, mortgage maturities lengthened, and debt-to-income ratios rose. Credit absorbed what incomes could not. Rather than forcing prices lower, weakening affordability pushed households deeper into debt remain competitive in the market.

This distinction matters because it changes how the problem is understood. A supply shortage can theoretically be eased through more construction over time. A financialised housing system is far harder to correct because rising prices become embedded in lending, household wealth, government revenues, and political expectations across the economy.

The simultaneity of these movements across advanced economies points toward a common denominator. Over the same decades that housing valuations accelerated, interest rates declined persistently and financial systems deepened their exposure to property markets. Housing inflation therefore emerged not primarily as a supply phenomenon, but as a financial phenomenon. The forces driving prices had changed by then.

Once housing became fully integrated into the financial architecture, price growth was no longer governed solely by income and supply. It was shaped by monetary conditions, bank lending standards, and policy incentives. The question was no longer how many homes were built, but how much buyers could borrow. That shift changed the anchor of the housing market. Prices were no longer disciplined mainly by what households earned. They were increasingly sustained by what lenders were willing to finance.

That shift altered the entire structure of stability. When credit becomes the engine of price formation, stability becomes tied to continued access to borrowing at favourable rates, and affordability ceases to anchor valuations. Instead, valuations begin to anchor the system itself. The danger is subtle but profound. Once economies become dependent on permanently elevated property values, governments and central banks face growing pressure to protect prices even when distortions become increasingly obvious.

## *Credit as the Engine of Price Inflation*

The decisive shift occurred when housing became fully embedded in the modern credit system. Declining interest rates altered the basic arithmetic of ownership. As borrowing costs fell, the same monthly payment could support a larger loan. Buyers did not suddenly earn more; they gained access to larger balances, and sellers adjusted prices upward accordingly. What appeared at first to be improved affordability gradually translated into permanently higher valuations.

Mortgage debt expanded in parallel. In many advanced economies, household mortgage debt as a share of GDP rose materially from the 1990s onward.[6] Banks increased their exposure to residential lending because property-backed loans were perceived as secure and were often favoured under regulatory frameworks. For financial institutions, mortgage lending increasingly appeared safer and more predictable than many forms of business lending. Cheaper credit did not resolve the affordability problem; it postponed its visibility. Higher leverage made prices sustainable so long as interest rates remained low and employment remained stable. The new environment reshaped expectations.

Over time, households adapted to these conditions both financially and psychologically. Larger mortgages gradually stopped feeling unusual. Thirty-year loans became normal, while rising prices encouraged the belief that ownership would eventually justify the burden. Expectations of future gains also reduced concern about the debt required to enter the market.

As rates declined over successive decades, valuations rose to levels that could only be supported by continued access to inexpensive financing. The system increasingly depended not on rising incomes, but on the continuation of low borrowing costs. Housing markets became less sensitive to underlying wages and more sensitive to central bank policy, credit availability, and investor expectations.

At the same time, housing increasingly attracted investors. As returns on government bonds and other low-risk assets fell, property emerged as a substitute store of value. Institutional capital entered markets previously dominated by owner-occupiers, rental portfolios expanded, and housing shifted from a consumption good to an investment vehicle within diversified portfolios. Demand was no longer anchored solely in shelter but in yield, collateral, and balance-sheet expansion. Homes increasingly functioned as financial assets expected to generate returns as safer investments produced little income.

This transformation altered the nature of stability. When property prices rise steadily, consumption is reinforced through wealth effects, borrowing feels manageable, and political pressure eases. Households spend more confidently, lenders extend credit more freely, and governments face fewer immediate pressures to confront deeper structural weaknesses. When prices stall or fall, the reverse occurs and housing begins to amplify rather than absorb financial shocks. What had once provided stability became a source of vulnerability across the system. The response was to reinforce the conditions that had created the problem.

As interest rates approached their lower limits and central banks injected more money into the financial system, property values became increasingly dependent on continued support. A system built around rising prices cannot easily tolerate prolonged rate increases, because policies aimed at controlling inflation or reducing fiscal pressures risk destabilizing the foundations on which household wealth and bank lending depend. No single decision created this dependence.

This dependence developed gradually and often invisibly. Year after year, falling rates and expanding credit appeared to stabilize the system, even as they quietly increased its long-term fragility. What felt sustainable during periods of low inflation and rising asset prices became far more vulnerable once borrowing costs began to rise again.

Credit therefore did more than inflate housing prices; it redefined the limits of adjustment and made stability contingent on financial conditions that could not normalize without triggering correction. The longer the system relied on cheap credit to support elevated valuations, the narrower the path toward normalization became without significant disruption.

## *Locked-In Advantage and the End of Neutral Entry*

Rising property values did more than inflate balance sheets. They reshaped incentives across the advanced world. For existing owners, appreciation delivered wealth without additional labour. Equity accumulated through time and market conditions rather than productivity alone, and in many cases gains in property values exceeded wage growth over extended periods.

Housing increasingly functioned not only as shelter but also as a store of value and a substitute for traditional saving. For many households, ownership itself became one of the primary ways wealth was accumulated and preserved.

For those already inside the market, rising prices reinforced security. For those outside, they raised the threshold for entry. Deposit requirements increased alongside valuations, and in many advanced economies the required down payment grew far faster than median household savings.[7]

Access to ownership increasingly depended on parental assistance, inherited wealth, or exceptional earnings. Entry ceased to be broadly neutral. The ability to purchase a home increasingly reflected existing financial advantage rather than steady progress through work and saving alone.

This shift altered social expectations. Ownership no longer functioned as a predictable milestone of adulthood. It became a dividing line shaped by timing, geography, and family background. For younger households in particular, ownership increasingly appeared less like a normal stage of life and more like access to an exclusive financial tier. The link between effort and access weakened as advantages accumulated for those who entered earlier in the cycle.

The divide was also generational. Older cohorts, who purchased property before the most dramatic price escalations, benefited from decades of appreciation. Younger cohorts faced elevated entry prices, higher debt burdens relative to income, and greater exposure to interest rate volatility. Many younger buyers entered markets at valuations that assumed continued low borrowing costs and continued price support. The same monetary conditions that enriched existing owners imposed greater risks on new entrants.

Over time, this widened more than a wealth gap. It widened a security gap. Older owners often accumulated equity as prices rose, while younger households increasingly accumulated debt in order to gain entry. One generation benefited from asset inflation; the other became increasingly exposed to it. Expectations of future gains also reduced concern about the debt required to enter the market. Homeowners form a substantial share of the electorate in most advanced economies. Policies that support property values are therefore rewarded, while policies that threaten valuations are resisted. Low interest rates support borrowers and sustain prices, tax systems in several countries favour ownership and leveraged investment, and mortgage lending often receives favourable regulatory treatment. Governments increasingly operated within political environments where falling house prices became difficult to tolerate electorally as well as financially.

As the system evolved, these choices insulated housing markets from downward correction. Protection, once justified as stabilization, became entrenched policy. The longer prices were defended, the more concentrated wealth became and the more difficult adjustment appeared with each passing year.

Falling valuations would not merely reduce paper wealth; they would affect consumption, bank lending, and electoral outcomes. A growing share of households came to rely on continued price stability for financial security, while governments relied on transaction taxes and property-related revenue, and banks relied on mortgage performance.

Adjustment therefore became politically hazardous even when imbalances were widely visible. Housing gradually ceased to function as a neutral market and instead became a protected asset class tied to fiscal health, financial stability, and political survival. What began as support for stability gradually evolved into protection of a fragile structure increasingly dependent on elevated prices and continued policy support.

The consequence was structural segmentation in which stability was preserved primarily for those who already owned appreciating assets while exclusion intensified for those who did not. Over time, this divide eroded social cohesion and complicated policy choices. When too many interests depend on prices not falling, the capacity for orderly correction diminishes. Adjustment becomes increasingly difficult.

The longer the imbalance persists, the harder it becomes to resolve without economic or political disruption. The pressures gradually become social as well as financial in their effects.

What begins as a financial imbalance therefore becomes something broader. Over time, the effects extend beyond markets and increasingly shape life opportunities, economic security, and social expectations. The consequences are ultimately measured not only in prices and wealth, but in people's ability to participate in the economic system itself.

## *The Human Cost of Exclusion*

The transformation of housing reshapes daily life in ways that extend beyond wealth statistics. For renters and aspiring buyers, sustained price inflation translates into delayed independence, prolonged insecurity, and constrained mobility. In many major cities across the advanced world, housing costs now absorb 30 to 40 percent of disposable income for renters, leaving limited room for saving, investment, or resilience in the face of economic shocks.[8] For many households, housing costs increasingly determine not only where they live, but how they live, when they form families, and whether long-term financial stability feels attainable at all.

As deposits rise faster than wages, the timeline to ownership lengthens. Years of disciplined saving may be overtaken by another surge in prices, and the goal recedes as it is approached. Entry becomes conditional not only on effort but on market timing and family support, altering expectations about work, security, and opportunity. What earlier generations often viewed as difficult but achievable increasingly feels uncertain even for middle-income earners with stable employment.

These pressures change behaviour. Household formation slows, marriage and childbearing are postponed, and geographic mobility declines as workers remain tied to high-cost regions or delay relocation altogether. Young adults remain with parents longer, shared accommodation becomes more common well into middle age, and financial dependence extends further across generations. When housing absorbs a large share of income, risk tolerance declines, entrepreneurship becomes less attractive, and labour flexibility diminishes across the economy.

The consequences accumulate at the macroeconomic level. High housing costs reduce disposable income available for consumption outside shelter, increase sensitivity to interest rate changes and employment disruptions, and constrain productivity growth by limiting labour mobility. Regions with elevated property prices often experience reduced workforce mobility, slowing adjustment to economic change. Workers become less willing or less able to relocate for employment opportunities when moving itself carries major financial risk.

The divide is not simply economic. It is psychological and political. Younger generations facing high prices and heavy debt increasingly see the system as tilted against them. The expectation that work and patience will lead to security begins to weaken, especially when ownership depends more on inheritance or family assistance. The problem is no longer seen solely as expensive housing, but as unequal access to stability itself. Its role within the economy had fundamentally changed.

Housing therefore ceases to be merely a market outcome. It becomes a symbol of unequal access to stability. Trust in institutions declines when opportunity feels unevenly distributed, and political polarization intensifies when large segments of the population feel excluded from asset ownership that others treat as routine. The social contract begins to weaken when younger and lower-income households no longer believe the economic system operates on broadly attainable terms.

The burden is not confined to renters. Highly leveraged new buyers face elevated exposure to interest rate increases, and even modest tightening can strain budgets when debt levels are high relative to income. What once appeared manageable under low-rate conditions becomes precarious when financing costs rise.

Stability at the household level becomes dependent on continued monetary accommodation. The same policies that supported rising prices also increased vulnerability once borrowing conditions changed. The resulting divide becomes increasingly self-reinforcing with each cycle of price growth.

Over time, exclusion and vulnerability reinforce one another. Those outside ownership remain exposed to rent inflation and limited asset accumulation, while those inside but heavily indebted remain sensitive to financial tightening.

The human cost therefore becomes a structural consequence of a model that tied stability to asset appreciation rather than income growth. When shelter becomes financially engineered, security becomes uneven and social cohesion weakens. The divide increasingly shapes how different groups experience the economy itself: one group sees rising asset values as protection, while another experiences rising costs as permanent instability.

## *From Stabilizer to Systemic Amplifier*

Housing once functioned as a stabilizing force. Gradual price appreciation supported household wealth without dominating it, mortgage lending was substantial but not overwhelming relative to bank balance sheets, and correction, when it occurred, did not threaten the foundations of the system. Housing cycles still created strain, but they did not carry the same potential to destabilize the broader economy. That balance has shifted.

In most advanced economies, residential mortgages now represent the largest single category of domestic bank lending.[9] Property values serve as collateral not only for home loans but for broader credit expansion. Pension funds, insurers, and sovereign balance sheets are increasingly exposed through mortgage-backed securities and real estate-linked assets. Housing is now deeply woven into the financial architecture.

The financial system no longer simply finances housing. It increasingly depends on housing remaining stable. As a result, housing market weakness can trigger wider financial stress.

When prices rise steadily, this integration reinforces confidence. Collateral values strengthen, lending appears secure, consumption benefits from wealth effects, and governments collect property-related taxes tied to transactions and valuations. Stability appears self-reinforcing. Rising prices create the impression that the system is functioning well because households feel wealthier, credit losses remain contained, and economic activity appears resilient. The process can also work in reverse with surprising speed.

When prices fall, the same linkages transmit strain rapidly. Collateral weakens, credit standards tighten, transaction volumes decline, fiscal revenues soften, and consumption contracts. The system becomes highly sensitive to valuation shifts because so much perceived wealth and credit capacity rest on property prices. The same structure that amplifies confidence during expansion amplifies stress during downturns.

Interest rate policy now operates within this constraint. Raising rates to address inflation increases borrowing costs for households and can slow price appreciation or reverse it. In highly leveraged housing markets, even moderate rate increases exert outsized effects on affordability and demand. Policymakers must therefore weigh price stability against the risk of destabilizing property markets that underpin household wealth and banking collateral. Central banks increasingly confront the trade-off between controlling inflation and protecting heavily indebted housing markets from abrupt correction.

This creates a policy trap. Rates cannot remain permanently suppressed without encouraging further price inflation and misallocation of capital. Yet tightening risks triggering declines that affect banks, borrowers, and government finances. The room for gradual adjustment narrows as valuations rise relative to income and debt accumulates relative to output.

The trap did not emerge suddenly. It developed gradually through decades during which rising property values appeared to support growth, strengthen household balance sheets, and reinforce financial stability. Over time, however, the system became progressively more dependent on conditions that could not easily be normalized without causing disruption.

Fiscal policy is entangled as well. In many jurisdictions, property transactions and real estate values contribute materially to government revenue. Local authorities depend on property taxes, while national governments benefit from transaction duties and capital gains. A sustained downturn in housing markets would strain these revenues just as social spending pressures rise. Governments therefore become exposed to the same housing cycles affecting households and banks.

Housing therefore magnifies both expansion and contraction. During periods of monetary easing, it channels liquidity into rising asset prices. During periods of tightening, it transmits financial strain into household spending and fiscal pressure. A system built around rising property values becomes increasingly sensitive to normalization, and housing shifts from stabilizer to amplifier of wider financial stress. What once absorbed economic shocks increasingly transmits them across the broader economy.

## *Why the Housing Divide Signals Collapse*

Housing sits at the intersection of debt, policy, and political will. It reveals how deeply the stability model that emerged across advanced economies after the early 1980s depended on asset appreciation rather than sustained income growth. Property markets absorbed falling interest rates, expanding credit, and policy intervention, converting them into rising valuations that reinforced confidence across households, banks, and governments. For decades, rising housing values helped create the appearance of expanding prosperity even as debt burdens steadily increased beneath the surface.

That model has limits. A system that relies on continuously elevated property prices cannot normalize without strain. If interest rates remain suppressed to protect housing, inflationary pressures and capital misallocation persist. If rates rise to restore monetary discipline, borrowing costs increase and valuations come under pressure. The policies required to preserve stability increasingly conflict with the policies required to restore balance.

In highly indebted housing markets, even modest corrections can weaken collateral, reduce lending, and compress consumption. Residential property often accounts for a large share of household wealth and remains central to domestic banking systems.[10] Governments are both fiscally and politically exposed to housing conditions. The dependence extends far beyond individual homeowners. Entire financial and public revenue structures become vulnerable when housing markets weaken.

Correction therefore carries consequences that extend beyond individual borrowers. Advanced economies responded to past downturns with monetary easing and credit expansion, reinforcing the central role of property markets in maintaining stability. The repeated interventions reshaped behaviour.

As the system evolved, tolerance for price correction gradually weakened. Valuations rose faster than income, debt expanded faster than economic output, and policy flexibility steadily narrowed. Each intervention helped stabilize conditions while deepening long-term dependence on elevated asset prices.

Housing was once viewed as one of the foundations of economic stability in advanced economies. It provided not only shelter, but also a pathway into the middle class, a store of long-term security, and a sense of participation in the broader economic system. For decades, rising homeownership reinforced the belief that each generation would gradually achieve greater financial stability than the one before it.

That assumption is beginning to weaken. In many advanced economies, housing no longer functions as a broad mechanism of inclusion. Increasingly, it separates those protected by rising asset values from those locked out by them. Access to ownership now depends not only on income, but also on existing wealth, family assistance, inheritance, and the timing of entry into the market. For growing numbers of younger households, the barriers increasingly appear structural rather than temporary.

The consequences extend beyond housing itself. Delayed household formation, declining affordability, rising financial insecurity, and widening generational divides are reshaping social and political attitudes across the advanced world. For younger households in particular, the problem is not simply that housing has become expensive. It is that a system once associated with stability and upward mobility increasingly feels closed to them. The weakening belief that effort alone can provide security carries consequences that extend far beyond property markets.

The breaking point need not arrive as a sudden collapse in prices. It can emerge through prolonged stagnation, reduced mobility, political polarization, and declining confidence in institutions. Societies do not become unstable only when markets crash. Instability can also build gradually as frustration, exclusion, and distrust accumulate over time.

When large segments of the population feel excluded from asset-based security, social cohesion weakens. When banks, households, and governments depend on valuations that cannot adjust without disruption, policy choices narrow. Over time, the effects do not remain confined to property markets. They begin to alter expectations, behaviour, political trust, and belief in the fairness of the economic system itself.

Housing therefore does not merely illustrate the end of stability. It helps bring it about. A system structured around protecting ever higher asset prices cannot absorb shocks, cannot rebalance without pain, and cannot extend security broadly. The longer correction is delayed, the more fragile the structure beneath the appearance of stability becomes.

As correction finally asserts itself, whether through monetary tightening, fiscal stress, or external shock, the adjustment will not remain confined to property markets. It will test the financial, political, and public revenue foundations of the advanced world. Shelter, once viewed as a stabilizing anchor, has become a structural fault line as pressures build beneath the surface. What began as a source of security increasingly functions as financial vulnerability for many households.

As the ground beneath economic security begins to shift, the consequences extend far beyond housing itself. They begin to reshape how societies define opportunity, fairness, and stability.

For much of the post-war era, homeownership served as one of the principal mechanisms through which households accumulated wealth and shared in economic progress. As access to ownership becomes increasingly uneven, that role begins to weaken. The result is not only a widening divide between owners and non-owners, but a growing challenge to the assumptions that once underpinned social mobility. Questions that initially appear to concern housing increasingly become questions about the future distribution of wealth, opportunity, and economic security. The issue is therefore no longer simply where people live, but how economic opportunity is created and sustained across society.

Housing is no longer simply shelter. It has become one of the defining structural pillars of the modern financial system.

# 11

## THE GREAT EXPANSION OF INEQUALITY

Inequality is often treated as a social issue. In advanced economies, it has become something more dangerous: a growing threat to the stability of the system itself. The issue is no longer confined to differences in income or wealth. It increasingly affects how societies understand fairness, opportunity, and economic legitimacy.

For much of modern history, widening inequality accompanied periods of visible breakdown, surging during depressions, industrial decline, or financial crisis when hardship made the divide impossible to ignore. As economies recovered, inequality was expected to ease or at least stabilize. Crisis exposed imbalance, while recovery was expected to restore a measure of equilibrium. The old rhythm no longer held.

Since the early 1980s, however, this historical pattern has begun to reverse. Advanced economies entered a new phase of economic management defined by debt expansion, financial market support, and prolonged central bank intervention. The goal was to stabilize growth, prevent severe downturns, and protect financial systems from collapse. In many ways, those policies succeeded. Markets recovered, recessions became less severe, and large financial breakdowns were repeatedly avoided.

In recent decades, developed economies have relied on debt expansion, asset price support, and prolonged monetary intervention to maintain stability. During this period, inequality in many advanced economies widened not during collapse, but during periods officially described as stable. Employment has remained relatively high. Financial systems have continued to function. Asset markets have expanded dramatically.

Yet beneath that appearance of stability, the distance between those who own capital and those who rely primarily on labour income has widened steadily. Stock markets, housing prices, and financial wealth rose far faster than wages in many advanced economies. Households that already owned assets benefited disproportionately, while those attempting to build wealth primarily through income found it increasingly difficult to keep pace over time. Rising asset prices rewarded existing ownership far more than productive work or disciplined saving. The gap between those who owned appreciating assets and those dependent mainly on wages steadily widened.

This divergence unfolded during periods of relative calm, and that distinction matters. When inequality rises during crisis, it is often viewed as temporary damage that recovery may eventually repair. When it rises during stability, however, it becomes embedded in the structure of the economy itself. The imbalance gradually stops looking temporary and begins to feel permanent. The concentration of wealth illustrates the point.

In the United States, the share of wealth held by the top decile has increased markedly since the early 1980s, and today the top ten percent of households hold close to ninety percent of equities, while the bottom half hold only a small fraction.[1] Comparable concentration appears across other advanced economies, particularly in economies where financial markets play a dominant role in growth and wealth creation.

Meanwhile, median real wage growth has been modest relative to financial asset values, and since the 2008–2009 global financial crisis, major equity markets in advanced economies have more than tripled in value, while household income has grown far more slowly.[2] For many households, everyday living costs continued to rise even as financial markets surged far ahead of ordinary earnings and wage growth. The divide between financial wealth and everyday economic experience became increasingly difficult to ignore across society.

This divergence did not emerge from collapse but from the mechanisms designed to preserve stability, as the policies used to prevent crisis also reshaped how gains were distributed across society. The same interventions that helped stabilize financial systems also increased the value of assets that were already unevenly owned. Over time, inequality became less a temporary side effect of instability and more a built-in feature of how stability itself was maintained.

## *Inequality in an Era of Stability*

Modern inequality is therefore not the residue of breakdown. It emerged from the way stability itself was maintained through expanding debt, rising asset prices, and prolonged monetary intervention. The same policies that prevented systemic crisis also concentrated ownership in fewer hands. The system remained functional, but the gains produced within it became increasingly uneven across society.

As long as asset prices rise and institutions continue to function, the economy appears stable on the surface. Financial markets expand, unemployment remains relatively contained, and severe downturns are repeatedly eased through policy support. For many households, however, life beneath those headline figures feels increasingly different from the official image of stability.

Asset owners benefit from rising equity markets, appreciating property values, and expanding financial wealth. Those relying primarily on wages experience a slower and more difficult path. Earnings often struggle to keep pace with housing costs, healthcare, education, and other essential expenses. The economy continues to grow, yet participation alone increasingly fails to provide the same sense of progress or security that earlier generations expected. The implications are broader than they first appear in everyday life.

But stability built on widening divergence carries a hidden cost. When gains accrue narrowly and participation no longer guarantees progress, confidence in the system's fairness begins to erode. People may still accept unequal outcomes for long periods, but they become less willing to accept a system that appears permanently tilted toward those who already own assets.

Stability depends not only on functioning markets, but on whether people believe the system remains fair. In practical terms, this means that people accept uneven outcomes because they believe effort still leads to advancement. The expectation is not that everyone prospers equally, but that advancement remains broadly attainable through work, saving, and participation. The principle matters as much as the outcome.

When the connection between effort and advancement weakens, public confidence weakens with it. If home ownership, retirement security, and financial stability increasingly depend on inherited wealth or prior ownership, the perception of equal opportunity gradually loses credibility. Inequality at sufficient scale and duration begins to undermine the political and social foundations that allow economic stability to persist.

The advanced world is now testing the limits of how much divergence a system can absorb while still calling itself stable. The danger is not simply that wealth has become concentrated. It is that large segments of society increasingly feel disconnected from the mechanisms through which security and advancement are created.

## *Debt and Ownership Concentration*

The widening of inequality since the early 1980s did not occur by accident. It followed from the way advanced economies chose to preserve order. When growth slowed or financial stress emerged, governments borrowed more to sustain spending and cushion downturns. Central banks reduced interest rates and supplied liquidity to prevent contraction. These measures helped stabilize economies during periods of strain, but they also reshaped how wealth accumulated over time. Asset ownership increasingly became a more powerful driver of financial advancement than income growth or productive work alone.

During deeper crises, central banks also purchased financial assets directly in what became known as quantitative easing.[3] These purchases typically included government bonds and, in some cases, corporate bonds and other financial securities. The goal was to lower long-term interest rates, support financial markets, and encourage borrowing and investment.

These responses were not reckless. In moments of severe stress, they were necessary to prevent systemic failure, since without intervention several advanced economies could have faced banking collapses, deeper recessions, and extended financial panic. At the same time, repeated intervention also reshaped prosperity.

By pushing asset prices higher, these policies increased the value of financial assets already held mainly by wealthier households. Lower interest rates increase the present value of financial assets.[4] Bond prices rise. Equities reprice upward. Real estate becomes more valuable as financing costs fall.

When these conditions persist for years rather than months, valuations adjust structurally across financial markets and property markets alike. Households that already own stocks, bonds, or real estate see the value of those assets rise steadily, often with little additional effort. Ownership itself becomes increasingly valuable.

At the same time, ownership is not evenly distributed. In the United States, equity ownership is heavily concentrated among higher-income households, leaving much of the population with limited exposure to rising financial markets.[5] Similar patterns appear across many other advanced economies, where pension wealth and financial assets are also concentrated among upper-income households, to varying degrees.

When governments and central banks support asset markets, the benefits therefore flow primarily to those who already hold claims on them. The gains are not distributed evenly across society because access to appreciating assets is itself uneven. Over time, this dynamic quietly widens the distance between asset owners and those dependent mainly on wages.

Meanwhile, households relying mainly on wages experience a different effect. Lower rates may support employment, but they also compress returns on savings. Asset prices rise faster than earnings, and entering housing and financial markets becomes increasingly expensive. For younger and lower-income households in particular, the cost of entering the ownership economy rises steadily over time.

Debt plays a central role in this process. Public borrowing sustains demand during downturns. Corporate borrowing finances share buybacks, acquisitions, and financial restructuring. Household borrowing bridges the gap between stagnant incomes and rising living costs. Each layer of debt reduces immediate pressure while also helping sustain higher asset prices.

Over time, stability itself becomes increasingly tied to elevated market valuations. Pension systems depend on investment returns. Governments rely on manageable financing costs. Corporations adapt to low interest expenses and rising asset prices. Withdrawal becomes disruptive, and the system gradually adjusts to the very conditions that widen divergence. What began as temporary stabilization increasingly evolves into permanent dependence.

The policies used to prevent downturns therefore also reinforce ownership concentration. As markets rise, households that already own financial assets and property benefit disproportionately, while those attempting to enter these markets face rising barriers. Gradually, wealth and ownership become more concentrated, and the gains from growth become increasingly uneven across society.

The result is not sudden disruption, but a gradual separation between those positioned inside appreciating markets and those attempting to enter them. The system continues to function, yet the experience of economic progress becomes increasingly unequal. Debt-supported stability preserves order in the short term while steadily reshaping who benefits from it. The longer this process continues, the more difficult it becomes to separate economic stability from rising inequality.

## *Compounding and the Locking-In of Divergence*

Once ownership concentration is reinforced by policy and sustained borrowing, inequality ceases to be cyclical and instead becomes cumulative, and the reason lies in simple arithmetic. The process no longer depends on a temporary boom or crisis. It becomes self-sustaining.

Financial assets generate returns on existing wealth. Dividends are reinvested. Capital gains increase the base on which future gains are calculated. Even modest annual returns compound over time, allowing households that own significant assets to see their wealth expand automatically as markets rise.

Compounding is powerful because each gain builds upon the last, allowing existing wealth to generate additional wealth that then produces further returns in the future. As this process continues, the distance widens between those who own appreciating assets and those who do not.

Labour income does not compound in the same way. Wages tend to grow incrementally and often struggle to keep pace with increases in housing, healthcare, and education costs. Income supports consumption, while wealth supports accumulation. Most households relying primarily on wages must use a large share of earnings simply to maintain living standards rather than build lasting financial assets.

Over extended periods, this difference produces widening gaps even without economic stress. Since the 2008–2009 global financial crisis, major equity indices in advanced economies have more than tripled, while over the same period median real incomes have grown far more slowly.[6] Housing values in many cities have risen faster than household earnings, and in many major cities across advanced economies house price-to-income ratios are now above levels seen before the 2008 crisis.[7]

These differences may appear manageable year to year, but over a decade or more they become structural. A household whose wages rise slowly cannot easily keep pace with assets appreciating far faster than income growth. Saving for ownership becomes progressively more difficult as the target continues to move further away for younger households.

Compounding transforms advantage into distance. Those who already hold appreciating assets see their net worth expand with limited additional effort, while those who do not must save from income that grows slowly relative to asset prices. Entry into ownership becomes increasingly dependent on inheritance, early access, or high levels of borrowing.

Over time, timing itself becomes a major source of advantage. Households that entered housing and financial markets earlier benefit from rising valuations, while later entrants face higher debt burdens and greater financial risk simply to acquire similar assets. Ownership increasingly reflects prior access rather than present productivity alone.

This process is self-reinforcing. Rising valuations increase the value of assets used to secure loans, which supports additional borrowing, and additional borrowing supports further price increases. Participation becomes increasingly tied to prior ownership because existing assets help generate access to additional credit and future gains.

Importantly, none of this requires a recession or financial panic. Employment can remain solid. Output can expand. The system can appear to function normally, yet the relationship between participation and progress weakens. People continue working, consuming, and participating in the economy, but advancement feels increasingly uneven and difficult to attain.

When gains are driven primarily by asset ownership rather than productive contribution, perceptions of fairness begin to shift. Effort no longer guarantees mobility, while timing and initial position matter more than participation alone. The economy increasingly rewards what households already own rather than what they produce.

Gradually, divergence hardens into structure. It becomes embedded in housing markets, retirement systems, corporate balance sheets, and the growing role of inherited wealth across generations. What began as a policy response to stabilize the system evolves into a framework that steadily directs gains toward those who already own assets.

Inequality therefore becomes not merely a by-product, but a built-in feature of how the system operates. The longer the process continues, the more difficult it becomes for societies to preserve the belief that opportunity remains broadly accessible. As that belief weakens, social cohesion and trust in the fairness of the economic system begin to erode as well.

## *When Divergence Undermines Public Consent*

Economic systems do not rest on output alone. They rest on acceptance. For decades, advanced economies maintained broad public confidence because most citizens believed that participation would eventually lead to advancement. People accepted inequality because they believed the system still offered a path toward greater security and opportunity over time.

The promise was not equality of outcome, but fairness of opportunity. People could tolerate gaps in wealth if mobility remained plausible. They could accept rising markets if wages grew over time. They could accept borrowing if it supported growth. As long as living standards improved broadly across society, the system retained legitimacy even when outcomes were uneven beneath the surface.

This belief allowed public institutions to function without constant challenge. Legitimacy, in practical terms, means that citizens accept the rules of the system even when outcomes are uneven. It reflects a broader belief that effort is rewarded, that advancement remains possible, and that markets are not permanently tilted beyond reach.

This acceptance also allows governments to borrow, central banks to intervene, and corporations to operate without constant political upheaval. Economic management becomes far more difficult once large segments of the population begin questioning whether the system still operates fairly.

When divergence becomes entrenched, that acceptance begins to weaken. If asset ownership determines advancement more than participation does, mobility appears constrained. If housing becomes unattainable without family wealth, the narrative of equal opportunity loses credibility. If wages trail far behind asset values for extended periods, confidence in the balance and fairness of the system gradually erodes.

This shift is gradual rather than sudden. Trust does not collapse overnight. It weakens through repeated experience, as younger cohorts delay homeownership, households carry larger debt burdens to secure basic assets, and retirement security feels increasingly uncertain for those without exposure to financial markets or appreciating assets.

As the process continues, patience declines and public frustration intensifies. Political discourse becomes more polarized, while redistribution becomes more contentious and central bank independence, once widely accepted, comes under growing scrutiny. Fiscal policy becomes trapped between rising obligations and declining tolerance for austerity. The more unequal the system becomes, the harder it is to sustain broad agreement about how economic burdens and rewards should be shared. The effects reach into public confidence.

This is not primarily a moral reaction but a structural shift. As large gains flow repeatedly toward asset owners while living costs rise for much of the population, distrust gradually accumulates. A system that delivers concentrated gains while asking broader society to absorb rising pressures eventually begins to lose consent.

As consent weakens, institutions become less capable of managing stress. Stability depends on more than functioning markets. It also depends on a broad belief that outcomes remain legitimate. Even sound policy becomes harder to implement once trust in institutions begins to erode.

Inequality at scale therefore does not simply coexist with stability. It gradually strains the social and political foundations that sustain it. The danger is not merely economic imbalance, but the slow erosion of the public confidence on which modern economic systems depend. Once confidence begins to fracture, restoring legitimacy becomes far more difficult than preserving it in the first place. As the process continues, the system becomes increasingly vulnerable to political division, public distrust, and resistance to economic adjustment.

## *When Inequality Limits the Capacity to Stabilize*

Modern stability has depended on flexibility. Governments borrowed to cushion downturns. Central banks lowered rates to support demand. Asset markets absorbed liquidity and transmitted stimulus. For decades, this approach helped keep the system stable without triggering systemic breakdown. During recessions and financial crises, these tools often prevented far deeper economic damage and financial panic.

But this framework also depended heavily on public tolerance. When borrowing rises, citizens must accept higher public debt. When central banks intervene, households must accept prolonged low interest rates and support for financial markets. When inflation accelerates, voters must tolerate some erosion in purchasing power during periods of adjustment. Stability requires room to manoeuvre politically as well as financially.

Entrenched inequality gradually reduces that room. In a system where wealth gains are heavily concentrated, further asset support appears less neutral. Market intervention begins to look like favouritism. Fiscal expansion appears to reward those already positioned to benefit. Monetary easing seems to inflate housing and financial markets further beyond reach. Policies once viewed as stabilizing increasingly appear to many households as reinforcing inequality itself.

This perception matters because confidence in economic management depends in part on whether the public believes intervention benefits society broadly rather than mainly protecting financial wealth. As outcomes become more unequal, support for future rescue measures becomes harder to sustain.

Economic downturns in unequal societies often generate stronger resistance to stabilization efforts. Calls for redistribution intensify, political coalitions fracture, and legislative gridlock becomes more common. As economic stress collides with political fragmentation, the consensus needed for coordinated action begins to weaken. Policies that once appeared temporary or widely accepted become far more politically contested.

At the same time, elevated debt levels reduce the ability of governments to borrow freely during future downturns. After decades of borrowing to preserve stability, public debt burdens in several advanced economies are now substantially larger relative to national income than in earlier periods. Public debt levels in several advanced economies now exceed 100 percent of national income, leaving less room for large-scale borrowing without political resistance or market concern.[8]

Central banks face similar limits. Years of low rates and asset purchases have increased the sensitivity of markets to policy shifts.[9] When inflation rises, tightening becomes disruptive. When growth slows, renewed easing risks reinforcing the very divergences that weakened public acceptance in the first place.

Inequality therefore constrains both sides of the stabilization equation. It reduces political tolerance for intervention while increasing economic dependence on it. The system becomes simultaneously more fragile and more difficult to support.

A system built on stability supported by rising asset prices becomes increasingly difficult to adjust. If policymakers withdraw support, stock and housing prices can fall, weakening household wealth, corporate balance sheets, and government finances. If they continue support, inequality deepens as existing asset owners benefit disproportionately.

Either path carries risk. What once helped stabilize the economy gradually begins to generate new forms of instability. The tools used to manage downturns become progressively less effective and more politically contentious.

High public debt makes additional borrowing more difficult both financially and politically. Political polarization weakens the ability to coordinate responses during crisis. Confidence in public institutions becomes more fragile when large segments of the population feel excluded from economic gains. The system loses flexibility precisely when it needs flexibility most.

Inequality does not cause collapse on its own, but it weakens the system's ability to respond effectively when shocks occur. Over time, the capacity to stabilize weakens not because governments and central banks lose their tools entirely, but because the political and social foundations supporting those tools begin to erode.

## *From Divergence to Breaking*

Inequality without crisis can persist for years and coexist with rising markets and expanding output, yet it alters the character of stability in ways that are not immediately visible. The economy may continue growing while the experience of that growth becomes increasingly uneven. When gains are concentrated and advancement depends increasingly on ownership rather than participation, economic systems lose one of their central anchors: the belief that effort translates into security. Confidence begins to erode with it.

Once that belief weakens, the foundations of stability begin to shift. People continue working, consuming, and participating in the economy, but confidence in the fairness of the system gradually declines. The weakening often occurs slowly at first, through frustration that accumulates over years rather than through a single dramatic event.

Advanced economies have relied on three pillars to absorb shocks since the early 1980s: public borrowing, monetary intervention, and political consent.[10] Debt financed downturns. Central banks stabilized markets. Voters tolerated the trade-offs because growth, even if uneven, appeared to justify them.

Deep and persistent inequality now strains each of these pillars. High debt levels make further borrowing politically contentious and financially delicate. Prolonged intervention makes monetary policy less neutral and more contested. Concentrated gains make fiscal decisions more divisive. As the distance between ownership and opportunity widens, maintaining broad political agreement becomes increasingly difficult.

Social cohesion weakens as larger segments of society feel excluded from the mechanisms through which wealth and security are created. The issue is no longer simply unequal outcomes. It is the growing perception that advancement itself has become structurally uneven.

In earlier periods, economic downturns were often met with coordinated action and broad public support. Today, responses to economic stress occur in an environment marked by distrust, polarization, and reduced tolerance for further imbalance. Policy measures that once restored calm now trigger greater suspicion. Redistribution debates intensify, while public institutions come under growing scrutiny.

What makes this shift especially dangerous is that inequality no longer feels temporary. In earlier periods of instability, hardship was often understood as part of a cycle that would eventually reverse. Many households believed difficult periods would eventually give way to renewed opportunity and improving living standards.

Today, for many households across the advanced world, the divide increasingly appears structural and enduring. Wealth compounds through ownership of assets, while access to those assets becomes progressively more difficult for those outside the system of accumulated capital. The longer this process continues, inequality feels more permanent than cyclical.

Over time, this changes how societies understand fairness, opportunity, and economic legitimacy itself. When younger generations no longer believe that work alone can provide security, when home ownership becomes unattainable for large segments of the population, and when financial gains appear increasingly detached from productive activity, confidence in the broader economic order begins to weaken.

The consequences extend beyond income distribution. Inequality gradually reshapes political behaviour, weakens social cohesion, and erodes trust in institutions. Economic systems depend not only on markets and policy, but also on the belief that advancement remains broadly possible and that the rules governing society retain a degree of fairness and credibility.

When that belief weakens, polarization deepens and public frustration becomes more volatile. Distrust then begins to spread through political institutions, financial systems, and expectations about the future. The weakening may unfold slowly, but over time it reduces the ability of societies to absorb pressure with confidence and restraint.

Divergence therefore contributes not by producing immediate collapse, but by weakening the system's ability to absorb shocks and narrowing the margin for adjustment. When the next severe shock arrives, the system confronts it with higher debt, thinner public patience, and less room for compromise.

The danger is not simply that wealth has become concentrated. It is that large parts of society increasingly feel excluded from the mechanisms through which stability and security are created. Prosperity begins to appear selective rather than shared, while economic success feels increasingly detached from the everyday experience of work and living standards.

At that point, stability is no longer a baseline condition but a contested outcome. A society can tolerate inequality for long periods when living standards are rising broadly and opportunity remains believable. It becomes far more unstable when economic advancement appears permanently unequal and the distance between asset ownership and labour income continues to widen.

Under those conditions, distrust spreads gradually through institutions, political systems, and public expectations. The system does not fail all at once. It weakens progressively as confidence, flexibility, and social cohesion erode together.

The breaking of the advanced world will not begin with inequality alone. It will emerge when inequality intersects with fiscal strain, monetary constraint, and political fracture. By the time those forces converge, however, the groundwork will already have been laid. The weakening will have developed gradually beneath the surface, long before the full consequences become visible.

This is where inequality becomes more than a social issue. It becomes a structural pressure capable of weakening the cohesion that stable societies depend upon. The challenge is no longer simply how wealth is distributed. It is whether advanced economies can continue to sustain legitimacy when prosperity itself is experienced so unevenly.

The deeper question that follows is why modern economies have become increasingly unable to translate technological progress, financial expansion, and rising market wealth into broad-based improvements in productivity and living standards. That paradox lies at the centre of the next stage of the breakdown.

# PART IV

# THE FORCES OF BREAKDOWN

# 12

# THE PRODUCTIVITY PARADOX

For much of the modern era, technological progress functioned as capitalism's most reliable stabiliser. New inventions raised productivity, lowered costs, and expanded output. As firms became more efficient, wages tended to rise alongside them. Rising wages supported consumption. Consumption reinforced growth. Growth strengthened public finances. The system, for decades, reinforced itself, with innovation steadily underpinning economic stability.

In practical terms, technological progress improved everyday living standards for broad parts of society. As economies became more productive, households generally experienced rising incomes, greater security, and expanding access to consumption. Innovation strengthened confidence in the system because its benefits were widely felt rather than narrowly concentrated.

This was not accidental but reflected a transmission mechanism through which productivity gains flowed into labour markets, into household income, and from there into demand. In earlier eras, when workers produced more, their incomes generally rose as well. Those rising incomes then supported spending across the broader economy for many years thereafter.

Innovation therefore legitimised capitalism because its gains spread widely enough to reinforce both growth and social stability. History repeatedly demonstrated this pattern.

The factory floor, electrification, aviation, and computing each disrupted older industries, yet they also created employment on a scale large enough to absorb much of that disruption. Technological change often displaced older forms of work, but it also generated large numbers of new jobs and rising incomes across expanding industries and sectors.

During the mid-twentieth century, this relationship was visible in the data. In the United States and much of Western Europe, productivity and real wages moved broadly together. As output per worker increased, compensation followed. Between 1947 and the early 1970s, U.S. labour productivity and real median compensation rose at broadly similar rates, reinforcing a period of strong middle-class expansion.[1]

A similar pattern appeared across other advanced economies, including Western Europe and Japan, where productivity gains were broadly shared through rising wages and expanding employment. The gains were not evenly distributed, but they were broad enough to sustain a durable middle class. Growth expanded purchasing power, not merely corporate balance sheets. Economic expansion strengthened households as well as markets.

## *When Innovation Stabilised Growth*

That relationship acted as a stabiliser. When productivity rose, demand rose with it, and when firms became more efficient, households became more secure. Innovation strengthened private incomes before it required public intervention, allowing the system to absorb shocks because rising wages replenished the demand base. Growth reinforced itself because rising productivity translated into rising household purchasing power.

Over time, however, that transmission mechanism weakened. Productivity continued to rise, but the gains no longer flowed as directly into wages and household income. When productivity no longer feeds broadly into pay, the economy must rely on alternative means to sustain demand. The resulting gap was filled through other channels across the economy.

From the early 1980s onward, advanced economies increasingly depended on substitutes such as rising household borrowing, asset appreciation, and prolonged periods of low interest rates. In the United States, household debt rose from roughly 45 percent of GDP to nearly 100 percent by the eve of the 2008 financial crisis.[2] Consumption increasingly depended not only on income growth, but also on easier credit and rising asset values, and low borrowing costs.

Similar trends emerged across other advanced economies. In the United Kingdom, household debt climbed sharply from the late 1980s through the mid-2000s, reaching levels comparable to those seen in the United States.[3] In Canada and Australia, household debt continued rising even after the global financial crisis, driven largely by housing markets and prolonged low interest rates.

Consumption continued across these economies, but it was increasingly supported less by wage growth and more by credit expansion and rising asset prices. Housing and equity markets strengthened household financial positions and encouraged spending even where income growth remained modest. Across several advanced economies, housing prices rose significantly faster than incomes during the two decades preceding the global financial crisis.

This increase reinforced consumption through wealth effects and further weakened the direct relationship between productivity growth and household income. Rising property and stock market values increasingly substituted for the stronger wage growth that had supported earlier periods of economic expansion.

This shift altered the role of technology. Innovation continued and output continued to rise, but the stabilising loop between productivity and pay no longer functioned in the same way. Growth persisted, yet its benefits became less widely transmitted. Economic expansion increasingly depended on financial conditions rather than broadly rising incomes across the economy.

In that environment, technological progress took on a different character. It no longer automatically strengthened the system's foundations. Instead, innovation unfolded within an economy already burdened by debt and increasingly reliant on asset prices and credit conditions to maintain stability.

Technology did not create that fragility, but once the wage channel weakened, innovation ceased to function as a self-correcting force. The economy could now expand output without proportionately expanding financial security for large parts of the population over time.

That distinction matters because when a stabiliser weakens in an economy already carrying heavy debt, the consequences are not merely distributional but structural. The economy can continue to grow, but the foundations supporting that growth become less secure. Stability increasingly depends on borrowing conditions, asset prices, and continued financial support rather than on broadly rising household incomes.

## *The Break Between Productivity and Pay*

For much of the twentieth century, productivity growth and wage growth moved broadly together. As output per worker increased, compensation followed. The relationship was not perfect, but it was strong enough to sustain rising living standards across large segments of society and reinforce the expansion of a stable middle class. Economic growth translated into broader household security because workers shared in the gains created by higher productivity and rising wages.

That pattern began to shift in the 1970s. In the United States, labour productivity, essentially the amount of output produced per worker, has risen by more than 60 percent since the early 1970s, while real hourly compensation for typical workers has grown far more slowly, increasing by roughly 15 to 20 percent over the same period. In simple terms, workers have been producing far more, but their pay has not risen in proportion to what they produce. That gap has consequences.

This link matters because when workers produce more value, firms typically generate higher revenues and profits. In earlier decades, part of those gains flowed back to employees through higher wages, better benefits, and more stable employment. As incomes rose, households spent more, reinforcing demand and supporting broader economic growth. The economy strengthened from the middle outward because productivity gains circulated through wages and consumption.

The gap widened after 2000. Output continued to expand, but median wage growth did not keep pace. This divergence between output growth and worker compensation marked a structural shift in how growth translated into household income. The economy continued producing more, yet much of the population experienced far weaker income growth than earlier generations associated with periods of expansion.

This development, however, was not uniquely American. Across several advanced European economies, productivity continued to rise while real wage growth remained subdued, particularly since the early 2000s. In Germany, labour productivity increased steadily in the decades following reunification, yet real wages were largely stagnant between the late 1990s and the mid-2000s before recovering modestly in the 2010s.[4]

A similar pattern emerged in the United Kingdom. Productivity grew by roughly 20 percent between the late 1990s and the global financial crisis, while real median earnings stagnated after 2008.[5] The pattern varies in degree, but the broader shift is visible across the advanced world. Economies continue producing more output, yet the gains no longer flow into labour income in the same proportion.

This shift does not trigger immediate collapse. Instead, it creates a structural imbalance. When productivity feeds wages, rising output strengthens household purchasing power and reinforces demand. When that link weakens, growth no longer guarantees stronger consumption, and demand must increasingly be supported by other means such as borrowing and policy intervention. Other mechanisms filled the gap.

Over recent decades, those substitutes have included rising household borrowing, asset appreciation, and supportive monetary policy. Debt and rising asset values often compensated for weaker income growth. The substitution is subtle. Employment may remain relatively high, markets continue functioning, and headline growth persists. Yet the economy's internal stabiliser has weakened.

The system continues expanding without proportionately reinforcing the income base that once sustained it. Instead, growth increasingly depends on financial support mechanisms rather than on rising wages broadening purchasing power across society. That shift changes how economies absorb stress.

In an economy where rising output strengthens wages, downturns are cushioned by the accumulated gains of prior growth. By contrast, when output expands but income growth remains thin, households enter downturns more exposed. Household finances become more strained. Savings buffers are smaller. Debt burdens are heavier relative to income. than in previous decades.

Across several advanced economies, household savings rates declined in the decades leading up to the global financial crisis, while household borrowing increased, leaving households more vulnerable to economic shocks. Growth continues, but its ability to strengthen resilience declines. The economy appears stable on the surface even as underlying household resilience weakens.

This is the environment into which modern technological change now accelerates. In earlier eras, innovation reinforced the wage channel and supported broad income growth. Today, many of the most dynamic technologies increase economic output without requiring proportional increases in labour income.

As a result, the break between productivity and pay becomes more deeply embedded rather than temporary. Growth continues, but its stabilising effect weakens. The economy expands, yet broad-based financial security does not expand alongside it in the same way. Expansion increasingly occurs without comparable gains in household incomes and financial resilience.

This shift helps explain why technological progress can coincide with growing economic strain. The issue is no longer simply how much innovation occurs, but how that innovation is translated into jobs, incomes, and broader economic participation. Increasingly, those relationships are changing in ways that differ from earlier technological eras.

## *Capital Scaling Without Labour Scaling*

Many of today's most valuable technologies are capital-intensive rather than labour-intensive. They require large amounts of investment and computing infrastructure, but relatively fewer workers once the systems are built. Software platforms, digital infrastructure, and artificial intelligence systems can scale to millions or even billions of users without proportional increases in employment or labour demand.

Once built, these systems expand largely through code, data, and network effects, meaning the platforms become more valuable as more people use them. Revenue and market value can therefore grow extremely quickly without requiring equally large increases in payrolls or physical expansion.

Earlier waves of technological transformation looked very different. The automobile revolution did not simply produce cars. It generated employment across steel, rubber, glass, assembly lines, transport networks, dealerships, road construction, and suburban development. Electrification required vast workforces to build power stations, lay transmission lines, manufacture appliances, and redesign factories. Industrial expansion created large numbers of middle-income jobs as production scaled upward. The relationship was relatively straightforward.

Industrial growth required human scale. As output expanded, employment expanded alongside it. The economy produced more goods, but it also created mass purchasing power because rising production generated rising employment across many sectors.

At its mid-twentieth-century peak, General Motors employed more than 600,000 workers.[6] Many of today's largest technology firms, despite far larger market valuations in real terms, employ only a fraction of that number. Apple, Microsoft, and Alphabet each employ roughly between 150,000 and 220,000 workers, yet their market capitalisations exceed those of many traditional industrial giants by a wide margin.[7]

The contrast is striking. Modern technology firms can generate enormous revenues and financial valuations without employing workforces on the scale once associated with industrial expansion. Revenue and market value scale exponentially, while payrolls expand far more slowly.

This difference is often dismissed with a familiar historical argument. Automation has always generated anxiety. Mechanisation displaced artisans. Industrial machinery replaced manual labour. Computers eliminated clerical roles. Yet new industries eventually emerged, and employment adapted. Over time, technology created more jobs than it destroyed, and economies reorganised around new forms of production.

That historical pattern is real, but it depended on a crucial condition. Those earlier technological revolutions not only raised productivity; they also generated broad labour demand across expanding industries. Displacement in one sector was offset by large-scale job creation elsewhere. Workers leaving older industries could often move into expanding sectors that still required substantial human labour.

The structure of today's technological expansion is different. Digital platforms, cloud computing, and artificial intelligence increase output without requiring equivalent increases in employment. Many of the most profitable firms rely heavily on intellectual property, data control, and network dominance rather than large workforces. The relationship between employment and profitability continues to weaken.

Artificial intelligence extends this logic further by automating not only routine manual tasks but also cognitive and analytical functions once associated with middle-income employment. Technology is now moving beyond factory automation into areas once viewed as relatively protected white-collar work.

The issue is not that work will disappear overnight, but that income growth becomes less connected to output growth. When firms can expand revenue without expanding payrolls proportionately, productivity gains flow more heavily toward capital than labour. The economy can therefore become more productive overall while broad wage growth weakens.

In a low-debt economy with strong income growth, such a shift might be absorbed gradually. In an economy already carrying heavy debt and relying on steady consumption to service it, however, the implications become more serious. Broad wage growth supports household spending. Household spending supports corporate revenues. Revenues help support debt repayment across the system.

When innovation raises output without strengthening wages broadly, the spending power of households becomes thinner relative to the financial obligations resting upon it. The economy continues generating output, but the income needed to sustain consumption and debt repayment grows more slowly.

This is where capital scaling without labour scaling becomes systemic rather than merely distributional. If income growth concentrates while debt remains widely distributed, the burden of adjustment falls increasingly on households with limited financial buffers. Asset owners may benefit from rising valuations, but consumption across the broader economy becomes more sensitive to borrowing conditions and interest rates.

Technology does not create this vulnerability on its own. It interacts with an existing structure in which borrowing has long substituted for income growth. By weakening the wage channel further, it reduces one of the few natural stabilisers through which the economy once reinforced itself. The margin for absorbing economic shocks gradually narrows.

Growth continues. Innovation advances. Market valuations rise. But the economy's ability to absorb shocks through rising labour income weakens. In a system already stretched by debt and uneven income growth, that loss of resilience becomes increasingly important over time. The effects may not be immediately visible during periods of expansion and rising asset prices. They become far more apparent when financial markets begin to play a larger role in transmitting the gains from technological change.

This shift does not stop technological progress. It changes how its benefits are distributed throughout the economy. As labour income becomes less central to the transmission of growth, financial markets assume a larger role. The result is that economic gains increasingly depend on asset ownership as well as productive activity across the economy.

## *When Financial Markets Amplify Technological Gains*

Technological change over the past fifteen years, broadly since 2010, did not unfold in neutral financial conditions. It accelerated during an era defined by exceptionally low interest rates and unprecedented central bank support. Following the 2008 financial crisis, policy rates in the United States, the Eurozone, and the United Kingdom were pushed toward zero and held there for years, while central bank balance sheets expanded dramatically as authorities purchased government bonds and other financial assets to stabilise markets.[8]

These measures were introduced to prevent financial collapse, and in that objective they largely succeeded. Banking systems stabilised, borrowing costs fell, and financial markets recovered far more quickly than many policymakers initially feared. Yet the same policies also reshaped the environment in which modern technology firms operated and were valued. The shift was reinforced by extraordinary monetary support.

The U.S. Federal Reserve's balance sheet, for example, grew from under 1 trillion dollars before the crisis to roughly 4.5 trillion dollars within a few years, and expanded further after the pandemic.[10] Similar expansions occurred across other advanced economies. The European Central Bank's balance sheet increased several-fold during the same period, while the Bank of England's asset purchases expanded sharply through quantitative easing programmes in response.

When interest rates fall, the future profits investors expect companies to generate become more valuable in today's markets. Companies promising strong growth many years into the future therefore become worth far more in the present. This disproportionately benefits firms built around scale, intellectual property, and long-term technological dominance.

Technology companies fit that profile closely. Capital flowed aggressively toward innovation that could scale rapidly and generate large future returns, even when the broader economic benefits remained unevenly distributed. Venture funding surged. Equity valuations climbed. The largest technology firms increasingly dominated major stock indices.

Asset markets began pricing technological promise long before those gains translated into widespread income growth. Wealth accumulated rapidly on financial balance sheets. Market capitalisations expanded dramatically. Yet median wages did not accelerate in parallel. The gains appeared immediately in markets, but much more slowly in ordinary household incomes.

Between 2009 and 2021, for example, the S&P 500 rose more than fourfold, while real median household income in the United States grew far more modestly over the same period.[10] Similar patterns emerged across several advanced economies where stock markets and housing prices surged while wage growth remained subdued for many households. The benefits of expansion became increasingly uneven. Gains flowed more readily to those who owned appreciating assets than to those who relied on wages.

For households with substantial exposure to financial markets and property, rising asset values created significant wealth effects. Households owning stocks and real estate often felt financially stronger as markets rose. For those without such exposure, however, many of the gains remained largely invisible. The same financial conditions that stabilised markets also reinforced the concentration of wealth and asset ownership.

This dynamic gradually changed the meaning of economic strength. Market indices could rise sharply even while wage growth remained modest. Valuations could surge on expectations surrounding artificial intelligence and digital transformation even as purchasing power for many households remained under pressure in everyday life.

The economy increasingly looked stronger in financial markets than it felt in everyday life. Stability appeared robust because asset prices remained elevated, yet asset-driven stability is inherently conditional. It depends on valuations remaining high and borrowing costs remaining manageable.

When markets price future technological gains immediately while households experience adjustment and insecurity in the present, a gap opens between financial optimism and economic resilience. Technology thrives in such conditions because it promises scalable returns, yet the broader economy becomes more sensitive to financial cycles.

If valuations correct or borrowing conditions tighten, the stabilising effect of rising asset prices weakens quickly. The economy becomes more exposed because consumption and confidence increasingly depend on markets continuing to rise.

In earlier eras, technological gains reinforced wages and demand before they inflated asset prices. In the post-2008 era, the sequence often reversed. Asset markets priced transformation first, while broad income gains, if they arrived at all, followed much later in the process. The shift altered economic stability. Its consequences extended well beyond financial markets.

That inversion matters in an economy already carrying heavy debt because when rising asset prices support consumption and borrowing, stability becomes increasingly dependent on financial markets themselves. Economic resilience relies less on broadly rising incomes and more on elevated valuations continuing to hold.

The system appears strong so long as markets remain buoyant, but its resilience rests increasingly on financial conditions rather than durable income growth. Technology does not merely operate within this environment. It flourishes because of it, and in doing so deepens the economy's dependence on asset markets as a pillar of stability and growth. The arrangement remained stable only while financial conditions remained favourable.

## *Rising Rates and the Return of Fragility*

For more than a decade after 2008, exceptionally low interest rates reduced the immediate cost of debt across much of the advanced world. Governments could refinance large deficits at modest yields. Corporations borrowed heavily to fund acquisitions, share buybacks, and expansion. Households serviced mortgages and consumer loans at historically low rates. Low borrowing costs helped preserve stability in an economy where wage growth remained uneven and asset prices carried increasing weight.

Debt remained manageable because rates were suppressed. Asset valuations remained elevated because the future profits investors expected companies to generate were discounted very lightly. The entire structure held together because borrowing remained cheap and financial conditions stayed supportive.

Between 2008 and 2021, policy rates in many advanced economies remained at or near historic lows, while government debt levels rose significantly, including in the United States, the United Kingdom, and much of the Eurozone.[11] This combination allowed very high debt levels to remain serviceable despite modest income growth. The arrangement worked only while those conditions persisted.

That support, however, was never permanent. When interest rates begin to normalise, the mathematics of the system change quickly. Higher rates increase the cost of servicing public debt. They compress corporate margins where borrowing financed operations or shareholder returns. They reduce the market value investors place on distant future earnings, placing downward pressure on high-growth equity valuations.

Housing affordability also deteriorates as mortgage rates rise, while markets become more volatile. The same conditions that supported asset prices and borrowing during the low-rate era operate in reverse once money becomes more expensive.

In an economy anchored by broad wage growth, such adjustments can often be absorbed gradually. In an economy where income growth has lagged while debt burdens have risen, the margin for adjustment becomes much narrower. Households facing higher borrowing costs cannot rely on strong wage gains to offset them as they once could.

Governments carrying large debt loads must allocate more revenue toward interest payments rather than public investment or social support. Corporations that expanded during years of cheap money face tighter financing conditions. Pressure spreads across households, businesses, and governments alike.

By the early 2020s, government debt levels in many advanced economies had reached historically elevated levels, with public debt exceeding 100 percent of GDP in the United States and several European economies.[12] At the same time, corporate borrowing had also expanded significantly during the low-rate period, while household debt remained elevated in several countries, particularly those with strong housing markets.

These conditions meant that even modest increases in interest rates could produce amplified effects across financial positions throughout the economy. The system became more sensitive because debt accumulated during years when borrowing costs appeared permanently manageable across much of the economy.

At the same time, many of the technologies attracting very high valuations during the low-rate era depended heavily on expectations of sustained future growth. When rates rise, investors value those future profits less generously, and technology-related asset prices can adjust rapidly.

The combination matters because when productivity gains are concentrated and wage growth remains subdued, higher interest rates do not simply cool speculation. They tighten pressure on an economy already dependent on borrowing and elevated asset prices to maintain stability.

Debt servicing costs rise at the same time that asset values face downward pressure. The system therefore becomes more vulnerable to financial shocks. Technology does not create that sensitivity, but by concentrating gains and scaling without proportionate labour absorption, it weakens the economy's ability to offset tightening through stronger wage growth.

If incomes do not rise sufficiently, adjustment falls more heavily on balance sheets instead. Households reduce spending. Governments face greater fiscal pressure. Financial markets become more unstable at the same time.

In this environment, stability depends increasingly on careful calibration. Rates must remain high enough to contain inflation and preserve credibility, yet low enough to avoid widespread financial stress. That balancing act becomes far more difficult once debt levels are elevated and asset markets carry much of the economy's weight.

What once appeared to be flexibility gradually becomes constraint. The same tools that preserved calm during earlier periods now carry much larger trade-offs. As the corridor narrows, the probability of policy miscalculation rises.

Technology increases that sensitivity by weakening the wage channel and strengthening dependence on asset markets. increases that sensitivity. It does not trigger the reckoning directly, but it reduces the room in which it can still be avoided. The consequences are cumulative and increasingly difficult to reverse.

## *Technology and the Erosion of Economic Consent*

Economic systems do not rest on efficiency alone. They rest on acceptance. For much of the postwar era, technological progress strengthened that acceptance because innovation raised productivity, wages followed, and living standards improved across broad segments of society. Even when inequality existed, there remained a visible relationship between effort and advancement. Work still appeared to provide a credible path toward greater security and upward mobility. That expectation reinforced public confidence.

For much of the modern era, technological progress expanded both output and opportunity. Innovation disrupted older industries, but it also created rising incomes, broader prosperity, and confidence that future generations would benefit from continued economic advancement. People generally believed that technological progress would improve their lives rather than weaken their economic position over time.

When that relationship weakens, legitimacy begins to erode. If output rises while median incomes stagnate, households experience progress very differently from financial markets. If asset prices surge while housing becomes less affordable, stability begins to feel selective rather than broadly shared.

If employment persists but becomes more volatile, algorithmically managed, and less predictable, work no longer guarantees security in the same way. Technology intensifies these tensions not necessarily by eliminating employment outright, but by increasing uncertainty about future stability and opportunity.

The relationship between innovation and economic security therefore begins to change. Productivity may continue rising, yet the gains increasingly accumulate unevenly across labour, capital, and geography. Technological progress still transforms economies, but it no longer guarantees that financial security will expand alongside it for broad parts of society. Expectations often change before labour markets do on a large scale.

Artificial intelligence and automation do not need to eliminate employment entirely to destabilise expectations. It is enough for them to increase perceived risk. When middle-income roles appear vulnerable to software or machine learning systems, long-term planning becomes more cautious. When career ladders narrow and income volatility rises, risk-taking declines.

When economic gains concentrate in specific sectors and regions, geographic and generational divides widen. Some parts of the economy experience enormous technological wealth creation while others experience rising insecurity and weaker long-term prospects. Technology therefore ceases to function solely as a stabilising force.

It continues increasing efficiency and output, yet it also deepens the perception that the future may become less secure for large segments of the population. The concern is no longer simply whether jobs disappear, but whether stable middle-income security gradually weakens even while innovation accelerates.

Across several advanced economies, younger cohorts have already experienced slower income growth and lower rates of asset ownership compared with previous generations, particularly in housing markets. In countries such as the United Kingdom, Canada, and Australia, house price growth since the early 2000s has significantly outpaced income growth, making asset accumulation more difficult for younger households.[13]

These trends reinforce the perception that technological and economic progress no longer benefit all groups equally. For many younger households especially, innovation increasingly coexists with delayed ownership, heavier debt burdens, and greater uncertainty about future living standards.

Over time, the perception that innovation benefits a relatively narrow segment while exposing others to insecurity begins reshaping political behaviour. Trust weakens. Populist movements gain traction. Demands for protection, redistribution, or economic restriction increase. Political systems become more polarised as voters respond to economic strain.

Recent electoral shifts across several advanced economies have reflected growing dissatisfaction with inequality, stagnant incomes, and declining perceptions of economic mobility. This shift matters because modern stability depended not only on growth itself, but also on the belief that growth would remain broadly shared over time and across society.

Once that belief weakens, technological progress no longer reinforces social cohesion in the way it once did. Innovation may continue generating wealth and market expansion, yet confidence in the fairness of the broader system begins to erode.

In an economy already carrying heavy debt, these pressures become increasingly difficult to manage. Fiscal responses become harder when public finances are already stretched. Monetary responses become riskier when inflation remains a concern. The room for policymakers to stabilize the system narrows just as social pressures intensify and become harder to manage. Every part of the system adapts in response.

Technology therefore no longer operates as a neutral force inside the economy. It increasingly accelerates divergence in incomes, asset ownership, and perceptions of opportunity. Stability, once anchored by broad income growth and expanding opportunity, becomes more dependent on financial conditions and public narrative. That dependence remains largely invisible.

As long as markets rise and credit continues flowing, the system appears intact. Yet beneath that surface, social cohesion weakens gradually. The economy may continue generating impressive technological advances while confidence in long-term security quietly deteriorates.

History suggests that when economic systems cease translating growth into broadly felt improvement, political strain intensifies before financial breakdown becomes visible. Adjustment often begins in institutions and elections before it appears in bond markets. The early signs of instability frequently emerge socially and politically before they appear financially or economically.

Innovation may continue accelerating, yet the social foundations that once absorbed disruption weaken beneath it. The paradox is no longer that productivity has slowed, but that rising technological capability no longer produces the broad-based stability earlier eras of growth once sustained.

Technology does not guarantee such an outcome, but under current structures it increases its likelihood. Innovation will continue. Artificial intelligence will advance. Productivity may even accelerate. The question is no longer whether technology will progress, but whether its gains will reinforce the foundations of stability or further hollow them out.

In an economy where wage growth no longer anchors demand, where debt increasingly substitutes for income, and where asset prices signal strength more clearly than living standards, technological acceleration narrows the system's margin for error. Economies may become more technologically advanced while simultaneously becoming more financially and socially fragile.

Technology continues to raise productivity and expand economic possibilities. Yet it can no longer compensate for ageing populations, excessive debt, widening wealth disparities, or an economy increasingly dependent on rising asset prices. It does not create these pressures, but it can intensify them by separating productivity from broadly shared prosperity.

The challenge facing advanced economies is therefore no longer simply whether they can generate innovation, but whether they can ensure its benefits strengthen economic resilience rather than deepen existing vulnerabilities. That question becomes more pressing as another structural force gathers momentum: the demographic transformation reshaping the advanced world.

# 13

# THE DEMOGRAPHIC BREAKING POINT

For decades, advanced economies assumed that growth would continue because it always had. Output would rise. Tax revenues would grow. Debt would remain manageable because the economy itself kept getting larger.

What made that expansion possible was rarely discussed. Behind rising output and rising incomes stood a simple demographic reality: populations and workforces were expanding. Growing workforces generated more output, more spending, more tax revenue, and stronger support for public systems. Today, that demographic foundation is shifting. Across much of the developed world, populations are ageing rapidly while workforces are no longer expanding. In some countries, they are already shrinking.

The ratio of workers to retirees, once comfortably wide, is narrowing across Europe, Japan, and increasingly the United States. In many advanced economies, there were roughly five working-age adults for every retiree in the 1980s. In several countries, that ratio is now closer to three to one and continues to decline.[1] At first glance, this appears to be a slow-moving demographic change. In reality, it alters the economic arithmetic that supported growth, public finances, and debt sustainability for decades. The shift is already underway.

Across much of the developed world, the number of working age adults is no longer rising. In several major economies, it is already shrinking. Fertility rates in Europe, Japan, and parts of

East Asia have fallen far below the replacement level of 2.1 children per woman. Japan's fertility rate has hovered near 1.3 for years. South Korea's has fallen below 1.0. Italy and Spain remain well below replacement.[2] Even in the United States, where population growth once appeared relatively resilient, labour force expansion has slowed sharply compared with the 1980s and 1990s. The demographic engine that once supplied a steady flow of new workers is no longer operating with the same strength.

China, long viewed as a source of global labour expansion, has now entered population decline.[3] Eastern Europe has experienced sustained population contraction for years. These trends are not isolated developments. They represent a broad demographic shift across the advanced and ageing parts of the global economy.

At the same time, people are living longer. The share of citizens over sixty-five has risen steadily across advanced economies and continues to climb. In Japan, there are now fewer than two working-age adults for every retiree.[4] Germany, Italy, and much of Eastern Europe are moving in the same direction. The United States faces a similar shift as the baby boom generation moves fully into retirement. Longer life expectancy is one of the great achievements of modern society. Economically, however, it means that more retirees depend on a relatively smaller workforce to support pensions, healthcare systems, and public finances.

These trends do not reverse quickly. A society cannot produce a new generation of workers in response to rising debt or fiscal pressure. Demographic change unfolds over decades, and once it moves in one direction, it carries momentum. Population trends possess a stubborn persistence. Decisions about family formation made today influence labour markets twenty years from now and retirement systems forty years from now. The resulting pressures accumulate across decades rather than years. The effects are already largely locked in.

The age structure that now defines the advanced world will shape economic outcomes for a generation. The challenge is not merely that populations are ageing. It is that many of the institutions, promises, and financial structures built during an era of demographic expansion must now operate in a very different demographic reality.

## *The End of Demographic Tailwinds*

This shift alters the arithmetic of growth. Economic expansion depends on two broad forces: the number of people working and how productive they are. When the workforce grows by one or two percent per year, the economy benefits from built-in momentum.[5] A larger workforce generates more production, more consumption, more taxpayers, and more demand.

For much of the postwar era, advanced economies benefited from both forces at the same time. Workforces expanded while productivity improved, creating a powerful combination that supported growth, rising incomes, and expanding public revenues. Those conditions no longer prevail.

When the workforce stalls or contracts, that momentum begins to fade. Unless productivity accelerates dramatically, economic growth slows almost automatically. In most advanced economies, however, productivity growth has been modest for years. The two trends reinforce one another.

This is where the demographic challenge becomes more serious. A growing workforce can compensate for weak productivity growth. A shrinking workforce cannot. Once labour force growth fades, economies become far more dependent on productivity improvements to sustain expansion.

Slower growth changes everything. Debt that once appeared manageable becomes heavier when the economy expands at two percent instead of four. Pension systems designed for a broad base of workers begin to strain when the number of workers paying into the system shrinks while the number of retirees drawing from it rises. Public finances that relied on steady increases in tax revenue face increasingly difficult trade-offs.

Growth helped postpone a direct confrontation with these constraints for many years.

The stability model that emerged in the early 1980s assumed that expansion would smooth many of these pressures. Growth acted as a shock absorber. Rising incomes, expanding employment, and growing tax bases helped governments meet obligations without requiring constant adjustment.

This demographic shift is particularly significant because it interacts with the other pressures explored throughout this book. Rising debt becomes harder to sustain when growth slows. Asset values become more politically sensitive as populations age. Policy choices become more constrained as electorates increasingly prioritize preservation over change. What once appeared to be separate challenges increasingly reinforce one another. Slower growth makes debt more burdensome. Higher debt increases sensitivity to interest rates. Ageing populations make reform more difficult politically. The pressures accumulate rather than operate independently. over time.

This is not a cyclical slowdown but a structural turning point. Ageing does not cause crisis by itself, yet it reduces the economy's ability to absorb shocks. It leaves less room for error and makes policy mistakes more costly. When strain emerges elsewhere in the economy, the effects spread more quickly and prove harder to contain. A slower-growing economy has less capacity to recover from mistakes, absorb unexpected costs, or grow its way out of trouble when pressures build.

The demographic shift now underway therefore does more than slow advanced economies. It weakens one of the foundations that supported stability for decades. The boost that came from a growing workforce is fading, yet many economic institutions still operate as though it remains in place.

As that support disappears, the gap between expectations and reality begins to widen. Commitments made during decades of demographic expansion become increasingly difficult to sustain under conditions of slower growth and ageing populations. That is why ageing populations represent more than a social challenge. They are becoming an economic breaking point. The consequences extend beyond demographics, shaping growth, public finances, and financial stability.

## *Growth Without Expansion*

When an economy grows more slowly, its promises do not shrink with it. Pensions must still be paid. Healthcare systems must still function. Governments must still service existing debt. Households must still meet mortgage payments. Corporations must still deliver returns to investors.

Economic obligations do not automatically adjust when growth slows. The commitments made during periods of expansion remain in place even when the economy beneath them grows more slowly. In a period of expanding labour supply, these obligations are easier to sustain. More workers mean more income, more tax revenue, and more consumption. Growth carries much of the burden automatically when populations expand.

When the number of workers stalls or declines, that support weakens. If output rises at one or two percent instead of three or four, the gap between obligations and expansion widens. The economy continues moving forward, but with less momentum supporting an increasing number of commitments. The difference does not disappear. It must be financed. This is where borrowing begins to change character in fundamental ways.

In earlier decades, debt often accompanied expansion. Firms borrowed to build factories, develop technologies, and expand production. Governments borrowed during recessions and often reduced deficits during stronger periods. Households borrowed against rising incomes and expanding opportunity. Debt was frequently associated with future growth. Borrowing helped finance activities expected to generate additional income, production, or tax revenue.

In ageing economies, however, borrowing increasingly serves a different purpose. It sustains spending that growth no longer naturally supports. Governments borrow to maintain social programmes designed for a younger demographic structure. Corporations borrow to protect earnings and shareholder payouts in slower-growing markets. Households borrow to preserve living standards when income growth struggles to keep pace with rising costs. Debt increasingly fills the gap between expectations and economic reality. Financial positions expand even as the underlying growth engine weakens.

Japan illustrates this shift clearly. Since the mid-1990s, its working-age population has fallen from roughly 87 million to around 75 million, a decline of more than fifteen percent, with further declines projected in the decades ahead.[6] Over the same period, economic growth has averaged roughly one percent per year, reflecting the drag from a shrinking workforce. To cushion the slowdown, successive governments increased spending and issued debt. Public debt now exceeds 250 percent of national output, while the central bank holds a large share of that debt and has kept borrowing costs near zero for decades.[7]

Japan avoided collapse, but it did not restore sustained expansion. Instead, it demonstrated how an ageing society can maintain stability for long periods while becoming increasingly dependent on debt and policy support. This pattern matters because many advanced economies are now moving in a similar direction, albeit with larger populations and more globally connected financial systems.

When growth slows and debt rises simultaneously, the room for policy error becomes smaller. Even modest increases in borrowing costs can ripple through public finances, housing markets, corporate finances, and pension systems.

What makes this shift particularly significant is that many advanced economies are entering this phase at the same time. Europe is ageing. Japan has already aged. The United States is ageing more gradually but steadily. China is now ageing rapidly.

For decades, the global economy benefited from at least some major regions providing demographic momentum. That support is now fading across much of the developed and ageing world simultaneously. The shift from expansion to maintenance is subtle at first, yet over time it reshapes incentives. Governments become reluctant to reduce spending. Corporations hesitate to invest heavily in long-term projects with uncertain returns. Households focus more on preserving existing wealth than building new wealth for the future.

Borrowing becomes increasingly routine, filling the gap between what the economy naturally produces and what society expects it to provide. The economy continues functioning, but it increasingly relies on financial support mechanisms rather than demographic expansion to sustain itself.

The structure becomes more sensitive to shocks because it was built for a different demographic era. A society can carry high levels of debt when growth is strong. It struggles far more when growth is constrained by demographic arithmetic. When the next disturbance arrives, whether through inflation, energy shortages, geopolitical conflict, or financial instability, it encounters an economy already operating with slower underlying growth and larger fixed commitments.

In that environment, the appearance of stability becomes harder to maintain. Growth no longer absorbs strain automatically. Policy choices become more consequential. The margin for adjustment narrows.

The consequences become increasingly difficult to contain. What previously might have been manageable disruptions increasingly become tests of the system's resilience. Adjustment under those conditions is rarely gentle. It tends to unfold through prolonged stagnation, rising financial strain, or sudden corrections that expose vulnerabilities built up over many years. When growth no longer absorbs pressure, even relatively modest shocks can produce disproportionately large consequences for households and governments alike.

This is one of the ways demographic change exerts its influence. The effects are often gradual and easy to overlook, yet they reshape the financial environment in ways that become increasingly important over time.

## *Interest Rates in an Ageing World*

An ageing society does not only grow more slowly. It also saves differently. Older households tend to spend less on expansion and more on preservation. They prepare for retirement, medical costs, and uncertainty about the future.

As the population ages, a larger share of income is directed toward saving rather than spending. This shift is gradual, but over time it changes the balance between consumption, investment, and growth. An older population often generates more savings than the economy can easily channel into productive investment. Businesses facing slower demand hesitate to expand capacity. Governments focus more on maintaining existing commitments rather than building new ones. The shift has broader consequences.

The result is a simple imbalance: more money seeks safety than seeks opportunity. When savings exceed attractive investment opportunities, borrowing costs tend to fall. This pattern has unfolded across advanced economies for decades. Long-term interest rates have trended downward since the 1980s.[8] In several countries, inflation-adjusted government bond yields approached zero or fell below it during the years leading up to the pandemic.[9] Central banks reinforced this direction, but they were not acting against demographic forces. Ageing populations were already exerting steady downward pressure on borrowing costs by increasing the supply of savings relative to investment demand.

Lower rates ease pressure in the short term. Governments refinance large debts at modest expense. Mortgage payments remain manageable even when property prices rise. Financial markets adapt to the expectation that funding will remain inexpensive. Asset values climb because investors place higher values on future profits when borrowing costs are very low. When money is cheap, the future becomes more valuable in today's markets. Over time, however, the entire system adapts to this environment and becomes dependent upon it.

Public debt in many advanced economies now exceeds annual national output. Corporate borrowing expanded significantly during the years of near-zero rates. Housing markets in several countries depend more on low monthly payments than on low house prices to remain accessible. Pension systems and insurers built long-term projections around the assumption that financing conditions would remain favourable. Financial structures across the economy gradually came to depend on cheap funding. Financial positions across the economy were structured around the expectation of low borrowing costs.

When borrowing costs rise in an economy carrying this scale of obligation, the impact is not marginal. It spreads across sectors simultaneously. Governments refinancing large debts face rising interest bills. Homebuyers encounter sharply higher monthly payments. Property values adjust downward as affordability tightens. Pension calculations shift. Corporate strategies built on inexpensive financing become less viable. The pressure does not remain confined to one sector. It appears almost everywhere at the same time across the economy.

In a younger, faster-growing economy, higher rates can often be absorbed through expanding incomes and stronger demand. In an ageing, heavily indebted one, there is less underlying momentum to cushion the adjustment. Obligations accumulated under low-rate assumptions remain fixed even as financing costs change. The commitments remain, but the conditions that made them manageable begin to disappear.

Returning to the borrowing costs of the 1990s or early 2000s would therefore not feel normal today. The economy was structured differently then. Debt levels were lower relative to output. Asset prices were less dependent on expectations of future gains, and the boost that came from a growing workforce was still present. Demographic expansion provided support that today's ageing economies no longer possess. What once appeared to be a normal interest-rate environment would now expose how dependent the modern financial structure has become on low borrowing costs and abundant liquidity. What once supported stability now reveals fragility.

Higher rates in such an environment do not merely slow growth. They force a repricing of housing, public finances, pension promises, and corporate financial positions at the same time. Foundations that cannot tolerate ordinary strain are not stable foundations at all.

The deeper issue is not that interest rates are rising. It is that decades of ageing, slower growth, and rising debt have made the economy far more sensitive to any increase in borrowing costs.

## *Asset Values and Social Stability*

As populations age, the structure of financial security begins to change. In younger societies, income from work supports consumption and savings. In older societies, accumulated wealth plays a larger role. Retirement income increasingly depends on pensions, investment portfolios, and property values rather than wages. As the share of retirees rises, the stability of those assets becomes increasingly important not only for individual households but for society as a whole. Financial markets and property markets begin to carry a larger share of the responsibility for maintaining economic security in later life.

In many advanced economies, defined benefit pension systems have gradually given way to defined contribution plans tied directly to market performance. Public pension systems depend on financial returns to meet long-term obligations. Insurance companies rely on stable asset values to fund future payouts. Household retirement plans are tied to housing equity and investment accounts. This means that falling asset prices no longer affect only investors. They affect retirees, pension solvency, insurance systems, and confidence in future financial security. Falling property values reduce household wealth. Declining equity markets shrink retirement balances, while bond market repricing makes pension liabilities harder to fund.

In ageing societies, these shifts are not abstract financial adjustments. They affect spending decisions, retirement plans, and confidence in the future. Their influence extends well beyond financial markets. For this reason, asset markets have taken on a broader role than simple price discovery. They have become part of the social contract.

Over the past two decades, especially since the global financial crisis of 2008, property prices in many advanced economies have risen far faster than median incomes.[10] In several major cities, house prices have doubled or tripled while wages have grown modestly. Stock markets have reached repeated highs even during periods of weak productivity growth. These developments are often attributed to investor optimism or central bank policy. Both matter, but demographic change also plays a role. As populations age, more households become dependent on accumulated assets for retirement security. This increases the sensitivity of the economy to fluctuations in property and financial markets during downturns.

What might once have been viewed as a normal market correction increasingly carries wider social and political consequences. As more households approach retirement, preserving the value of accumulated wealth becomes politically sensitive. Policymakers understand that sharp declines in property or equity markets would reverberate far beyond financial headlines. They would affect retirees who depend on those assets for security. They would expose pension shortfalls. They would place additional strain on public finances already challenged by ageing populations. The incentive to support asset values therefore grows stronger as societies age.

This creates a tension. Rising property and financial values support retirement systems, strengthen household finances, and reassure older generations. At the same time, higher prices raise barriers for younger generations. Housing becomes harder to enter. Wealth becomes increasingly concentrated among those who already own assets. Younger workers are asked to finance public systems while facing higher barriers to ownership themselves. The same rising asset values that provide security for one group can reduce opportunity for another.

This dynamic introduces a subtle but important shift. Stability for one generation increasingly depends on rising asset values, while opportunity for younger generations becomes more constrained. The longer this imbalance persists, the more it shapes expectations and behaviour throughout the economy. Over time, younger households delay homeownership and family formation. Savings goals appear more distant. Intergenerational tensions increase, even if they are not always expressed openly. The mechanism used to preserve stability today can gradually undermine cohesion tomorrow.

Asset values in ageing societies therefore become intertwined with political stability. Once that linkage forms, allowing prices to fall significantly becomes more difficult. Policies and market adjustments that might once have been tolerated begin to appear threatening. This deepens dependency because if stability requires sustained asset values, and sustained asset values depend on supportive financial conditions, policy flexibility shrinks further. The result is a feedback loop. Rising asset values support stability. Stability reinforces policies that support asset values. Over time, the dependency strengthens, making adjustment progressively more difficult and politically sensitive.

Each effort to protect existing wealth reinforces the structure that made the system vulnerable in the first place. A society built around preserving accumulated wealth finds adjustment harder to accept, yet without adjustment the imbalances continue to grow as demographic ageing makes this tension more pronounced with each passing decade.

## *Politics in an Ageing Democracy*

Demographic change does not only reshape economies. It reshapes electorates. As the share of older citizens rises, the political centre of gravity shifts. Older voters tend to prioritise stability, predictable income, and the preservation of accumulated wealth. Younger voters are more likely to prioritise opportunity, affordability, and upward mobility. Neither set of priorities is irrational. Each reflects a different stage of life and a different relationship to economic risk. Over time, however, the balance between these priorities changes as societies age.

In ageing democracies, policies that protect existing assets often attract broad support. Policies that impose short-term disruption, even in pursuit of long-term repair, become more difficult to enact. This has profound consequences for economic adjustment. Measures that may appear economically sensible can become politically difficult when large numbers of voters depend on the arrangements those measures would disrupt. Reducing public debt may require spending restraint or higher taxes. Returning borrowing costs to more normal levels may depress property values. Reforming pension systems may require changes to retirement ages or future benefits. Each of these steps can be defended economically. Each also carries political risk.

Governments facing older electorates therefore have strong incentives to avoid policies that threaten near-term security. The pressure is not necessarily ideological. It is often demographic. The result is gradualism even when imbalances continue to build. Short-term calm is favoured over structural repair. Immediate stability takes precedence over reforms whose benefits may not appear for years. The longer difficult decisions are delayed, however, the larger the eventual adjustment often becomes. One policy area demonstrates this particularly well.

Immigration illustrates this constraint particularly clearly. Expanding the workforce through immigration can offset population decline and improve the ratio between workers and retirees. It can also ease pressure on pension systems, labour markets, and public finances. Countries such as Canada and Australia have used immigration policy to support labour force growth.[11] The United States has historically relied on immigration as an important source of workforce expansion as well. From a purely economic perspective, immigration represents one of the few direct tools available to address demographic decline.

However, ageing electorates also alter the political context in which immigration is debated. Older populations often place greater emphasis on stability and may be more cautious about rapid change. At the same time, housing shortages, infrastructure pressures, and concerns about public services can intensify resistance to large-scale immigration even when economic logic supports it. The challenge is that what may be economically beneficial can still be politically difficult.

Large-scale immigration can create tensions around housing affordability, infrastructure capacity, cultural integration, and public services. In societies already experiencing housing strain and cost-of-living pressures, those concerns become more politically potent. The economic case for immigration may strengthen as populations age, yet political resistance often strengthens as well. The workforce needs replenishment precisely when the electorate becomes less comfortable with the scale of change required to achieve it. The result is a structural contradiction. The economy benefits from more workers, while the political system becomes increasingly cautious about the adjustments needed to attract them.

An ageing democracy therefore tends to protect existing arrangements even when those arrangements become more difficult to sustain. It favours policies that preserve current asset values, benefit structures, and retirement expectations. It becomes more hesitant to implement reforms that redistribute costs across generations or impose near-term sacrifices in pursuit of longer-term gains for future generations.

Over time, this political posture interacts with slower growth and higher debt. Each constraint reinforces the others. Fiscal choices become more limited. Monetary policy becomes more sensitive. Public trust becomes more fragile. None of this produces immediate crisis. What it produces is rigidity. Rigid systems can function effectively during calm periods. They struggle when circumstances change rapidly. When external shocks arrive, whether economic, financial, geopolitical, or demographic, rigid systems tend to break rather than bend. This growing rigidity is particularly significant because advanced economies historically relied on flexibility and adaptation to preserve stability. As demographic pressures intensify, that capacity to adjust becomes more constrained.

Demography does not determine political outcomes, but it strongly influences incentives. In ageing advanced economies, those incentives increasingly favour preservation over adaptation. When preservation becomes the overriding objective, reform becomes harder, adjustment is delayed, and the eventual correction often becomes more abrupt. The challenge is that delaying adjustment does not eliminate underlying pressures. It merely allows them to accumulate beneath the surface until a larger disruption forces change under less favourable circumstances. The trigger is seldom the underlying cause.

## *When the Shock Arrives*

The forces described in this chapter do not create collapse on their own. An ageing population does not automatically trigger crisis. Countries can grow slowly for long periods. They can manage rising obligations through careful policy and gradual adjustment. The danger lies elsewhere. Demographic change weakens the economy's ability to absorb pressure when other problems emerge. It narrows the margin for error long before a crisis becomes visible.

However, the system that defined advanced economies after the early 1980s depended on continued growth. Larger workforces, rising output, and the expectation that tomorrow would be better than today helped sustain it. High debt appeared manageable. Rising asset values were easier to maintain. Political compromise was often less urgent because growth helped ease competing demands. Expansion created room to manoeuvre. When growth was strong, many economic pressures could be postponed, softened, or absorbed.

Demography has altered that foundation. In an ageing society, growth slows unless productivity rises dramatically. Obligations continue accumulating even as expansion weakens. Borrowing becomes increasingly routine. Interest rates remain lower than in earlier eras. Retirement systems become more dependent on stable financial markets. Political incentives increasingly favour preservation over disruption.

These forces do not operate independently. They reinforce one another. Slower growth increases reliance on borrowing. Higher debt increases sensitivity to interest rates. Ageing electorates make reform more politically difficult. Dependence on asset values raises the stakes of market corrections. Separate vulnerabilities increasingly form a single structure.

Together, these dynamics reshape the stability model that defined the advanced world. This structure can function in calm conditions. It becomes far more difficult to manage under stress.

When inflation resurfaces, higher borrowing costs expose commitments accumulated during years of cheap funding. When financial markets correct sharply, retirement balances and pension assumptions weaken simultaneously. When energy prices rise or geopolitical conflict disrupts trade, slower-growing economies have less flexibility to absorb the shock. The system remains stable until it is asked to absorb something large.

In a younger, faster-expanding economy, adjustment can be spread across a growing workforce and rising incomes. In an ageing one, the base is narrower and more fixed. The burden therefore concentrates more quickly. The room for policy error becomes smaller. Tolerance for short-term pain declines.

Demography therefore acts as an amplifier of breakdown. Pressure emerging in one area of the economy travels faster and cuts deeper elsewhere. Slower growth makes existing debt harder to sustain. Dependence on asset values makes market corrections more destabilising. Political resistance makes reform slower and less decisive. The shock itself may come from somewhere else. Demography determines how well the system can withstand it. The process unfolds differently, through gradual accumulation rather than sudden disruption.

Yet demographic change does not produce sudden crisis. It reshapes economies gradually, narrowing growth, increasing fiscal pressure, and altering the balance between workers, retirees, and the state. Unlike financial cycles, demographic shifts cannot be reversed quickly through emergency programmes or stimulus measures. Once populations age and labour forces stagnate, the effects unfold across decades. There is no equivalent of a central-bank rescue for demographics.

The breaking point, when it comes, is unlikely to resemble past recessions. It will not be a temporary contraction followed by a rapid rebound. Instead, it will mark a recognition that the old stability model no longer fits the demographic reality of the advanced world.

A society that cannot grow through expansion must grow through productivity and reform. If it relies instead on rising debt and protected asset values, the adjustment does not disappear. It accumulates. Ageing ensures that accumulation cannot continue indefinitely without eventually forcing difficult adjustments. The transition has already begun.

The advanced economies are therefore entering a period in which slower growth is no longer cyclical, but structural. The assumptions that defined the post-1980 era, expanding workforces, rising consumption, and steadily growing tax bases, are beginning to weaken. What emerges in their place is a more constrained economic environment in which pension obligations, healthcare costs, fiscal pressures, and demographic realities increasingly collide.

Economic systems can adapt relatively quickly to financial shocks. Demographic structures cannot. A society cannot produce a new generation of workers in response to rising debt, fiscal strain, or weakening growth. Once demographic momentum fades, the effects carry forward across decades, narrowing flexibility and making adjustment progressively more difficult. The demographic challenge is not temporary. It becomes part of the operating environment and shapes behaviour across the economy.

This is where demography intersects most directly with the central theme of this book. Stability in advanced economies was built during a period of expanding populations, rising labour force participation, and broad demographic support for growth. As that momentum fades, the foundations beneath that stability begin to weaken as well. When the next major shock arrives, it will meet an economy with slower growth, heavier obligations, and stronger political resistance to change. Under those conditions, preserving stability becomes far harder than before.

The demographic breaking point does not announce itself loudly. It emerges gradually through slower growth, rising dependency, weaker fiscal flexibility, and growing strain between economic promises and demographic reality.

The moment of recognition arrives when the tools that once restored calm no longer work as effectively as before. What once appeared manageable begins to feel structurally constrained. The problem is no longer a temporary shortage of growth, but the disappearance of the demographic conditions that once made growth easier to achieve.

# 14

# DEMOCRACY MEETS ARITHMETIC

Advanced economies face a problem that is neither cyclical nor temporary, yet one that their political systems struggle to confront. Growth has slowed across much of the developed world, with long-term growth in many advanced economies falling from approximately 3 percent a year in the late twentieth century to closer to 1–2 percent in recent years.[1]

For decades, slower growth could be offset by expanding borrowing, lower interest rates, and favourable demographic conditions. Those supports are now weakening at the same time. The result is a growing tension between what economies can realistically deliver and what societies continue to expect.

At the same time, populations are ageing, and pension and healthcare obligations are rising automatically as demographics shift. In many advanced economies, the share of the population over 65 is projected to rise from roughly one in five today to closer to one in four over the next two decades.[2]

This shift unfolds gradually, but its financial consequences accumulate year after year. More retirees mean higher spending commitments even when economic growth remains subdued.

Public debt levels, already elevated after the global financial crisis, increased sharply again during the pandemic.[3] Interest costs, once suppressed by exceptionally low rates, are now consuming a growing share of government revenue. The change is gradual rather than dramatic, but it steadily narrows the room available for future policy choices.

Money that once funded public services, infrastructure, or investment is increasingly directed toward servicing existing obligations. What was once manageable is becoming progressively more difficult to sustain.

Compounding this, the global environment has become more expensive. Supply chains are being reorganised for security rather than lowest cost. Defence budgets are increasing. Industrial policy has returned. The transition to new energy systems requires large upfront investment and sustained financial commitment across the wider economy.

Each of these developments may be justified on its own merits. Together, however, they place additional demands on public finances already under pressure. Defence spending alone is increasing across many advanced economies, with several European countries committing to raise military spending toward or above 2 percent of GDP in response to rising geopolitical tensions.[4] These choices may be justified on strategic grounds, but none of them come without financial consequences.

The arithmetic that emerges is difficult to avoid. Long-term growth is slower. Baseline spending commitments are higher. The room to expand borrowing without consequence is smaller than it was a decade ago.

At the same time, government debt across advanced economies has risen sharply, with debt-to-GDP ratios in several major economies now exceeding levels last seen during wartime or the immediate post-war period.[5] The challenge is not simply that governments face difficult choices. It is that many of the choices required to restore balance impose visible costs on voters who have become accustomed to decades of relative stability.

That tension sits at the heart of the modern advanced world. Economic reality increasingly points toward restraint, while democratic politics continues to reward relief, protection, and postponement. The collision between those two forces, democratic expectations and economic arithmetic, is becoming one of the defining pressures of the age. That tension leaves governments with increasingly difficult choices.

## *The Adjustment No Government Can Sell*

Restoring balance would require a series of difficult and politically uncomfortable choices. Governments would need to raise taxes meaningfully. They would need to slow the growth of pension and healthcare commitments or increase retirement ages. Public sector wages and government benefits would need to grow more slowly than inflation for an extended period.

Asset prices that have been supported by years of exceptionally low interest rates would need to adjust to levels consistent with higher borrowing costs. In some cases, economies would need to accept recession as part of the process of restoring balance between demand and supply.

None of these measures are politically attractive because each imposes visible costs on identifiable groups. Someone pays more tax. Someone receives lower benefits than expected. Someone sees the value of a home or investment fall. Someone faces weaker employment prospects during a downturn.

These are not abstract policy choices. They represent visible reductions in income, wealth, or public support. The political difficulty therefore becomes immediately apparent.

What elected government can campaign on lower household purchasing power, reduced benefits, falling property values, and tighter public spending? What party can win by promising deliberate contraction in living standards today in exchange for greater stability tomorrow?

The economic logic may be clear. The political incentives are far less accommodating. Democratic systems are designed to respond to present conditions. Voters experience current prices, current wages, and current employment. They do not experience future debt burdens or long-term fiscal pressures with the same immediacy or political urgency. That creates a powerful political bias against adjustment.

The costs of adjustment are visible and immediate. The benefits are often delayed and uncertain. The risks created by sustained borrowing and delayed reform unfold slowly and often invisibly until they become unavoidable. The incentives therefore become misaligned. The economy requires long-term restraint, but politics rewards short-term relief.

This tension sits at the centre of the modern advanced world. Economic reality points toward restraint, yet political incentives reward expansion. Adjustment is economically necessary, yet politically toxic. The difficulty is not that solutions are unknown, but that many of the available solutions require sacrifices that democratic systems struggle to ask voters to accept voluntarily.

## *Why Democracies Delay*

Democratic systems do not fail because leaders misunderstand arithmetic. They struggle because electoral incentives reward postponement rather than restraint. Most policymakers understand that debt cannot rise faster than growth indefinitely and that long-term obligations eventually need to be funded. The challenge lies not in recognising the problem, but in taking actions that carry immediate political costs and uncertain rewards. Politics operates on a different timetable.

Election cycles are short, while debt accumulates over decades. Voters react more strongly to visible losses than to abstract risks. A reduction in benefits is immediate and measurable, while increased borrowing is spread across time and often across generations.

The political cost of restraint arrives quickly. The cost of borrowing arrives later. The political cost of cutting spending is concentrated, whereas the cost of issuing debt is dispersed and less visible. This asymmetry shapes behaviour.

Governments that attempt rapid fiscal consolidation, reducing deficits through spending cuts or higher taxes, often face backlash before any long-term benefit becomes visible. In the aftermath of the global financial crisis, several European governments that implemented austerity measures were voted out before debt levels had meaningfully improved. The political consequences were immediate and often severe.

Countries such as Greece, Italy, and Spain experienced political upheaval following austerity measures, reinforcing the perception that fiscal restraint carries immediate political costs.[6] For many political leaders, the lesson was straightforward: voters punish present pain more reliably than they reward future stability.

The same pattern appeared in the 1970s. Inflation accelerated across advanced economies, yet decisive tightening was repeatedly delayed. Policymakers feared unemployment and social unrest more than rising prices. It took years of declining purchasing power before firm action was taken, and when tightening finally occurred, it triggered deep recession. Rather than eliminating the adjustment, the delay increased its eventual cost.

More recently, during the pandemic, fiscal expansion across advanced economies reached levels not seen outside major wars. Governments acted to prevent collapse. In several advanced economies, fiscal support during the pandemic reached double-digit percentages of GDP, stabilising incomes and preserving employment.[7] The response bought valuable time.

These measures were largely successful in preventing immediate economic damage. Yet they also reinforced a broader expectation that governments could respond to major challenges through large-scale spending when necessary. The lesson for many political leaders was not caution, but the belief that large-scale intervention is both possible and popular during periods of stress. Although these episodes differ in context, they share a common thread. Democratic politics rewards policies that reduce present pain and punishes policies that impose immediate sacrifice for future stability.

The structure of modern electorates reinforces this pattern. Ageing populations vote at higher rates than younger cohorts. Retirees depend on public transfers, government benefits and support payments, and stable asset values.

Policies that threaten pension adjustments or property prices can therefore encounter considerable resistance. In many advanced economies, older voters now represent one of the largest and most politically engaged voting blocs, making benefit reductions particularly difficult.

At the same time, asset ownership has become concentrated among groups with significant political influence. Measures that might reduce property or financial asset values therefore face resistance from powerful constituencies as well.

The result is not paralysis but bias. Political systems tilt toward expanding commitments rather than reducing them. Promises accumulate more easily than they are withdrawn, and borrowing becomes the tool that allows competing demands to be satisfied without forcing immediate choices.

Denial, in this context, does not imply ignorance. Policymakers recognise limits. Voters sense pressure. Yet both respond to incentives that favour postponement rather than contraction.

The problem is not a lack of awareness. It is the absence of strong incentives to act early. Over time, this pattern becomes self-reinforcing. Each episode of postponement raises the level from which future correction must occur. Each round of borrowing increases sensitivity to interest costs. Each avoided reform narrows the space for gradual change and honest political debate.

The political system adapts by reframing limits rather than confronting them directly. Structural slowdown becomes temporary weakness. Fiscal strain becomes investment. Dependence on borrowing becomes flexibility. The language changes, but the arithmetic does not. When incentives consistently reward delay, adjustment is not avoided. It simply accumulates over time.

The result is not the avoidance of economic reality, but its gradual accumulation beneath the surface until adjustment becomes increasingly difficult to postpone, and the eventual choices As the room for adjustment narrows, political incentives begin to change. become more constrained and more politically contentious. Governments rarely accept those limits passively. Delay becomes the path of least political resistance. The response increasingly shifts from accepting limits to attempting to overcome them. The next stage is not restraint, but the search for new sources of expansion.

## *Turning Limits into Ambition*

When adjustment becomes politically dangerous, it is rarely presented as adjustment. Instead, it is framed as transformation or renewal. The language changes because the politics change. Voters are far more receptive to promises of improvement than to discussions of sacrifice, and governments therefore tend to present difficult realities through the language of opportunity, reform, and national renewal.

Slower growth is described as transition. Rising costs are framed as investment. Expanded public spending is justified as resilience. Industrial subsidies are presented as competitiveness. Each of these arguments may contain strategic logic and many are supported by legitimate economic or geopolitical concerns. Yet they also serve another purpose: avoiding more difficult conversations about limits, trade-offs, and affordability.

In a world of geopolitical tension and supply chain disruption, governments can credibly argue that security requires redundancy. Production must be relocated. Critical materials must be secured. Energy systems must be redesigned.

These initiatives require substantial public funding and long planning horizons. They also carry higher costs than the globally integrated system they are intended to replace. For example, the re-shoring of supply chains and diversification of critical industries often involves higher production costs than globalized supply systems, placing additional pressure on government budgets and consumer prices.

In earlier decades, such costs might have forced sharper political choices. Today, they are often absorbed through additional borrowing. The language emphasizes sovereignty, resilience, and security rather than rising costs or growing debt burdens. The objectives may be valid, but the financial implications remain.

Industrial policy follows a broadly similar path. Governments increasingly support industries considered strategically important, whether semiconductors, advanced manufacturing, clean energy, or critical minerals. Government support for strategic industries is frequently presented as an investment in future prosperity. It may well be. Yet it also allows public spending to substitute for slower private-sector growth, helping preserve the appearance of economic dynamism despite subdued productivity growth.

This reframing extends beyond fiscal policy. Central banks, faced with the tension between containing inflation and preserving employment, increasingly speak of balancing objectives rather than prioritizing price stability. Interest rate increases become gradual, and the possibility of reversal remains open, as policymakers attempt to slow inflation without triggering recession. The goal is understandable. Policymakers seek to avoid unnecessary damage. The challenge is that delaying difficult adjustments can make them larger later.

None of these choices are irrational in isolation. Taken together, however, they form a broader pattern. When long-term limits tighten, political systems often respond by expanding goals rather than narrowing commitments. Security is added alongside growth. Equity is added alongside efficiency. Climate transition is added alongside fiscal responsibility.

Each objective has merit. The difficulty arises when all of them are pursued simultaneously while economic growth is slowing. The cumulative burden grows faster than the economy itself. The room for honest debate narrows.

As priorities multiply, difficult choices become harder to acknowledge openly. Instead of admitting that some promises cannot be sustained simultaneously, governments expand the frame. Borrowing allows governments to promise more than the economy can realistically support. The narrative emphasizes strength, resilience, and renewal, even as the arithmetic becomes less forgiving.

Political language increasingly focuses on what can be achieved rather than what may need to be sacrificed. Economic limits are no longer treated as boundaries that require restraint, but as obstacles to be managed through strategy and spending. Yet strategy does not eliminate cost. It redistributes and often increases it. The political consequences soon follow.

In this environment, restraint is increasingly portrayed as weakness rather than prudence . Calls for spending discipline can be positioned as undermining national resilience, economic competitiveness, or social cohesion. The political space for openly advocating sacrifice therefore narrows. The result is not immediate instability, but a steady expansion of commitments in an economy whose growth capacity is slowing. The promises become larger even as the resources available to support them grow more slowly.

## *Borrowing Instead of Choosing*

When governments expand commitments without matching revenue, the difference is financed through borrowing. This is not unusual. Governments have always borrowed during wars, recessions, and periods of exceptional strain. What has changed is the scale, persistence, and purpose of that borrowing. Increasingly, debt is used not only to respond to emergencies but also to avoid difficult choices about taxes, spending, and competing priorities.

Since the 1980s, public debt levels across advanced economies have risen steadily relative to national income. The increase accelerated after the global financial crisis and again during the pandemic. Government debt now exceeds 100 percent of GDP in several major advanced economies, including the United States and parts of Europe, while Japan's public debt has risen to more than 250 percent of GDP.[8] Even where debt levels are lower, they remain well above those that prevailed before the 2008 crisis.

For years, the cost of servicing that debt remained subdued because interest rates were exceptionally low. Governments could issue bonds at minimal expense. In some cases, borrowing costs fell below the rate of inflation, reducing the real burden over time. Borrowing appeared inexpensive, and postponing reform appeared relatively painless. This environment reduced the visible cost of delay, as expanding spending did not immediately crowd out other priorities because interest payments remained manageable.

That period has ended. As interest rates have risen, debt servicing costs, the interest payments governments make on outstanding debt, have increased rapidly. In the United States, for example, interest payments on federal debt are projected to become one of the largest components of government spending over the coming decade.[9]

Similar pressures are emerging across many other advanced economies. Funds that might have supported infrastructure, education, or healthcare are increasingly directed toward servicing past obligations, reducing the resources available for future growth and investment. The trade-offs become increasingly difficult. The incentives, however, do not.

Yet the political logic remains largely unchanged. Cutting existing programs remains unpopular. Raising taxes significantly remains politically risky. Borrowing therefore continues to bridge the gap between commitments and available revenue.

Debt functions as a powerful political shock absorber. It allows governments to maintain benefits, expand spending, and avoid choosing between competing priorities. Pensioners continue to receive payments. Strategic industries receive support. Defence budgets expand. Social programs are maintained. The difficult trade-offs are deferred rather than resolved. Much of that burden fell on monetary policy.

Central banks have played an important role in sustaining this dynamic. During periods of stress, they purchased government bonds to stabilize markets and prevent disorder.

Following the global financial crisis and the pandemic, central bank balance sheets in several advanced economies expanded dramatically, reinforcing expectations that authorities would intervene when needed. These actions prevented panic and supported recovery. They also helped create confidence that governments could continue borrowing without facing immediate consequences, even as debt levels continued to rise and fiscal pressures gradually accumulated.

The interaction between fiscal expansion and monetary support created a reinforcing cycle. Governments issued debt to finance commitments. Central banks maintained conditions that kept borrowing manageable. Markets adapted to the expectation that authorities would intervene to prevent severe disruption. Asset valuations increasingly reflected that expectation. As long as borrowing costs remained low, this arrangement appeared sustainable and politically manageable.

When rates rise, however, the tension becomes visible. Higher interest payments reduce the government's ability to respond to new problems. Attempts to reduce borrowing through spending cuts risk slowing the economy. Efforts to contain inflation through higher interest rates further increase borrowing costs. Each solution creates pressure elsewhere in the system, narrowing the available policy options with each intervention.

Borrowing does not eliminate the need for correction. Instead, it postpones it and increases the scale of the eventual adjustment. Each additional round of borrowing raises the starting point for the next crisis, while each delay increases dependence on continued confidence in government finances and central bank credibility. The choice is not between adjustment and no adjustment, but between adjustment now and potentially larger adjustment later.

The longer difficult decisions are postponed, the more commitments accumulate and the fewer options remain available. What begins as a manageable imbalance can gradually evolve into a structural constraint that affects fiscal policy, monetary policy, and economic growth simultaneously. The challenge is that delay often creates the appearance of stability even as underlying vulnerabilities continue to build.

Periods of apparent stability can therefore be misleading. The absence of immediate crisis is often interpreted as evidence that underlying pressures have eased, when in reality they may simply have been deferred. By the time those pressures re-emerge, the adjustment required is usually much larger.

## *Delay Makes the Reckoning Harder*

Postponement changes the scale of the problem. When borrowing replaces difficult choices, commitments continue to expand while the capacity to sustain them grows more slowly. Pension promises compound. Healthcare obligations rise as populations age. Subsidy programs become embedded. Defence expenditures become structural rather than temporary. The commitments continue accumulating even when the economy's ability to support them grows more slowly.

Households and businesses adapt to higher levels of public spending and continued government support. What begins as temporary assistance gradually becomes part of the expected economic landscape. Over time, the economy reorganizes around this structure. Asset prices reflect expectations of continued intervention. Property values incorporate the legacy of years of exceptionally low borrowing costs. Pension funds assume return targets that depend on stable markets. Corporations plan investment decisions on the assumption that public demand and government support will remain relatively firm. The longer these assumptions persist, the more difficult they become to reverse.

In this environment, even modest tightening can produce amplified effects. Higher interest rates affect mortgage payments, corporate refinancing, and government budgets simultaneously. A policy shift that once might have slowed excess demand now interacts with a much larger stock of outstanding debt. The economy becomes more sensitive because there is simply more debt resting on the same foundation.

Debt increases exposure and alters behaviour. Governments become cautious about imposing recession because downturns sharply reduce tax revenue while increasing spending on unemployment benefits and social support. Central banks hesitate to tighten aggressively because financial markets, households, businesses, and public finances have all become more sensitive to higher rates. Businesses delay investment when policy direction appears uncertain. Households reduce spending as borrowing costs rise. The system becomes more cautious because the consequences of mistakes become larger.

Demographics further reduce flexibility. Ageing societies devote a rising share of resources to retirees. Younger workers carry a growing tax burden. In many advanced economies, the number of workers supporting each retiree has been declining steadily, placing increasing pressure on public finances.[10] Political resistance to benefit reform intensifies as electorates grow older. Dependence on government benefits and support payments increases, reducing tolerance for economic contraction. The need for adjustment rises at the same time that the political willingness to accept adjustment weakens, making reform increasingly difficult.

The result is cumulative. Baseline spending rises. Debt grows. The room for gradual correction shrinks. What might once have been addressed through steady restraint now requires sharper and more disruptive measures.

Markets adapt as well. Investors increasingly assume that authorities will intervene to prevent severe disruption. Financial valuations incorporate expectations of continued support. When those expectations are challenged, adjustments can occur rapidly, with prices moving faster than policy responses. Confidence often builds slowly and weakens quickly when assumptions are challenged by changing conditions.

Deferring adjustment therefore does not stabilize the system. It changes the nature of the eventual adjustment. The correction becomes larger because the imbalances become larger. The adjustment becomes more difficult because the commitments become more deeply embedded. What could once have been addressed gradually increasingly requires sharper and more disruptive measures.

Delay does not eliminate the reckoning. It makes the reckoning harder. The longer adjustment is postponed, the more dependent the system becomes on continued support and favourable conditions. What begins as a temporary response gradually evolves into a permanent expectation. Over time, preserving stability requires increasingly larger interventions to achieve the same result. The margin for error narrows, while the costs of maintaining the existing structure continue to rise.

## *Central Banks Cannot Shield Forever*

For more than a decade following the 2008 global financial crisis, central banks cushioned instability through low interest rates and large-scale bond purchases. These measures prevented financial collapse after the global financial crisis and supported recovery during the pandemic. Markets gradually came to expect intervention whenever stress intensified. Borrowing costs remained low. Financial conditions stayed supportive. Confidence was reinforced by the belief that authorities would act when necessary. For many years, that belief appeared justified. Financial crises were contained. Markets recovered. Governments continued borrowing at manageable cost.

This protection, however, has limits. Central banks can cushion financial stress, but they cannot remove the underlying economic pressures that create it. Central banks can provide liquidity during a crisis, ensuring that financial markets continue functioning. They can calm panic and stabilize conditions when confidence suddenly disappears. What they cannot do indefinitely is finance expanding government commitments without consequences.

When inflation rises persistently, purchasing power erodes. Households feel the pressure through higher prices. Public confidence weakens. Pressure builds for tighter monetary policy. At that point, interest rate increases become increasingly difficult to avoid. The longer action is delayed, the greater the risk that inflation becomes embedded in wages, prices, and expectations. Once that occurs, restoring stability typically requires more aggressive measures and greater economic disruption.

Raising interest rates in a heavily indebted economy affects multiple parts of the system simultaneously. Mortgage payments rise. Businesses face higher refinancing costs. Governments pay more interest on outstanding debt. The same tool used to fight inflation increases financial pressure throughout the economy. If central banks tighten decisively, recession becomes more likely. If they hesitate, inflation may become more deeply embedded. Either path carries economic and political consequences.

The dilemma is straightforward but uncomfortable. Tightening risks slowing growth and increasing unemployment. Delaying action risks further erosion of purchasing power and confidence. Elected officials often prefer gradual adjustment because the immediate costs of recession are highly visible. Central banks understand that aggressive tightening can destabilize financial markets that have adapted to years of exceptionally low rates.

This creates tension between price stability and financial stability. Containing inflation often requires tighter financial conditions, yet tighter financial conditions can place stress on borrowers, markets, and public finances. It also creates tension between central bank independence and political pressure. When higher interest rates slow growth, weaken housing markets, or increase unemployment, demands for relief intensify. When inflation remains elevated, demands for stronger action increase instead. The pressure comes from both directions at once. Act too aggressively and financial stress can spread through the economy. Act too cautiously and inflation may become more deeply entrenched. The room for error becomes increasingly narrow as debt levels rise and growth slows.

The belief that central banks can indefinitely shield economies from fiscal expansion depends on two conditions: inflation remaining contained and financial markets continuing to absorb growing amounts of government debt. When either condition weakens, the room for manoeuvre narrows quickly.

The return of inflation in recent years exposed this constraint. Inflation in several advanced economies rose to levels not seen in decades following the pandemic, forcing central banks to raise interest rates more rapidly than markets had anticipated.[11] Financial conditions tightened. Stress emerged in sectors that had adapted to low borrowing costs. Governments faced rising interest payments almost immediately. The limits of monetary support became visible. More than a decade of intervention had helped stabilize markets and support economic activity, but it had not removed the underlying pressures created by rising debt and slower growth. As those pressures intensified, monetary policy became less effective at shielding the economy from difficult trade-offs and painful adjustments.

Central banks could still provide liquidity when needed. They could still influence financial conditions. What they could not do was eliminate the underlying tension between expanding public commitments and slower economic growth. Monetary policy can delay reckoning, but it cannot eliminate it. Low interest rates can ease financing pressures and support economic activity for a time, but they cannot permanently offset slower growth or rising obligations. Eventually, the underlying arithmetic prevails despite supportive financial conditions.

When public commitments expand faster than the economy's capacity to support them, central banks eventually face choices that involve economic pain. The longer those choices are postponed, the narrower the available options become.

## *When Adjustment Is No Longer Optional*

Democratic systems can postpone adjustment for long periods. They can distribute costs across time, reframe limits as strategy, and rely on borrowing and monetary support to cushion pressure. What they cannot do is suspend economic reality indefinitely. Eventually, financial, demographic, and fiscal constraints begin to assert themselves regardless of political preference. Political flexibility steadily diminishes.

As obligations expand and borrowing accumulates, tolerance narrows. Markets require compensation for risk. Interest payments absorb a larger share of government revenue. Inflation erodes real incomes and weakens public confidence. Currency values adjust when confidence declines, reflecting growing concerns about long-term sustainability. The pressure builds gradually. Then it begins to appear in multiple places at once.

The breaking point does not arrive because leaders suddenly change their views. It arrives when the mechanisms that allowed postponement lose effectiveness. If investors demand higher returns to hold government debt, refinancing costs rise quickly.[12] If inflation persists, central banks must tighten further or risk damaging credibility. If tightening triggers recession, fiscal deficits widen automatically as tax revenues fall and support payments increase at the same time.

Each response creates pressure elsewhere in the system. The margin for error shrinks as economic, fiscal, and political constraints begin to converge. Policymakers have less flexibility to absorb setbacks than they once did. The choices become narrower and the consequences become larger. Decisions that might once have been made gradually increasingly need to be made under pressure. The ability to determine the timing and pace of adjustment begins to erode.

At that stage, adjustment is imposed through market pressure, currency depreciation, or forced fiscal contraction rather than deliberate political choice on policymakers' terms.

The political system loses the ability to determine timing and shape. It reacts to events instead of directing them. Control gradually shifts from policymakers to circumstances.

The defining feature of the post-1980s era was the belief that advanced economies could absorb shocks without threatening the system itself. Borrowing smoothed downturns. Monetary policy contained panic. Global integration reduced costs. Political leaders promised stability and, for long periods, were able to deliver it.

That model depended on conditions that are no longer fully present. Growth has slowed. Demographic pressures have intensified. Global integration has weakened. Debt burdens are larger. Interest rates are no longer negligible.[13] Many of the supports that sustained stability for decades are becoming weaker simultaneously. Public expectations, however, remain anchored to the earlier era of stability. When expectations remain high and capacity has diminished, tension builds.

Stability does not end with immediate collapse. Instead, the buffers that once absorbed strain gradually weaken and erode over time, allowing pressure to spread more easily across the system. Trade-offs can no longer be deferred without consequence. Denial, once manageable, becomes destabilizing. The challenge is no longer simply economic. It becomes increasingly political and social as well across advanced societies. The transition is already under way.

Advanced democracies are entering a period in which expectations formed during decades of expansion are colliding with slower growth, rising pressure on government finances, and narrowing room for manoeuvre. Governments are expected to preserve living standards, support ageing populations, maintain social stability, strengthen national security, finance energy transitions, and protect households from economic shocks, often simultaneously. Each objective may be reasonable on its own. The difficulty is that the economy's capacity to support all of them is no longer expanding as rapidly as before.

The challenge is compounded by the nature of democratic politics itself. Electoral incentives reward relief more readily than restraint, particularly after decades in which borrowing and monetary support softened the immediate consequences of economic weakness. The longer adjustment is delayed, the narrower the political space becomes. Trade-offs that once appeared manageable become increasingly contentious as governments struggle to reconcile public expectations with economic capacity.

Promises made during an era of expansion become harder to sustain in an era of constraint. Adjustment will still come. The question is whether advanced democracies will confront constraints early enough to shape the process gradually, or whether growing pressures will narrow those choices over time.

The challenge emerging across the advanced world is no longer simply whether economies can continue expanding under rising debt burdens. It is whether democratic systems built during a long era of abundance, growth, and expanding expectations can adapt to a world increasingly defined by limits, trade-offs, and structurally slower growth. That question lies at the heart of the coming reckoning for advanced economies.

# 15

## WHEN ENERGY BECOMES THE LIMIT

From the mid-1980s through the early 2020s, advanced economies operated on a powerful assumption: economic stability could be managed through financial tools. When growth slowed, interest rates could be cut. When markets stumbled, liquidity could be supplied. When recession threatened, fiscal support could be deployed. Policymakers believed downturns were problems of demand and confidence. Adjust the financial settings and expansion would resume for another cycle.

For a long time, this belief appeared justified. From the mid-1980s through the Global Financial Crisis of 2008, and again during the 2010–2019 expansion, inflation trended downward, borrowing costs fell steadily, and output expanded across the advanced world. Global GDP more than doubled between 1990 and 2019.[1] Financial markets deepened and broadened. Business cycles became milder. The period was often described as the Great Moderation.

Yet this stability rested on conditions that were rarely acknowledged. Energy was abundant. Real energy prices, adjusted for inflation, were generally lower and less volatile than in the 1970s. Oil supply expanded through new extraction technologies and geopolitical realignment. Natural gas production increased sharply in North America after the shale revolution. Electricity grids expanded and global trade reduced input costs across supply chains throughout much of the world.

Cheap energy and falling borrowing costs moved together. That combination created the impression that expansion could be managed primarily through financial tools. If inflation appeared, rates could rise. If recession threatened, they could fall. The physical foundation of the economy was treated as stable background rather than as an active constraint. Over time, many came to believe that stability could be maintained largely through financial management. The energy, resources, and infrastructure that supported that stability received far less attention because they appeared plentiful and reliable.

This is where economics meets physics. Beneath interest rates, markets, and government budgets lies a simpler reality. Every unit of output requires energy. Goods must be mined, processed, transported, refrigerated, heated, and assembled. Data centres require electricity. Hospitals, factories, and logistics networks operate through constant energy conversion. Every modern activity depends on turning energy into useful work.

Money represents a claim on production, but production itself depends on physical inputs. When energy becomes unstable or expensive, financial management loses its reach. Liquidity cannot drill wells. Lower rates cannot refine fuel. Budget deficits cannot compress geological timelines.

Financial tools can influence demand, confidence, and credit conditions. They cannot create energy supplies that do not exist.

The early twenty-first-century economy is rediscovering that finance operates within physical limits. What we are now witnessing is not merely a temporary spike in prices but the collision between a financial system built on high debt and rising physical constraints. That collision matters because many of the forces discussed throughout this book depend on energy. Growth, inflation, borrowing costs, household finances, business competitiveness, and political stability are all affected by its cost and availability. As a result, it is helping bring the era of policy-managed stability to an end across advanced economies. The shift unfolded gradually.

By the early 2020s, that era had begun to weaken. For decades, policymakers assumed that financial tools could smooth disruptions and sustain growth. As energy becomes more constrained and volatile, that assumption is being tested. The economy is rediscovering a reality that was never repealed: finance can distribute resources, but it cannot replace the physical foundations upon which economic activity depends. As energy becomes more expensive, less predictable, and increasingly shaped by geopolitical rivalry, the limits of financial management become more visible across the economy.

The question is no longer whether policymakers can manage demand. It is whether a highly indebted economic system can adapt when one of its most important physical foundations becomes less reliable than it was during the era of stability.

## *Why Finance Cannot Replace Energy*

Energy is not simply another sector of the economy. It is the foundation upon which all economic activity depends. Every industry, from manufacturing to healthcare, relies on continuous energy conversion. When energy becomes unstable, the effects spread quickly across the entire system. Unlike many economic inputs, energy sits upstream of almost everything else. When its cost rises or supply becomes uncertain, the effects cascade through production, transportation, food systems, industry, and household budgets simultaneously.

During 2021 and 2022, this reality forced itself into view. In Europe, natural gas prices rose several fold after supply disruptions and geopolitical conflict. Electricity prices followed. At the peak in late 2022, energy accounted for more than half of headline inflation in parts of the euro area, even though energy represented a much smaller share of household consumption baskets.[2] In the United Kingdom and parts of continental Europe, household energy bills doubled or tripled within a single year.[3] In the United States, gasoline prices rose above four dollars per gallon nationally, levels that historically coincide with economic slowdown and weaker consumer spending.

For many households, the impact was immediate and highly visible. Energy is not a discretionary purchase. Families can postpone holidays, restaurant meals, or major purchases. Heating, electricity, and transport are far harder to avoid

The consequences extended beyond households. Germany, Europe's industrial engine, faced a sudden surge in energy costs after Russian gas supplies declined. Chemical producers, steel manufacturers, and industrial firms began cutting output or relocating production abroad. BASF, one of the world's largest chemical companies, announced plans to reduce operations in Germany and expand investment elsewhere, citing persistently high energy costs.[4] German industrial production weakened, highlighting how energy instability can quickly translate into broader economic slowdown.

These were not isolated price adjustments. They moved through entire production chains. Higher fuel costs raised transportation expenses. Fertilizer prices surged because natural gas is a key input in its production. Food prices followed. Manufacturing margins compressed. Airlines, logistics firms, and heavy industry faced rising operating costs at the same time consumers faced higher utility bills. Energy operates as a multiplier. When its cost rises, it touches almost every other price in the economy.

The United Kingdom provided another illustration. In 2022, household energy bills surged sharply, forcing governments to introduce emergency price caps and support programs. Small businesses, including restaurants, manufacturers, and local retailers, reported energy bills doubling or tripling within months. Some firms reduced operating hours or closed entirely.

The episode revealed how quickly an energy problem can become an economic problem and then a political problem. Rising bills strained household finances, pressured public budgets, and increased demands for government intervention.

From the mid-1980s through the late 2010s, advanced economies benefited from the opposite dynamic. Real energy costs were generally contained. Global supply chains expanded. Trade integration reduced input expenses. Inflation trended downward. Falling interest rates reinforced that environment by lowering financing costs across households, businesses, and governments. Cheap energy and cheap money reinforced one another. Together they created a powerful tailwind that allowed higher levels of borrowing to be sustained without triggering persistent inflation.

That era has now ended. Energy is no longer helping keep costs down as it once did, and supplies are increasingly affected by a combination of geopolitical tensions, ageing infrastructure, changing environmental priorities, and the years required to bring new projects online. Since the late 2010s and early 2020s, energy markets have become tighter. Demand remains structurally high in advanced economies and continues to rise across emerging markets. When energy costs stop falling and begin rising, the assumptions underlying the stability model begin to change. A system built around cheap energy and declining rates cannot adjust easily to expensive energy and higher borrowing costs.

The stability of the past forty years was not purely the product of wise management. It was reinforced by a highly supportive physical environment that kept costs relatively low. As those conditions become less favourable, the financial system built on top of them becomes more fragile as well.

The challenge is that many of the mechanisms used to support growth, contain inflation, and stabilize markets ultimately depend on reliable and affordable energy. When that foundation becomes less dependable, pressures that once remained manageable can spread more quickly through the wider economy. The economy is therefore being forced to confront a reality that remained largely hidden during the era of abundant energy and falling costs.

Energy provides perhaps the clearest example. It reveals that economic limits are not only financial but also physical, rooted in the resources that sustain production, transport, and modern life

## *Energy Is the Foundation of the Economy*

Energy usually enters public debate only during disruption. When fuel prices surge or supply chains are threatened, headlines follow. Once prices ease, attention fades. This episodic focus creates a misleading impression that energy matters only during crises. In reality, energy influences economic activity every day, whether it attracts attention or not.

This episodic focus obscures something fundamental. Energy is not another sector of the economy. It is the operating system that enables all other sectors to function. When energy costs move, production costs move. When production costs move, inflation follows. When inflation rises, interest rates adjust. When interest rates adjust, debt burdens change. What begins as an energy issue can therefore travel quickly through the entire economic system. This chain reaction illustrates why energy sits at the centre of modern economic stability.

Consider a typical day in a modern economy. Food often travels long distances before reaching supermarket shelves. Hospitals rely on uninterrupted electricity. Data centres process vast quantities of information around the clock. Factories depend on continuous power to operate machinery and maintain production schedules. None of these activities can occur without reliable and affordable energy at the scale required.

For decades, policymakers treated energy as a background condition rather than a driving force. That assumption worked when energy remained abundant and relatively inexpensive. From the 1980s through the late 2010s, advanced economies benefited from stable and relatively cheap energy inputs, reinforcing confidence in financial management as the primary stabilization tool for sustaining growth. When energy remains reliable and affordable, attention naturally shifts toward interest rates, fiscal policy, and financial markets because those appear to be the variables driving economic outcomes.

As energy markets become more constrained and more volatile, that assumption becomes harder to sustain. The economy is being reminded that finance operates on top of a physical foundation. Financial decisions influence how resources are allocated, but they do not eliminate the need for energy, raw materials, transportation, and infrastructure.

Energy cannot be replaced by credit. Financial tools can influence demand, but they cannot increase supply. Central banks can encourage borrowing. Governments can increase spending. Neither can generate additional electricity, expand refining capacity, or accelerate major energy projects simply by creating more money in the short term.

This distinction becomes increasingly important as economies become more leveraged and more dependent on stable input costs. When the physical foundation becomes less reliable, financial tools become less effective. The economy does not stop responding to them, but they become less capable of overcoming underlying constraints. Their limits become increasingly apparent. The consequences extend far beyond energy markets

## *When Energy Drives Inflation, Policy Tools Fail*

Inflation is often treated as a problem of excess demand. Too much spending chases too few goods. Raise interest rates, reduce borrowing, slow demand, and prices stabilize. That framework works when inflation is primarily financial, but it works far less well when inflation begins with supply constraints.

The distinction matters because the cure depends on the cause. If inflation is driven by excessive spending, reducing demand can be effective. If inflation begins with shortages or rising production costs, the problem becomes much harder to solve through monetary policy alone.

Energy shocks behave differently from demand booms. The 1970s illustrate why. When oil prices surged, advanced economies experienced both rising inflation and rising unemployment.[5] Growth slowed even as prices accelerated. The shock came from the cost side of the economy rather than from overheating demand. Businesses faced higher operating costs even as growth weakened. Households paid more for fuel and heating even as economic activity slowed.

Following the oil supply disruptions, energy prices surged and inflation accelerated across advanced economies. Growth slowed at the same time unemployment increased. The result was stagflation, a combination that conventional monetary policy struggled to address. Higher interest rates eventually reduced inflation but at the cost of deep recessions and financial strain. Inflation was eventually contained, but only after significant economic pain.

A similar dynamic emerged in 2021 and 2022. Energy costs rose first. Food, goods, and services followed. In the United States, gasoline prices above four dollars per gallon have historically coincided with economic slowdowns, and the 2022 surge reinforced that pattern.[6] Consumer confidence declined, discretionary spending softened, and inflation spread beyond energy into broader categories.

When inflation is rooted in supply limits, higher interest rates may slow spending, but they do not remove the underlying shortage. Factories do not produce more fuel because borrowing becomes expensive. Shipping routes do not shorten because mortgage rates rise or borrowing becomes more expensive. Higher rates can reduce demand. They cannot create additional energy supply. Interest rates can cool housing markets and reduce discretionary spending, but monetary tools cannot expand physical supply in the short term.

This difference becomes decisive in a system burdened by large debt loads. In the 1970s, public and private debt levels were far lower than they are today. Governments had more fiscal flexibility. Households were less exposed to long-term mortgage obligations. Corporate finances were not as dependent on continuous refinancing at low cost as they are today. The economy had more capacity to absorb higher interest rates without destabilizing other parts of the system.

By the early 2020s, the situation had reversed. Public debt in many advanced economies exceeds national income. Households rely heavily on property markets supported by years of low borrowing costs. Corporations have grown accustomed to refinancing at minimal interest expense. Government budgets assume manageable debt servicing.

When energy prices rise in such an environment, the pressure spreads quickly. Input costs increase. Profit margins compress. Real household incomes decline. Tax revenues soften as growth slows. At the same time, higher inflation pushes central banks to raise rates. Interest payments rise across governments, firms, and households, tightening the system from multiple directions at once. The economy faces a double squeeze. Energy costs rise while borrowing costs rise as well.

When energy instability collides with large debt burdens, stress accumulates across government finances, corporate earnings, and household finances. Each sector becomes more sensitive to shocks, and small disturbances begin to produce outsized reactions. The issue is not simply higher prices. It is the gradual loss of resilience to future shocks.

For decades, advanced economies relied on falling borrowing costs and moderate input prices to cushion disturbances. When one factor shifted, the other often provided relief. The old balancing mechanism is now weakening. Energy volatility pushes inflation higher at the same time that debt levels limit how far rates can rise without triggering financial strain. As a result, policymakers have less room to act. The tools still work, but less effectively in a high-debt, high-energy-cost economy.

Under these conditions, instability does not require a dramatic external event. A winter supply disruption, a refinery outage, or a geopolitical escalation can become more consequential because the system is already stretched. Energy shocks in a low-debt world created recession and inflation. Energy shocks in a high-debt world threaten government finances, financial market stability, and political cohesion at the same time. That is what makes the current environment fundamentally different from many previous energy cycles. The consequences extend well beyond short-term inflation.

## *The Return of Higher Costs*

Advanced economies are undertaking one of the largest energy transitions in modern history. Since the 2010s, and accelerating after 2020, they have pursued an ambitious shift toward lower-emission energy systems, greater resilience, and reduced dependence on traditional fuels.

The objectives are understandable. The scale of the challenge is often less appreciated. Every major energy transition in history has taken decades. Coal did not disappear when oil emerged. Oil did not eliminate coal. New systems scale slowly because infrastructure must be built, supply chains developed, grids upgraded, and capital deployed at enormous scale. During these transitions, old and new systems overlap. Historical energy transitions, such as the gradual shift from coal to oil, suggest that energy systems are rarely replaced quickly. More often, societies operate two systems simultaneously for long periods, increasing complexity and cost during the transition.

Today the transition is unfolding under financial and political pressure. Investment in fossil fuel capacity is often discouraged through regulation, environmental targets, and investor mandates. Meanwhile, renewable systems have not yet reached the scale required to fully replace legacy supply, particularly in heavy industry, aviation, shipping, and base-load electricity generation. This creates a difficult balancing act. Existing energy systems remain essential even as policymakers seek to reduce reliance upon them while alternatives continue to expand.

When existing supply is constrained before alternatives are fully operational, available energy capacity tightens. Prices become more volatile. Investment cycles grow more erratic. Producers hesitate to commit long-term capital when policy signals are uncertain. Consumers face fluctuating bills that undermine confidence.

The challenge is not simply producing more clean energy. It is maintaining reliable and affordable energy throughout the transition. This is not an argument against transition. It is a recognition of arithmetic. If demand remains high while supply becomes more fragile, price stability erodes.

Geopolitics compounds the challenge. Energy supply is being shaped more heavily by strategic competition. Sanctions, export restrictions, and resource nationalism have become common. Countries are rethinking reliance on single suppliers. Security now competes with efficiency. The lowest-cost solution is no longer always viewed as the safest one. Throughout much of the stability era, the global energy system was organized largely around minimizing costs. Today, it is being reorganized around resilience, redundancy, and security.

Re-shoring and diversification may enhance resilience over time, but they often raise costs in the short and medium term. Redundant supply chains are more expensive than tightly optimized global ones. Strategic reserves tie up capital. Domestic production may be safer but less efficient. Resilience often costs more than efficiency. Building backup capacity and reducing dependence on single suppliers usually comes at a higher price.

From the 1980s through the late 2010s, advanced economies benefited from a global system built to keep costs as low as possible. Energy and goods flowed across borders with relatively limited friction. That model supported low inflation and reinforced monetary flexibility. The new environment prioritizes security and resilience. These goals are legitimate, but they are not costless. When underlying costs are rising by design, inflation becomes less cyclical and more persistent. Price pressures no longer disappear as easily when demand slows because some of the pressures originate from how the system itself is being reorganized.

The global liquefied natural gas (LNG) market provides another example of this shift. Following the 2022 Ukraine conflict, European countries rushed to secure liquefied natural gas supplies. LNG prices surged dramatically as Europe competed with Asia for cargoes.[7] Developing economies such as Pakistan and Bangladesh struggled to secure fuel, leading to power shortages and rolling blackouts.[8] An energy shortage in one region quickly became an energy problem for many others. The episode demonstrated how supply constraints in one region can ripple across the global system, increasing volatility and raising costs worldwide.

These pressures do not operate in isolation. They interact with debt, government finances, and political stability, creating a more vulnerable economic environment. Governments then face difficult choices. They can protect consumers through subsidies and government support payments, which increase public borrowing. They can allow prices to adjust fully, which risks social backlash. They can tighten monetary policy to suppress demand, which raises interest payments on debt. None of these options restores the low-cost environment of the past, and each shifts the burden somewhere else in the system rather than removing it entirely.

The transition therefore introduces a new reality for advanced economies. The challenge is no longer simply producing enough energy. It is doing so while maintaining affordability, reliability, fiscal stability, and political support at the same time. Achieving all of these objectives simultaneously is considerably harder than many policymakers initially assumed. The difficulty is that progress in one area can often create new pressures in another. Efforts to improve resilience, reduce emissions, strengthen energy security, and contain costs do not always move in the same direction without compromise.

As these tensions accumulate, the economic environment becomes less forgiving. Trade-offs that once appeared manageable become increasingly difficult to avoid, setting the stage for a broader return of economic constraints. Energy is one example of a wider shift now taking place. The assumptions that allowed advanced economies to postpone difficult choices are becoming harder to sustain as economic constraints steadily re-emerge. What once appeared to be permanent flexibility increasingly proves to have been conditional. The limits that shaped earlier generations are beginning to assert themselves once again.

## *When Economic Limits Return*

From the mid-1980s through the early 2020s, advanced economies operated within unusually favourable conditions. Energy was broadly available. Global trade reduced costs. Borrowing costs fell steadily. Inflation was contained. When shocks occurred, central banks intervened and markets stabilized. The combination appeared remarkably durable. Stability came to be viewed not as a temporary outcome of favourable conditions, but as the normal state of affairs. This sequence created confidence in a model. Stability seemed manageable. Financial tools appeared sufficient. Debt expanded because it could be serviced at ever lower cost.[9] Asset values rose because discount rates declined. Governments ran deficits because markets absorbed them.

That framework depended on a quiet premise: that essential inputs would remain stable and inexpensive. Few people focused on that premise because it rarely appeared threatened. Modern economies were built on the assumption that energy would remain abundant, reliable, and relatively cheap.

That premise no longer holds. Energy markets are tighter. Supply chains are more fragmented. Geopolitical rivalry shapes access to resources.[10] Rules and policy changes alter investment decisions. Underlying costs are rising rather than falling. The era of steadily declining input costs that supported globalization and financial expansion is weakening. The environment that helped sustain the stability era is becoming less supportive on several fronts.

When essential inputs become unstable, the financial system built on top of them cannot remain untouched. Credit cannot substitute for energy. Central banks cannot fine-tune a system facing physical constraints. Political systems also come under strain when essentials become unstable. Financial systems can absorb many forms of stress. They cannot permanently detach economies from material reality. These are not rhetorical observations. They describe how the system actually works.

If governments carry large debt burdens, higher interest rates quickly strain budgets.[11] If households rely on property markets supported by low rates, tightening reduces affordability and suppresses activity. If corporations depend on cheap refinancing, rising costs compress investment, hiring, long-term expansion, and future growth. The effects do not remain isolated. Pressure emerging in one area quickly spreads to others.

When energy shocks occur in such a system, policymakers confront conflicting pressures. They can contain inflation and risk financial instability. They can protect financial markets and tolerate higher prices. They can support households and expand public borrowing. Each choice has consequences, yet none restores the conditions of the previous era. The challenge is no longer choosing the ideal outcome. It is deciding which costs are most acceptable.

What makes this environment more difficult is not simply higher energy prices in isolation. It is the interaction between energy volatility, elevated debt, ageing populations, weakened productivity growth, and rising geopolitical rivalry. Each of these pressures has been explored in earlier chapters. The difference today is that they are arriving together rather than one at a time. When several pressures hit simultaneously, economies have less room to absorb shocks and recover from setbacks.

The era of falling costs and expanding cheap credit is over. What follows is unlikely to be a single dramatic collapse. Instead, it is a period in which trade-offs become unavoidable and policy mistakes become more costly.

Energy is not the sole cause. It is one of the forces that exposes the limits of the existing model. Rising debt, ageing populations, weaker productivity growth, and geopolitical tensions also play important roles. The economy does not float above physical reality. It rests on it, whether we acknowledge it or not. Economic outcomes inevitably reflect that dependence.

When energy becomes scarce or more expensive, growth slows and expectations must adjust. Modern economies remain deeply dependent on stable flows of energy, resources, transportation, and industrial production, even when financial systems create the appearance of insulation from those constraints. The lesson is not that finance, technology, or policy no longer matter. It is that all of them operate within boundaries imposed by physical reality. Those boundaries can be deferred for a time, but they cannot be ignored indefinitely. The real question is not whether limits will shape policy, but how societies respond when growth encounters those limits. The outcome depends on whether adjustment unfolds gradually or arrives suddenly.

The era of stability did not end because policymakers forgot how to manage economies. It is ending because the financial, demographic, political, and physical conditions that once made stability easier are becoming less favourable at the same time. The pressures discussed throughout this book are no longer developing in isolation. Increasingly, they are reinforcing one another, making economies more vulnerable to disruption and reducing the margin for error available to policymakers.

# PART V

# THE BREAKING POINT

# 16

## WHEN STABILITY BECOMES FRAGILITY

Few words carry more reassurance in modern economic life than stability. It appears constantly in official statements, market commentary, and policy briefings, invoked as both a goal and a verdict. Stable markets are described as healthy. Stable prices are presented as proof of control. When volatility is low, confidence rises and policymakers speak of resilience. Calm is treated as evidence that risk has been mastered.

Yet in heavily indebted economies, long stretches of calm markets are rarely proof that risk has vanished. More often, they suggest that risk has not disappeared but has instead been deferred into the future. This distinction is important because stability and resilience are not the same thing. A system can appear stable for years while becoming progressively more vulnerable beneath the surface and less resilient.

Since the early 1980s, advanced economies have learned how to calm markets quickly when trouble appears. When markets trembled, interest rates were lowered. When borrowing became harder to obtain, central banks injected money into the financial system. When asset prices such as stocks, housing, and bonds fell sharply, policymakers stepped in quickly and forcefully. Each intervention restored order, and each episode reinforced the belief that severe breakdown could be prevented. By the early 2020s, total debt across advanced economies had risen to levels exceeding 250 percent of GDP, more than double the levels seen in the early 1980s, illustrating how stability increasingly relied on expanding debt and financial obligations rather than underlying resilience.[1] Dependence became structural.

The success of these interventions created a powerful impression. If instability repeatedly disappeared after policy action, it became increasingly easy to assume that instability itself had become manageable. Over time, this pattern reshaped expectations. Stability stopped being the result of strong foundations and became the product of continuous intervention.

Volatility was no longer something to endure and correct. It became something to suppress. That shift altered the character of the system. In an economy burdened by high debt, volatility is not merely discomfort. It is discipline. It forces losses to be recognized, leverage to be reduced, and prices to reflect risk.

When volatility is consistently contained, those adjustments do not disappear. They accumulate. The pressure is no longer released through periodic correction. Instead, it builds quietly beneath the surface, often hidden by the appearance of calm.

Economic breakdown rarely begins with visible chaos. It often begins with extended calm that masks rising strain. When stability depends on continuous support, calm itself can become an early warning sign. What appears reassuring may in fact be signalling growing dependence on conditions that cannot be maintained indefinitely without consequence.

The advanced world has come to rely on this policy-driven calm. What once absorbed shocks now postpones them, and the longer volatility is suppressed, the greater the adjustment required when suppression fails. The breaking point does not announce itself in advance. It forms gradually beneath years of apparent control, steady markets, and confidence that intervention will always arrive when needed.

What eventually emerges is not the sudden appearance of fragility, but the gradual revelation of fragility that had been accumulating all along. The vulnerabilities were present long before they became visible. Stability often concealed them, allowing pressures to build beneath the surface until they could no longer be ignored or postponed. That is how stability gradually came to be mistaken for strength.

## *When Stability Replaced Strength*

In the decades following the Second World War, roughly 1945 to the early 1970s, stability followed performance. When productivity rose, wages expanded, and growth was broadly shared, confidence emerged naturally. Markets reflected underlying strength, and calm was largely the consequence of resilience rather than its substitute.

Economic stability was supported by expanding productive capacity, rising incomes, and improving living standards. Confidence rested on what the economy was producing rather than on expectations of policy support.

In those decades, output expanded steadily. Real wages rose alongside productivity. Public debt burdens, though elevated after the war, declined relative to income as growth outpaced interest costs. Stability rested on expanding capacity and rising living standards across much of society.

Volatility existed, but it was not viewed as a systemic threat. Periodic recessions forced adjustment, excesses were corrected, and losses were recognized. Stability was not permanent, but it was grounded in economic fundamentals. The system was expected to absorb setbacks and recover. Short-term instability was accepted as part of maintaining long-term resilience and preserving the system's capacity to adapt.

Beginning in the 1980s, financial markets grew larger relative to the real economy, gradually altering the relationship between growth and stability. Debt levels climbed across households, corporations, and governments, while asset prices became increasingly central to public perceptions of prosperity and economic success in everyday life. The economy became progressively more dependent on maintaining confidence.

As debt and financial obligations grew, policymakers became less willing to tolerate downturns. The consequences of falling asset prices were no longer confined to investors. Housing markets, pension funds, banks, government budgets, and household savings all became more vulnerable when financial instability emerged.

Stability gradually ceased to be the result of economic strength and became a policy objective in its own right. Preventing market stress increasingly took precedence over allowing prices to adjust. Downturns that once cleared excesses were treated as dangers that required rapid intervention.

The objective gradually shifted from building resilience to preserving stability. Each crisis reinforced this approach. The lesson absorbed by institutions was not that leverage should be reduced, but that instability must be contained faster and more decisively. That lesson gradually reshaped the system itself.

Once stability becomes the goal rather than the outcome, the system changes character. Losses are delayed, debt is rolled forward, and intervention becomes increasingly routine. Markets begin to assume that severe declines will be met with support.

Eventually, behaviour adapts to those expectations. Borrowing appears less risky. Asset valuations become more dependent on continued stability. Financial markets come to expect intervention when stress emerges. This shift did not occur through recklessness. It emerged through rational responses to immediate threats. Policymakers acted to prevent deeper harm, but over time the avoidance of volatility increasingly replaced the cultivation of resilience across the system.

Stability was no longer earned primarily through performance but was increasingly maintained through intervention. Unlike resilience, however, intervention requires continuous support. What had once been a self-reinforcing product of economic strength increasingly became a condition that required ongoing management to sustain. As a result, periods of calm came to depend less on underlying resilience and more on the ability of policymakers to contain instability when it emerged. Periods of calm became increasingly manufactured rather than earned. The absence of turbulence did not necessarily signal underlying strength

## *An Unnatural Calm*

Since the early 2000s, and particularly after 2009, the persistence of unusually calm financial markets has been striking by historical standards. Yet beneath that calm, debt, intervention, and hidden weaknesses continued to build.

The contradiction is important. Financial markets often appeared increasingly stable even as many of the forces that create instability were becoming more pronounced.

Long expansions in earlier periods, such as the 1960s and the 1990s, were marked by periodic corrections. Markets fell sharply, borrowing became harder to obtain, and debt growth slowed. Excess risk was forced out of the system. These episodes were uncomfortable, but they served a purpose. They reduced imbalances before those imbalances became large enough to threaten the system itself.

By contrast, in the years leading up to the global financial crisis, measures of market volatility fell to unusually low levels even as borrowing across the financial system expanded rapidly. Between 2004 and 2007, the VIX index, often described as a gauge of market fear, averaged well below its long-term historical norm.[2] At the same time, US household debt rose from roughly 80 percent of GDP in the late 1990s to nearly 100 percent by 2007.[3] Bank debt and financial obligations expanded aggressively, while housing prices rose far faster than incomes.

The calm suggested confidence. The underlying trends pointed toward growing vulnerability. A similar pattern reappeared during the 2010s. After 2009, volatility declined again and remained subdued for much of the decade. Yet global debt continued to climb despite the calm.

By 2019, total global debt had risen above 320 percent of global output.[4] Public debt in many advanced economies exceeded 100 percent of GDP outside of wartime conditions.[5] Corporate borrowing reached record levels in several countries, while household debt remained elevated even as markets appeared stable. The appearance of stability and the accumulation of risk increasingly moved in the same direction. Even major disruptions were absorbed with unusual speed.

In early 2020, global equity markets fell by more than 30 percent within weeks as the pandemic spread.[6] In previous eras, declines of that scale were often followed by prolonged adjustment. Instead, markets rebounded rapidly. Within months, major United States indices had recovered their losses and moved to new highs.

This recovery was not accidental. Central bank intervention was swift and large. In the United States, the Federal Reserve balance sheet expanded from under 20 percent of GDP before the pandemic to more than 35 percent within a year.[7] Similar expansions occurred at the European Central Bank and the Bank of Japan. Policy rates were cut to near zero, while governments deployed fiscal support on a scale rarely seen outside wartime.

The speed of the recovery reinforced an increasingly powerful belief: severe market declines would be met with equally severe policy responses. Markets drew a clear conclusion. When stock markets decline sharply, when borrowing becomes harder to obtain, or when financial conditions tighten, authorities intervene forcefully and quickly. Deep and prolonged declines appear unlikely to be tolerated, even when underlying risks remain.

Historically, however, long stretches of low volatility have often preceded large corrections. Calm in the late 1920s was followed by an equity collapse of nearly ninety percent from peak to trough.[8] In the mid-2000s, narrow credit spreads masked mounting weakness in mortgage markets until the adjustment unfolded abruptly in 2008 and spread globally.

The pattern does not guarantee a future crisis. It does suggest that calm and safety are not always the same thing. The mechanism is familiar. When declines are repeatedly cushioned, borrowing expands. When losses are delayed, debt and financial obligations grow larger, more complex, and harder to manage. The eventual adjustment does not disappear. It is postponed. And what is postponed often becomes more difficult.

The key question is therefore no longer whether markets appear calm. It is whether that calm reflects strong foundations or continued support. If stability depends on intervention, then calm depends on continued policy support rather than underlying strength. That distinction becomes increasingly important because support mechanisms themselves are not unlimited. Policy responses did not remain isolated events.

## *From Rescue to Expectation*

Since the late 1980s, including the 1987 market crash, the early 2000s technology collapse, the 2008 financial crisis, and the 2020 pandemic, each major disruption has been met with increasingly decisive intervention.

After the technology bubble burst in the early 2000s, interest rates were cut aggressively. After the global financial crisis, policy rates in major economies were pushed to near zero and held there for years. Central banks purchased government bonds and other assets on a massive scale to stabilize markets.

These measures prevented deeper collapse, but they also reshaped expectations. When investors come to expect that sharp market declines will be met with rapid rate cuts, central bank support, and asset purchases, risk is assessed differently. Borrowing becomes easier to justify. Holding through downturns feels safer. The cost of caution rises relative to the perceived cost of risk-taking throughout the system. What begins as emergency support gradually becomes embedded in market expectations and investment behaviour.

Asset values begin to reflect not only projected earnings and productivity, but also the likelihood of policy support. When interest rates remain near zero for extended periods, valuation models mechanically produce higher prices. When central banks signal that they will act quickly to prevent disorderly market conditions, investors incorporate that signal into their decisions. The nature of risk nevertheless changes.

Risk is not eliminated. It is increasingly shifted into the future. Volatility that might once have occurred gradually is postponed. Corrections that could have unfolded over several years are compressed into shorter episodes and then reversed. Debt that might have been reduced during downturns is rolled forward instead into future cycles.

The incentives throughout the system begin to change. Behaviour that once appeared cautious gradually appears unnecessary, while greater risk-taking becomes easier to justify.

If borrowing costs remain low and market declines are repeatedly cushioned, increasing debt appears rational. Governments finance deficits more easily. Corporations refinance and expand their financial obligations. Households stretch further to purchase homes whose prices are supported by low rates and abundant credit.

As debt builds, the system becomes increasingly dependent on the conditions that encouraged the borrowing in the first place. What appears prudent at the individual level can create vulnerability at the system level.

When an economy expands at roughly 2 percent per year but total debt grows faster, stability depends increasingly on borrowing costs remaining suppressed. If effective interest rates rise by even one or two percentage points on debt levels exceeding 100 percent of GDP, the additional interest burden can amount to several percentage points of national income each year. A simple illustration makes the point.

For a government with debt equal to 120 percent of GDP, a 2 percentage point rise in average borrowing costs implies interest payments equal to roughly 2.4 percent of GDP annually.[9] That shift competes directly with public spending, social programs, and investment, demonstrating how small changes in rates can produce outsized effects in heavily indebted systems. The consequences spread well beyond higher borrowing costs. Income is redirected from borrowers to creditors. Consumption slows. Investment hesitates. The government's ability to respond to problems narrows when flexibility matters most.

The margin for error shrinks. The system gradually begins to feed on itself. Low volatility encourages borrowing. Rising debt increases dependence on continued calm. Dependence on calm strengthens expectations of intervention.

The relationship becomes self-reinforcing. It appears stable, but beneath that stability dependence on continued support steadily grows. What began as rescue gradually becomes expectation, and expectation gradually becomes dependency.

## *Debt Becomes the Fault Line*

Debt now sits at the centre of the modern economic system. Debt influences investment decisions, shapes government policy, and affects the stability of financial markets. More importantly, it determines how the economy responds when conditions begin to deteriorate and pressures begin to build.

Since the early 1980s, steadily falling interest rates have made borrowing cheaper across governments, firms, and households. Each downturn was met with lower rates and expanding debt and financial obligations. Each recovery began with higher debt levels than the one before.

By the early 2020s, public debt in many advanced economies exceeded 100 percent of GDP.[10] In some cases it is significantly higher. Corporate borrowing has reached record levels relative to output, while household debt remains elevated in countries where housing prices have outpaced income growth for years. Combined public and private debt burdens are historically high outside periods of war or post-war reconstruction.

The importance of debt, however, is not simply its size. What matters most is how it changes the behaviour of the entire system. High debt does not automatically create crisis. What it does create is sensitivity. When debt burdens are modest, rising interest rates slow activity but rarely threaten solvency. When debt burdens are large, even small increases in borrowing costs can destabilize governments, businesses, and households. What once absorbed shocks now begins to amplify them.

Debt changes the economy's tolerance for stress. A system carrying modest debt can often withstand higher rates, temporary recessions, or periods of market volatility without serious disruption. A system carrying very large debt burdens reacts differently. Movements that were once manageable become more consequential. Small disturbances begin producing larger effects.

As debt grows, policy choices narrow. Raising rates to contain inflation risks straining government finances and corporate refinancing. Cutting rates to relieve pressure risks reigniting inflation or weakening currencies. Expanding central bank support further risks increasing dependence on policies that already face diminishing effectiveness. The challenge is not simply that every option carries costs. It is that the costs become larger as debt accumulates and flexibility declines.

The threshold for instability changes as well. In a lightly indebted system, volatility is disruptive but manageable. In a heavily indebted one, volatility can trigger forced selling, funding stress, fiscal strain, and declining confidence in quick succession. Fragility increases quietly as obligations accumulate. The system becomes less resilient even while appearing stable.

There is another complication. Debt compounds regardless of calm. Interest accrues. Maturities must be refinanced. Governments roll over debt continuously. Corporations depend on access to capital markets. Stability therefore requires financial markets to function smoothly and borrowing costs to remain tolerable. If financing conditions change abruptly, adjustment becomes far more difficult. Time does not reduce the obligation. It merely changes when the obligation must be confronted.

Heavily indebted systems rarely unwind gradually. They tend to remain stable until financing conditions shift. This is why suppressed volatility becomes increasingly dangerous. The larger the debt base, the more sensitive the system becomes to disruption, and the more essential calm appears. The more essential calm becomes, the more intervention is required to sustain it over time.

Debt therefore acts less like a source of strength and more like a fault line. It may remain hidden for years, but once pressure begins to build, the entire structure becomes increasingly sensitive to stress. In this way, fragility becomes embedded within apparent stability long before it is recognized.

## *When the System Runs Out of Flexibility*

Since the 2008 financial crisis, the global economy has repeatedly absorbed strain by lowering interest rates, expanding central bank balance sheets, and increasing debt. For more than a decade, this approach stabilized markets and supported growth.

Yet the flexibility that made this possible is no longer unlimited. The tools remain available, but the room to use them is shrinking. Policies that once restored stability now face growing constraints and diminishing effectiveness.

Interest rates in advanced economies cannot fall much below zero without distorting financial institutions and savings behaviour. The period of near-zero rates that followed the 2008 crisis was extraordinary rather than normal, and repeatedly returning to that environment carries increasing side effects. Pension funds struggle to generate returns. Banks face pressure on profitability. Savers see purchasing power erode. What once stabilized markets increasingly creates new vulnerabilities of its own elsewhere in the economy.

Inflation imposes another constraint. When prices are rising persistently, cutting rates or injecting additional money into the financial system risks reinforcing the problem rather than alleviating it. Central banks that once faced deflationary pressure now confront the opposite challenge. The ability to cushion markets while maintaining price stability has become more limited. The room for manoeuvre is narrower than it was during the decade following the global financial crisis.

Fiscal pressures are becoming more visible as well. Since the global financial crisis, and particularly after the pandemic, public debt ratios that were once cyclical have increasingly become structural. Deficits persist even during periods of expansion, while interest payments rise as debt is refinanced at higher rates. The government's ability to respond to new challenges gradually narrows as more resources are directed toward existing commitments and interest costs.

Demographics add another layer of pressure. Ageing populations in many advanced economies increase pension and healthcare obligations while slowing labour-force growth.[11] This trend, visible for decades in Japan and increasingly across Europe and North America, reduces the growth that once helped dilute debt burdens. Slower growth makes existing obligations harder to sustain. The pressure does not arrive through a dramatic crisis. It accumulates gradually, year after year.

These constraints do not operate independently. Higher debt increases sensitivity to interest rates. Ageing populations reduce growth. Slower growth makes debt harder to manage. Inflation limits policy flexibility. Each constraint strengthens the effect of the others. What might be manageable in isolation becomes far more difficult when multiple pressures emerge simultaneously. The result is a system that becomes progressively less adaptable as challenges accumulate and interact.

The system is now more indebted, less flexible, and more dependent on confidence than at any point since the early 1980s. Suppressing volatility requires policy support. Intervention expands debt and financial obligations. Expanded debt increases sensitivity to interest rates. Rising sensitivity limits the scope for further intervention when stress emerges. The system gradually tightens around its own constraints. Measures that once created flexibility increasingly reduce it, as each intervention leaves behind higher debt and greater dependence on favourable conditions. The room for policy error steadily narrows.

If growth remains modest while interest payments rise, more income must be directed toward servicing debt. Less remains available for consumption, investment, and public services. Political support for austerity is limited. Acceptance of higher inflation is also limited. Public and market appetite for repeated rescues is weakening as well, particularly after the extraordinary interventions undertaken during the crises of 2008 and 2020.

The range of politically acceptable options narrows as economic pressures increase. Stability now rests on a delicate balance between competing pressures. It depends on interest rates that are low but not inflationary, deficits that are large but not destabilizing, and interventions that are forceful but not confidence-destroying. Maintaining that balance grows harder as debt accumulates and flexibility declines.

This balance can hold for a time, but it does not become easier to maintain. At some point, one constraint begins to overwhelm the others. Interest rates rise faster than expected. Inflation proves harder to contain. Bond markets demand higher compensation and currency pressures intensify. What once could be managed gradually begins to adjust more abruptly.

As a result, a correction that might once have unfolded slowly can cascade through financial markets with much greater force. The system becomes increasingly brittle.

## *When Constraints Become Breaking Points*

The breaking point does not arrive because policymakers fail to act. It arrives because the tools that once restored calm no longer operate with the same freedom. The policies that stabilized markets for decades become less effective as debt rises and policy flexibility gradually erodes. Each intervention achieves less than it once did while carrying greater costs and risks as its effectiveness steadily declines.

When confidence can no longer offset arithmetic, the system adjusts. When a system built on suppressed volatility adjusts, it rarely does so gently. Years of postponed corrections compress into shorter and more disruptive periods. Asset prices supported by low rates reprice. Borrowers that depended on cheap financing face rising costs. Governments confront larger interest burdens. The pressures no longer remain isolated.

What was once absorbed gradually begins to emerge all at once. For decades, policymakers learned how to smooth volatility and stabilize markets. Each intervention reinforced the belief that instability could be contained, while each recovery strengthened confidence that downturns could be avoided.

The success of stabilization gradually became one of the system's defining assumptions. Yet stability built on continuous intervention is inherently fragile. When calm depends on low rates, expanding debt and financial obligations, and rising leverage, the system becomes dependent on conditions that cannot persist indefinitely. The longer calm is maintained through intervention, the more sensitive the underlying structure becomes. What appears resilient increasingly depends on the continuation of unusually favourable conditions.

The final adjustment rarely announces itself in advance. It often begins with a shift in financing conditions, a sustained rise in interest rates, or a weakening of confidence in policy effectiveness. At first, these developments may appear manageable. Markets wobble. Borrowing costs rise. Policymakers respond.

The difference is that the responses no longer produce the same results they once did. If constraints have tightened sufficiently, the familiar tools restore less stability than before and confidence weakens rather than strengthens. Years of suppressed volatility leave markets poorly prepared for sustained adjustment. Investors accustomed to rapid recoveries face prolonged declines, governments accustomed to cheap borrowing confront rising interest costs, and corporations reliant on refinancing encounter tighter financial conditions.

Financial stress gradually spreads into the broader economy. Households become more cautious. Businesses become more reluctant to expand. Markets become more sensitive to shocks that might once have been absorbed with relatively little disruption. Behaviour begins to change because the assumptions that supported stability begin to weaken. The transition from stability to fragility is rarely dramatic at first. It unfolds gradually, then accelerates. Calm gives way to uncertainty. Uncertainty gives way to repricing. Repricing gives way to adjustment, bringing broader economic and financial strain.

This progression is not inevitable in timing, but it is structural in nature. The longer volatility is suppressed and debt accumulates, the more sensitive the system becomes. When adjustment finally occurs, it reflects years of postponed correction and accumulated imbalances.

For decades, stability appeared to strengthen the system. In reality, stability built on intervention gradually reduced resilience. Calm masked growing imbalances. Low volatility encouraged higher leverage. Rising debt increased sensitivity to interest rates. The paradox lies at the heart of the modern advanced economy. The very policies that succeeded in preserving stability also increased dependence on continued stability over time.

When the limits of intervention are finally reached, calm gives way to a more volatile environment. Market declines become harder to reverse. Borrowing costs remain elevated. Policy responses become less effective. Confidence weakens.

The greatest danger emerges when confidence in stability itself begins to erode. Systems that long appeared resilient can weaken rapidly once investors, households, and institutions begin to doubt that volatility will remain temporary or that policymakers can still restore calm with the same authority as before. In heavily indebted economies, stability depends not only on growth but also on continued access to affordable financing. When that access tightens, adjustments occur quickly. Asset prices fall. Debt burdens rise relative to income. Fiscal pressures intensify. Economic growth slows. Fragility that developed quietly becomes visible at last.

The breaking point does not emerge from a single event. It emerges from the cumulative effects of years of suppressed volatility and rising debt. Calm that once appeared to signal resilience reveals itself as conditional stability.

When that condition changes, the system adjusts. Confidence gives way to caution. Stability gives way to fragility. What had seemed permanent begins to look conditional, and assumptions that once appeared secure are reassessed.

What appears strongest at the end of a long period of stability is often where hidden vulnerabilities have had the most time to accumulate and deepen.

The lesson is not that stability is undesirable. It is that stability sustained primarily through intervention can gradually weaken the mechanisms that make systems resilient. The advanced world spent decades learning how to suppress volatility. It may now be entering a period in which volatility performs the adjustment that was postponed for years.

That is how stability becomes fragility.

# 17

# WHEN TRUST BREAKS STABILITY FRACTURES

Modern economies do not function on money alone. They function on belief. People accept a currency because they believe it will hold value tomorrow. Investors buy government bonds because they believe repayment is credible. Businesses hire and expand because they believe the rules will remain stable long enough to justify risk. Citizens tolerate high public debt because they assume the system, though imperfect, is broadly manageable.

At its core, the system runs on confidence. People accept money, buy bonds, and invest because they believe the system will still work tomorrow. When that confidence weakens, even institutions that once appeared strong can begin to look vulnerable with surprising speed.

From the 1980s through the early 2000s, advanced economies did not need to defend this belief openly because it was embedded in institutions, legal systems, and long periods of relative stability. Trust was not debated. It was assumed. That assumption now carries greater weight than before, particularly in highly indebted economies where confidence itself becomes a source of stability.

By the early 2020s, total public and private debt across advanced economies had reached historically elevated levels compared with overall economic output.[1] Highly indebted systems rely on trust in ways that less indebted systems do not.

When debt is modest, mistakes can be corrected without threatening credibility. When debt becomes large, confidence becomes as important as repayment because governments are judged not only on whether the numbers add up but also on whether markets and citizens believe obligations can be managed.

This shift is visible across the advanced world. In the United States, federal debt held by the public rose from roughly 35 percent of GDP in 2007 to around 100 percent in recent years, while debt levels in many European economies also climbed significantly following the 2008 financial crisis and the 2020 pandemic.[2] As debt rises, confidence increasingly carries the burden that fiscal flexibility once absorbed. Trust becomes the buffer between growing obligations and visible instability.

## *Trust as the Last Stabilizer*

In such systems, trust absorbs pressure that would otherwise force adjustment. Trust allows governments to keep borrowing instead of cutting spending, allows central banks to expand their role without immediate resistance, and allows voters to accept deficits on the promise that limits will be addressed later. As long as confidence holds, difficult choices can be delayed and growing strains can remain largely hidden from view. Over time, confidence becomes a policy resource rather than simply a public sentiment. The more heavily it is relied upon, the harder it becomes to rebuild.

The breaking point in advanced economies will not begin with an accounting threshold. It will begin when enough people question whether the system still deserves their confidence. Historically, these shifts rarely begin with a spreadsheet or a debt ratio. They emerge when institutions appear more capable of stabilizing markets than improving living standards, and when the gap between what people are told and what they experience begins to widen. The events of 2008 illustrate this dynamic with particular clarity.

During the 2008 financial crisis, governments across the United States and Europe moved quickly to stabilize banks and financial markets. These actions prevented systemic collapse, but they also created a lasting perception that financial institutions received extraordinary support while households faced unemployment, falling incomes, and foreclosures.

The stabilization worked, yet the distribution of outcomes altered trust. For many citizens, the system appeared capable of protecting markets more quickly than protecting livelihoods. That perception lingered long after the crisis passed and gradually transformed trust from something assumed into something evaluated and therefore more fragile during periods of stress.

Once trust becomes something people evaluate rather than assume, perceptions of fairness begin to matter as much as economic performance. Stability may still exist, but confidence increasingly depends on whether people believe the benefits and burdens of that stability are being shared fairly.

## *Stability for Some, Exclusion for Others*

Since the early 1980s, advanced economies have delivered rising asset values alongside rising debt. Stock markets climbed to repeated highs. Housing prices increased far faster than wages in most major cities. Government debt expanded without an immediate rise in borrowing costs. Central banks intervened repeatedly to steady markets during periods of stress.

These developments were often presented as signs of resilience. Markets recovered quickly after crises. Financial systems remained intact. Recessions were softened. Yet the benefits of this stability were not distributed evenly. The gains increasingly accrued to those who already owned assets.

In many advanced economies, the majority of equities are owned by a minority of households. Homeownership rates are far higher among older generations than among younger ones. Those who already owned assets benefited from falling interest rates and rising valuations, while those trying to enter faced higher prices and heavier borrowing.

The scale of this shift is visible in housing affordability. In the United Kingdom, average house prices were roughly three to four times average earnings in the 1980s, but have risen to around eight times earnings in recent years.[3] Similar patterns emerged in Canada, Australia, and parts of the United States, making homeownership harder for younger households.

Consider two households separated by a generation and shaped by very different economic conditions. One purchased a home in the early 1990s when prices were modest relative to income and interest rates, though high, fell steadily for decades. As rates declined and asset prices rose, that home increased several times in value, mortgage payments became manageable relative to income, and equity accumulated almost automatically.

The other household reached adulthood during an era of already elevated prices and low rates. By the time it could consider buying, prices had risen far beyond income growth, meaning a similar home required far more debt relative to earnings, while rent consumed a larger share of income and savings earned little return. Entry into ownership required either substantial borrowing or family assistance.

Both households participated in the same economy but experienced stability differently. For homeowners and investors, rising asset prices reinforced confidence in the system. For renters and first-time buyers, those same trends raised the cost of entry and made stability appear increasingly exclusionary.

Over time, this divergence alters perception. Official statements describe strong markets and healthy financial positions, yet households facing higher rents, elevated mortgage burdens, and weaker savings returns do not experience that strength as security. The issue is not envy but whether the system appears to work for everyone, not just some.

This divergence became particularly visible after the 2008 financial crisis and again following the 2020 pandemic, when housing prices in cities such as London, Toronto, Sydney, and parts of the United States rose far faster than incomes.[4] Older homeowners experienced large increases in wealth, while younger households faced rising rents and higher barriers to ownership. Policies designed to stabilize markets also contributed to rising valuations, meaning what appeared as stability for asset holders often translated into exclusion for those trying to enter the system.

When the rewards of stability accrue disproportionately to those already inside the system, trust begins to depend on who benefits from that system. People begin to ask whether the rules operate equally or whether they primarily protect those who already possess wealth and assets.

If markets rise after central bank intervention and those gains are concentrated among asset owners, neutrality is questioned. If public debt expands while public services feel strained, fiscal management is questioned. If younger generations face higher barriers than previous generations at the same stage of life, fairness is questioned. When these questions accumulate, confidence in institutions begins to weaken.

Institutions depend not only on technical competence but also on the belief that outcomes are not systematically skewed. When that belief weakens, confidence in governments and central banks begins to erode. The stability model starts to look less like a shared achievement and more like a system that produces different outcomes for different groups.

Trust in institutions and trust in economic management reinforce each other. When economic outcomes feel uneven, institutional credibility absorbs the strain. As confidence weakens, policymakers face growing pressure to deliver stability through action rather than persuasion, increasing reliance on intervention when deeper problems remain unresolved. The distinction between emergency measures and normal policy begins to blur. The longer this pattern persists, the more deeply it becomes embedded. Intervention gradually shifts from response to routine.

## *When Intervention Becomes the System*

During genuine crises, forceful intervention strengthens trust. When banks fail and markets freeze, decisive action restores order. Lowering interest rates, providing emergency funding, and stabilizing credit markets prevent panic from spreading. In those moments, public support is strong because the threat is visible and immediate and action appears necessary.

The difficulty arises when emergency measures remain in place long after the emergency fades. Following the 2008 financial crisis and again during the 2020 pandemic, interest rates in major advanced economies were pushed toward extremely low levels and remained there for extended periods. Central bank balance sheets expanded dramatically and, in many cases, never returned to earlier levels after the crisis.

The scale of this shift is striking. The U.S. Federal Reserve's balance sheet grew from under $1 trillion before the 2008 financial crisis to more than $8 trillion following the pandemic, while similar expansions occurred at the European Central Bank, Bank of England, and Bank of Japan.[5] What began as temporary crisis measures gradually became permanent features of the financial system in many advanced economies.

As intervention became routine, the character of institutions changed. Central banks were once perceived as guardians of price stability. Governments were expected to manage budgets within visible limits. Markets were expected to discipline excess through repricing. Over time, however, the boundaries between markets and policymakers began to blur as investors increasingly anticipated policy support during periods of stress.

When markets fell sharply, investors came to expect policy support. When borrowing costs rose, pressure mounted for central banks to lower interest rates again. When governments faced fiscal strain, central banks purchased large quantities of public debt, indirectly easing that strain. Each step may have been justified in isolation, but together they altered expectations.

Support gradually shifted from being an emergency response to becoming part of the system itself rather than the exception.

This shift became especially visible in the United Kingdom in 2022, when government bond markets reacted sharply to large unfunded tax cuts and increased borrowing plans.[6] Yields rose rapidly, triggering losses in pension funds that relied heavily on leveraged government bond strategies and forcing some funds to sell assets quickly to meet collateral demands.

The Bank of England intervened by temporarily purchasing government bonds, calming conditions and restoring order. The episode demonstrated how quickly financial stability could come to depend on policy action and how readily markets assumed authorities would intervene to prevent disorder. What was intended as a temporary safeguard also reinforced a broader expectation that support would be available when stress emerged.

Markets increasingly responded not only to earnings and productivity but also to anticipated policy actions. Risk was not eliminated but pushed into the future as imbalances accumulated between interventions. Instead of allowing periodic correction, asset prices rose further relative to income, debt levels increased across the public and private sectors, and fiscal deficits widened without immediate penalty.

Institutions were no longer viewed solely as referees but increasingly as participants in market outcomes. Once that perception takes hold, neutrality is questioned. Decisions that were once regarded as technical begin to look political, particularly when asset prices rise after policy action and inflation spreads costs across the broader public.

The result is not immediate revolt but gradual scepticism. What policymakers promise and what households experience begin to diverge. If institutions appear able to stabilize markets more quickly than living standards, citizens begin to question whom the system is designed to protect. The more stability depends on intervention, the more confidence depends on continued intervention as well.

As this dependency takes hold, policy choices begin to narrow. Once stability depends on continued support, policymakers face a difficult choice: withdraw support and risk instability, or maintain it and deepen dependency. Policymakers find themselves choosing between short-term calm and long-term credibility, a tension that gradually reduces policy flexibility and increases systemic fragility.

## *Economic Strain, Political Fracture*

Economic strain rarely announces itself in official reports. It appears instead in daily trade-offs, when rent absorbs a larger share of income than expected, when grocery bills rise faster than wages, when public debt climbs yet public services feel stretched, and when markets reach record highs while household finances feel tight. Individually, these pressures appear manageable, but collectively they alter political behaviour and reshape how citizens interpret stability.

Those whose wealth has risen with asset prices often prefer continuity because the system, despite imperfections, has delivered gains. Those who struggle to accumulate assets or secure housing are more likely to demand change, often seeking visible disruption rather than incremental reform. This divergence is not rooted in temperament but in economic position. When one group benefits from rising valuations and another confronts rising costs, they no longer evaluate stability in the same way. One sees resilience, while the other sees exclusion, and over time this difference reshapes political incentives and public expectations.

Since the 2010s, political outcomes across advanced economies have reflected this growing divergence, particularly following the 2008 financial crisis and the 2020 pandemic.

Voters frustrated by housing affordability, stagnant incomes, and rising living costs increasingly supported parties promising structural change. Across Europe and the United States, populist and anti-establishment movements gained traction during periods when asset prices rose while wage growth remained modest, illustrating how prolonged economic strain can reshape political alignment.[7]

Parties that promise fiscal restraint face resistance from voters who rely on public spending, while parties that promise intervention face resistance from those who fear inflation or higher taxes. Central banks that tighten policy to contain inflation are accused of harming workers, while those that loosen policy to support growth are accused of fuelling inequality. As economic pressures intensify, nearly every policy choice begins to produce visible winners and losers.

Political division does not arise from economic conditions alone, but persistent divergence between asset growth and income growth deepens existing tensions. When opportunity feels uneven, frustration attaches itself to institutions, and trust that was once broadly shared begins to fragment. Institutions that once commanded broad acceptance increasingly face suspicion from multiple directions. Courts are viewed through partisan lenses, central banks are accused of favouring markets, and legislatures are seen as protecting incumbents rather than addressing underlying problems. Trust in institutions becomes harder to sustain.

The result is fragmentation that makes compromise harder, slows decision-making, and weakens the ability of governments to respond to economic stress. Stable democracies depend on compromise, while highly indebted systems depend on credible fiscal adjustment. When polarization intensifies, both become more difficult to achieve. In that environment, postponing difficult choices becomes politically attractive, yet postponement in a highly indebted system allows underlying pressures to continue building.

As political division grows, the capacity to manage debt responsibly weakens. Investors begin to question not only whether the numbers add up but also whether policymakers remain willing to address the problem. Economic strain and political fracture then begin reinforcing each other, creating a feedback loop in which declining trust makes effective policymaking harder, while delayed decisions further undermine confidence.

## *The Intervention Trap*

As economic pressure builds, governments and central banks respond, which is precisely what they are designed to do. Weak growth invites stimulus, financial stress invites liquidity support, and rising borrowing costs invite reassurance. Each intervention is typically justified as necessary to preserve stability. In the short term, these actions often succeed, as markets steady, credit continues to flow, and panic is avoided.

Repeated intervention, however, alters expectations. Investors begin to assume that sharp downturns will be softened. Governments learn that borrowing can be extended without immediate penalty. Households come to expect that severe contractions will be mitigated. Over time, support becomes expected rather than exceptional, and stability increasingly depends on help arriving when needed.

The regional banking stress in the United States in 2023 illustrated this dynamic, when several mid-sized banks faced pressure and authorities moved quickly to guarantee deposits and provide liquidity facilities.[8] The response stabilized markets and prevented broader panic, yet it also reinforced expectations that policymakers would intervene quickly to prevent instability, strengthening the perception that financial systems operate with an implicit safety net.

This expectation stabilizes behaviour for a time but also raises the stakes. Each round of intervention must be at least as convincing as the last. If stimulus measures shrink, markets react negatively. If central banks hesitate, volatility increases. Governments that signal restraint often encounter political resistance. The system gradually becomes conditioned to continued support rather than periodic adjustment as pressures build. The focus moves from resolution to preservation.

Instead of correcting imbalances, policy increasingly delays correction. Structural pressures are smoothed rather than resolved, while repricing is postponed rather than allowed to occur. The immediate effect is calm. The cumulative effect is dependence. As dependence rises, credibility carries greater weight because markets increasingly rely on policymakers to maintain stability.

If inflation rises after prolonged stimulus, confidence in monetary discipline weakens. If public debt continues to climb without a credible path to control, fiscal promises lose force. If political division blocks reform, official assurances begin to sound less convincing. As confidence weakens, larger interventions are required to achieve the same stabilizing effect.

Larger interventions, however, raise new questions. How much more can be borrowed? How long can interest rates remain below market pressures? Who ultimately bears the cost? As these questions move beyond specialists into the broader public, confidence in policymakers begins to weaken. Policy tools become less effective because they depend heavily on belief. The same actions achieve progressively less.

When belief weakens, policy still functions but produces smaller results and greater controversy. Stabilization becomes more expensive both politically and financially. The system eventually reaches a point where intervention is both necessary and increasingly doubted, creating a trap in which reliance on support deepens vulnerability while withdrawing support risks instability. By then, confidence becomes the final line of defence.

## *The Final Buffer*

Highly indebted advanced economies can operate longer than expected because confidence delays repricing. Investors continue to buy government debt because they believe repayment is secure, citizens often tolerate deficits because they assume adjustments will come later, and markets remain orderly because participants expect institutions to respond quickly to stress. Confidence allows those assumptions to persist even as pressures continue to build. It delays the visible consequences of structural strain.

Trust therefore acts as a buffer between structural weakness and visible disruption. It allows debt to compound without immediate penalty and gives policymakers room to postpone politically costly decisions. As long as confidence holds, difficult adjustments can be postponed, but the underlying pressures do not disappear. They continue to build as debt accumulates, populations age, and borrowing costs gradually rise.

Public debt in many advanced economies now stands at levels previously associated with wartime, while ageing populations increase pension and healthcare obligations and growth rates remain modest compared to earlier decades.[9] When debt is large and growth is limited, stability depends heavily on the belief that management remains credible. If that belief weakens, adjustment can accelerate quickly as investors demand greater compensation for risk and fiscal choices narrow.

The Eurozone debt crisis between 2010 and 2012 demonstrated how rapidly confidence can shift once credibility weakens.[10] Countries such as Greece, Italy, and Spain experienced rising borrowing costs as investors questioned fiscal sustainability, and although European Central Bank intervention stabilized markets, the episode revealed how quickly trust can deteriorate when doubts emerge about credibility.

Adjustment does not require panic but rather growing caution. Investors shorten time horizons. Households reduce spending. Political leaders become more reluctant to compromise. Elections become more volatile, public frustration deepens, and reassurance from governments and institutions gradually loses its ability to calm anxieties. Each reaction reinforces uncertainty, making the system more sensitive to disturbances that might previously have been absorbed with little disruption. What changes first is not the economy itself but how households, businesses, and investors respond to it.

The breaking point therefore emerges not from a single event but from a change in behaviour. When stability is assumed, high debt and persistent deficits can appear manageable. When stability begins to be questioned, those same conditions appear far more hazardous. The shift may be gradual at first, but once confidence begins to weaken, adjustment tends to accelerate.

Confidence can buy time, but it cannot change the numbers. Debt continues to grow, interest payments rise, and demographic pressures build as ageing populations increase pension and healthcare obligations.[11] For years, belief allows governments to postpone difficult choices, reassuring markets and voters that stability can be maintained without meaningful adjustment. Delay changes timing, not reality.

Yet postponement does not eliminate pressure. It merely shifts it into the future. As borrowing expands and growth remains modest, the gap between promises and fiscal reality gradually widens. What once appeared manageable begins to feel heavier, and policies that once reassured begin to lose credibility. People continue working, spending, investing, and participating in daily economic life, yet beneath the surface confidence weakens as more households begin questioning whether the system still works in their interests.

When confidence weakens, the arithmetic reasserts itself. Investors demand higher compensation for risk. Political divisions complicate adjustment. Policymakers discover that options once available have narrowed. Economic problems no longer feel temporary. The pressure becomes social and political as well as financial, and institutions that once absorbed strain begin to lose the confidence that allowed them to stabilize them.

This is how stability ends. Not through a sudden collapse from strength, but through the gradual exhaustion of confidence after years of debt and denial. The breaking point rarely arrives as a single event. It emerges when belief can no longer carry the weight placed upon it, when people begin losing faith in the system itself, and when that moment arrives, the advanced world begins to discover that stability was never permanent, only postponed.

# 18

# THE BREAKING OF THE OLD MODEL

Since the early 1980s, advanced economies operated under a workable formula. When growth slowed, borrowing increased. When financial stress appeared, interest rates were lowered. When markets fell sharply, central banks intervened. When fiscal gaps widened, refinancing remained affordable.

Over time, this evolved into a policy strategy that appeared to make downturns manageable and growth easier to sustain. Governments and central banks increasingly relied on lower interest rates, expanded borrowing, and financial support to cushion economic weakness. Investors and households began to assume that shocks would be temporary and that policymakers would stabilize conditions when stress emerged. What began as a series of responses to individual crises gradually became an established approach to managing economic instability.

This approach did not eliminate recessions or volatility, but it reduced their duration and softened their impact. Debt rose, yet servicing costs remained manageable. Asset prices recovered quickly after shocks, and political pressure eased once markets stabilized. Downturns were seen less as moments requiring structural adjustment and more as temporary interruptions that policy could manage. Each intervention left a more demanding starting point for the next.

By the early 2020s, total debt across advanced economies had reached historically high levels relative to output, while policy interest rates, after decades of decline, had little room left to fail further without significant side effects.[1] The path to this outcome was long and gradual.

For nearly four decades, this approach appeared to work. The global economy experienced recessions, financial crises, and market corrections, yet each episode was followed by stabilization and recovery. Interest rates declined, financial conditions eased, and debt expanded without triggering sustained instability. Success reinforced confidence in the approach itself. The result was growing confidence that policymakers could support growth whenever problems emerged. That confidence rested on important assumptions.

The difficulty is that the conditions supporting this approach were never permanent. The same forces that made borrowing easier, inflation easier to contain, and growth easier to sustain are now becoming less supportive. As those conditions change, the model that shaped the post-1980 economic era begins to encounter limits that can no longer be postponed.

## *The Model That Worked*

This approach worked because three conditions made borrowing easier and risk less visible.

First, interest rates trended downward over time. Each cycle began with rates high enough to cut meaningfully, and lower rates reduced borrowing costs while supporting asset values. In the early 1980s, policy rates in major economies were in the double digits as central banks fought inflation. By the 2010s, many advanced economies operated with near-zero interest rates, and in some cases negative yields.[2] This forty-year decline in borrowing costs allowed governments, corporations, and households to accumulate debt while keeping servicing costs manageable for many years.

Second, inflation remained contained across much of the advanced world. Globalization, technological change, and credible monetary policy kept price pressures subdued, allowing central banks to ease aggressively without destabilizing expectations. The period often described as the Great Moderation saw inflation fall from the volatile levels of the 1970s and early 1980s to relatively stable ranges around two percent in many advanced economies.[3] With inflation low and predictable, policymakers gained room to intervene repeatedly without triggering sustained price pressures.

Third, demographics were not yet binding. Ageing had begun, but the fiscal burden of pensions and healthcare had not fully matured. The working-age population remained large enough to support expanding debt. Large cohorts entered the workforce through the 1980s and 1990s, supporting economic expansion and providing a broad tax base. Productivity gains from technological change reinforced this dynamic, helping output grow even as borrowing increased.

Under these conditions, policymakers appeared to have considerable flexibility, and governments could borrow without immediate penalty. Corporations could refinance with relative ease. Households could service mortgages at declining rates. Central banks could intervene without triggering currency instability or sustained inflation. The system appeared capable of absorbing growing obligations without encountering obvious limits. Few saw reason to expect otherwise.

The constraints that normally force governments and borrowers to slow down appeared distant. Borrowing increased, but the cost of servicing that borrowing declined. Asset prices rose, improving household finances and encouraging further borrowing. Success reinforced confidence, and confidence encouraged behaviour that assumed favourable conditions would continue. The system began to feed on itself.

Lower interest rates supported asset prices. Rising asset prices strengthened household finances. Stronger household finances encouraged further borrowing. Growth appeared stable, and risks seemed manageable. What looked like a durable equilibrium was heavily dependent on conditions that were becoming increasingly difficult to sustain. That environment is now changing fundamentally.

## *When Higher Rates Expose Rising Debt*

The model relied heavily on declining or stable borrowing costs. For many years, borrowing remained cheap across advanced economies, allowing governments, corporations, and households to expand debt without immediate financial strain. Governments refinanced large debts at low rates, corporations extended maturities cheaply, and households locked in mortgages at historically low costs. Even as total debt rose, interest payments as a share of income appeared contained, reinforcing confidence that rising debt remained manageable under existing conditions.

This dynamic became especially pronounced after the global financial crisis of 2008. Central banks lowered interest rates to near zero and implemented large-scale asset purchases, pushing borrowing costs down across advanced economies.[4] Governments responded with fiscal expansion, corporations took advantage of cheap credit to refinance and increase leverage, and households benefited from historically low mortgage rates. The pandemic period reinforced this trend, with even larger fiscal programs financed at exceptionally low borrowing costs.

The longer this environment persisted, the more economic behaviour adapted to the assumption that borrowing would remain inexpensive.

That balance begins to shift when rates rise. In a low-debt economy, higher interest rates slow activity but do not necessarily threaten solvency. In a heavily indebted one, higher rates raise borrowing costs across governments, companies, and households at the same time, amplifying the impact across the entire economy. What once appeared manageable under exceptionally low rates begins to look very different when financing costs move higher.

When public debt approaches or exceeds national output, even modest increases in borrowing costs translate into large increases in annual interest expense. With debt levels now exceeding one hundred percent of GDP in several advanced economies, even small increases in average borrowing costs leave governments with less room in their budgets.[5] What was manageable at two percent becomes far heavier at five percent, forcing budget priorities to shift as defence, infrastructure, and social programs compete with rising debt service.

This shift occurs automatically as existing debt is refinanced at higher rates. No financial panic is required for the pressure to build. As older low-rate debt matures and is replaced with higher-cost borrowing, interest payments rise mechanically, tightening fiscal conditions even if economic growth remains steady. The pressure often develops quietly before becoming a political issue.

Corporations face a similar adjustment. Debt accumulated during years of cheap credit must eventually be refinanced at higher cost, narrowing profit margins and reducing financial flexibility. Investment plans are delayed, hiring becomes more cautious, and risk tolerance declines. Companies that depended on low financing costs discover that their business models are more sensitive to interest rates than previously assumed, particularly in sectors where borrowing increased significantly during the low-rate period, leaving them more exposed.

Households experience the shift more directly. Variable-rate loans reset, fixed-rate mortgages eventually roll over, and consumer credit becomes more expensive. As borrowing costs rise, a larger share of income is directed toward interest payments, reducing discretionary spending. In several advanced economies, higher mortgage rates have already slowed housing markets, reduced affordability, and dampened consumer demand, reinforcing the broader slowdown.

The cumulative effect extends beyond any single borrower. Higher rates shift money from borrowers paying interest to lenders collecting it, and in highly indebted economies borrowers are widespread. Governments, corporations, and households all carry obligations, and when borrowing costs rise, pressure spreads simultaneously across sectors. The result is not an isolated adjustment but a broad tightening of financial conditions across the economy as a whole. Pressure that begins in one sector rarely remains there for long in a highly indebted economy. The strategy depended on one central premise.

This approach assumed that rates could remain low without consequence. Once inflation or market forces push them higher, that assumption begins to weaken. When interest costs rise faster than growth, debt ratios cease stabilizing on their own, and borrowing no longer softens economic adjustments. Instead, higher debt amplifies the impact of rising rates, making downturns harder to manage and reducing the ability of policymakers to stabilize the cycle as pressures build.

## *Ageing Economies, Slower Growth*

Higher borrowing costs expose existing debt burdens. Population trends, however, determine whether economies can grow fast enough to reduce those burdens over time. Debt can remain manageable if growth expands the income base from which obligations are serviced. When output rises steadily, yesterday's borrowing appears smaller relative to today's production, allowing economies to stabilize debt without dramatic policy adjustments.

For much of the postwar period, advanced economies benefited from favourable demographics. Large working-age populations supported expanding output, while younger cohorts entered labour markets in significant numbers. The ratio of workers to retirees remained high enough to finance pension and healthcare systems without visible strain, and economic growth benefited from both labour force expansion and productivity gains. Demographic conditions quietly reinforced economic growth for decades, providing support that many policymakers came to take for granted as permanent.

That ratio is now shifting steadily as fertility rates decline and populations age. Across most advanced economies, birth rates remain below replacement levels, and in several countries the working-age population has already begun to contract.[6] Japan provides an early illustration of this transition, with fewer workers supporting a growing number of retirees over several decades. Europe faces similar trends, while fertility rates in countries such as Italy, Germany, and Spain remain below replacement levels, reinforcing the long-term demographic shift.

Fewer workers limit the pace at which output can expand unless productivity rises sharply enough to compensate. At the same time, public obligations tied to ageing increase automatically. Pension payments grow, healthcare expenditures rise, and long-term care systems require additional funding as populations age.[7] As tax revenues grow more slowly and spending commitments continue to rise, pressure on government budgets builds year after year, even without new programs or policy changes.

This shift is gradual but persistent. When growth is modest and fiscal obligations rise mechanically, keeping debt under control requires more difficult choices. Governments may need to raise taxes, restrain spending, or continue expanding borrowing, with each option carrying economic and political costs. In a younger, faster-growing economy, higher debt can be diluted through expansion, but in an ageing, slower-growing one, investors and voters become less confident that rising debt can be sustained indefinitely .without adjustment

Demographics do not cause breakdown in isolation, but they narrow the margin for error. Ageing populations reduce labour force growth, increase fiscal obligations, and make it more difficult to grow out of rising debt. When debt levels are already high and growth potential is constrained, governments and central banks have fewer options for stabilizing the economy without creating additional pressure elsewhere. The challenge is not any single demographic trend but the way several pressures reinforce one another over time. Together, these pressures steadily reduced the margin available for gradual adjustment.

This approach assumed that growth would provide time for adjustment. Favourable demographics helped deliver that growth for decades. As populations age and labour force expansion slows, that source of support weakens, reducing the ability of advanced economies to rely on growth alone to stabilize rising debt. The result is an economy that becomes more dependent on policy choices at precisely the moment when demographic support is fading. Inflation then introduces an additional constraint, making the adjustment process even more difficult. That calculation changed once inflation returned.

## *When Inflation Collides With Debt*

For many years, inflation remained low and predictable across advanced economies. Prices rose gradually, wage pressures were moderate, and central banks could lower interest rates during downturns without destabilizing expectations. This environment allowed governments, companies, and households to borrow more without facing immediate consequences, reinforcing the belief that debt could expand without creating sustained instability. The mechanism was simple.

Low inflation meant low interest rates, and low rates meant manageable borrowing costs. As a result, rising debt did not feel urgent. Following the global financial crisis, inflation remained persistently subdued even as central banks maintained highly accommodative policies.[8] Policymakers became increasingly confident that borrowing could expand without triggering sustained inflation, and financial markets adjusted to an environment in which low rates appeared durable. What had once seemed an unusual combination of low inflation and expanding debt gradually came to be viewed as normal.

When inflation accelerates meaningfully, however, policymakers face a different environment. Containing inflation requires higher interest rates, slower credit growth, and reduced liquidity, all of which place pressure on borrowers. Higher rates make existing debt more expensive to service, and as borrowing costs rise, governments face larger interest expenses, corporations refinance at higher cost, and households encounter more expensive mortgages and consumer credit. The same policies that once supported stability begin to expose vulnerabilities that had accumulated during years of cheap borrowing. Government finances come under increasing strain.

Fiscal deficits widen unless spending is reduced or taxes increased, creating conflicting pressures for policymakers. Price stability requires tighter financial conditions, while debt management favours continued accommodation. In a lightly indebted economy, this tension can be managed, as higher rates slow activity, inflation recedes, and the system absorbs the adjustment. In a heavily indebted economy, however, the same rate increases carry broader consequences, as higher borrowing costs affect not only new debt but also the servicing of existing obligations across the economy.

This creates a direct conflict between controlling inflation and keeping borrowing affordable. Governments must allocate more resources to interest payments, leaving less room for public investment and social programs. Corporations respond by reducing investment and hiring, while households cut discretionary spending as borrowing costs rise. The pressure spreads through the economy because the same rate increases affect governments, businesses, and households simultaneously.

For decades, this conflict was largely avoided because inflation remained contained. Policymakers could lower interest rates during downturns without triggering sustained price pressures, allowing debt to expand without immediate consequences. When inflation returns, however, that balance becomes harder to maintain. Higher interest rates may be necessary to restore price stability, but those same rate increases expose vulnerabilities created during years of cheap borrowing.

The result is a structural trade-off. If interest rates remain too low in order to protect borrowers and support growth, inflation risks becoming persistent and harder to control. If interest rates rise enough to contain inflation, debt burdens become more apparent, government budgets come under greater strain, and economic growth slows. Policymakers must choose between competing objectives, and each choice carries costs.

This approach relied on avoiding this conflict. It assumed that inflation would remain low enough for borrowing costs to stay manageable and for debt to expand without forcing difficult decisions. When inflation re-emerges after years of accommodation, that assumption weakens, and policymakers face trade-offs that were previously deferred.

As inflation, debt, and growth pressures interact, the room for policy manoeuvre narrows. Governments, central banks, and financial markets must adjust to an environment in which interest rates cannot remain low indefinitely and borrowing cannot expand without consequence. The challenge is no longer managing one pressure at a time but navigating several competing pressures simultaneously. The flexibility that defined earlier decades becomes harder to sustain as the trade-off between inflation control and debt management becomes increasingly visible.

## *The Convergence of Limits*

Each pressure on its own can usually be managed. High debt can remain sustainable if borrowing costs stay low. Ageing populations can be supported if growth remains strong. Inflation can be contained if household finances, corporate finances, and government finances remain resilient and policy flexibility remains intact. For much of the past four decades, advanced economies benefited from an environment in which these pressures did not occur at the same time, allowing policymakers to manage challenges sequentially rather than simultaneously.

Falling interest rates offset rising debt, making borrowing more manageable even as total obligations expanded.[9] Contained inflation allowed central banks to lower rates during downturns without destabilizing expectations. Demographic pressures developed gradually and could be deferred politically, as the fiscal burden of ageing populations accumulated slowly. Governments and central banks appeared to retain room to respond, and policy interventions repeatedly stabilized markets and supported recovery. across advanced economies.

This pattern became particularly visible after the global financial crisis. Central banks lowered interest rates, governments expanded borrowing, and asset prices recovered. The pandemic reinforced this dynamic, as large fiscal programs were financed at historically low borrowing costs while central banks maintained highly accommodative policies. Each episode strengthened the perception that policymakers could extend time and delay adjustment without immediate consequence.

Policymakers relied on borrowing and low interest rates to delay difficult choices. Borrowing supported growth. Lower rates reduced debt servicing costs. Rising asset prices strengthened household finances and improved confidence. These dynamics allowed economies to absorb shocks while postponing structural adjustments that might otherwise have been required. Time was repeatedly purchased, but the underlying pressures continued to accumulate. Borrowing bought time, but it did not resolve underlying imbalances, and as debt accumulated, the margin for policy flexibility narrowed.

That convergence is now shifting. Debt levels are high across governments, corporations, and households.[10] Demographic pressures are intensifying as populations age and labour force growth slows. Inflation has demonstrated that it can re-emerge after prolonged accommodation, requiring tighter financial conditions to restore stability. Political division in many advanced economies complicates fiscal adjustment, making it harder to implement spending restraint or tax increases when debt rises o elevated levels.

What makes the current environment different is not any single pressure but the way these pressures interact. Higher debt makes economies more sensitive to interest rates. Slower population growth makes it harder to expand the income base from which obligations are serviced. Inflation limits the ability of central banks to keep borrowing costs artificially low. Political division makes adjustment more difficult precisely when adjustment becomes more necessary for long-term stability.

As these pressures reinforce one another, policy options become more constrained. Higher interest rates to control inflation increase fiscal strain and slow growth. Fiscal expansion to ease social pressure complicates inflation control and can weaken confidence in government finances. Attempts to keep borrowing costs artificially low risk weakening the currency or creating financial instability, while delaying adjustment usually makes the eventual correction more costly.

This marks a turning point where the tools that worked for decades become less effective. For much of the post-1980s period, policymakers relied on falling interest rates, contained inflation, and favourable demographics to stabilize the economy. Now high debt, ageing populations, and inflation risks are pressing at the same time, reducing the ability of governments and central banks to offset one pressure with another.

Stabilization no longer means simply softening downturns. It increasingly involves choosing which pressure to confront first. Policymakers may need to accept slower growth to control inflation, tolerate higher borrowing costs to restore confidence in government finances, or implement difficult fiscal adjustments to stabilize debt. Each choice carries economic and political consequences, and none offers an easy resolution.

This is the breaking of the model. It does not require panic or sudden crisis but reflects simple economic arithmetic becoming unavoidable. When liabilities grow faster than income, when obligations rise as populations age, and when price stability requires tighter financial conditions, limits that once seemed distant begin to shape policy decisions directly and increasingly constrain policymakers.

Governments face harder choices about spending, taxes, and borrowing. Central banks must weigh supporting growth against controlling inflation. Investors demand clearer evidence that rising debt can be managed without destabilizing currencies or financial markets. Households experience the adjustment through higher borrowing costs, slower wage growth, and reduced fiscal support.

The era in which borrowing could absorb strain without immediate consequence begins to close, not because confidence disappears overnight, but because the numbers become harder to ignore as debt grows faster than income. Rising interest costs crowd out public priorities, currency pressures emerge when policy credibility weakens, and political tensions increase as governments confront difficult fiscal decisions.

When this approach can no longer extend time, these pressures move from theory to reality. Government budgets tighten, borrowing costs rise, and households bear the cost of adjustment. The model breaks not through a single dramatic event, but when financial, fiscal, and political systems finally confront limits postponed for decades.

# PART VI

# THE RECKONING

# 19

# WHEN LONG STAGNATIONS END

Throughout this book, the argument has unfolded in stages. The advanced world did not arrive at its present condition suddenly, nor was it shaped by a single crisis. Instead, the foundations of the modern system developed over several decades. Beginning in the early 1980s, declining interest rates, expanding credit, and increasing policy intervention helped stabilize successive downturns. Each cycle appeared to validate the belief that instability could be contained without requiring deep structural adjustment or meaningful sacrifice.

Over time, this approach evolved from temporary crisis management into a permanent feature of economic governance. Following the global financial crisis of 2008, central banks expanded their balance sheets to unprecedented levels, governments increased borrowing to sustain demand, and asset prices became increasingly central to economic confidence. Growth continued, but it did so alongside rising debt and expanding intervention. The system remained functional, yet it became steadily more dependent on support.

Since the early 2000s, and particularly in the period following the 2008 financial crisis, advanced economies have displayed many of the characteristics associated with prolonged stagnation. The pattern appears across multiple measures. Productivity growth slowed compared with the period from 1980 to 2007. Median income growth became more uneven. Asset prices rose faster than wages. Debt accumulated across households, corporations, and governments. The appearance of stability endured, even as resilience weakened beneath the surface. That apparent stability deserves closer scrutiny.

This chapter examines how such conditions evolve and, ultimately, how they end. Long periods of managed stability rarely conclude through gradual improvement. Instead, they follow a recognizable pattern that has appeared repeatedly across twentieth- and early twenty-first-century economic history. The process is rarely dramatic at first. More often, it unfolds slowly, as weaknesses that were once hidden become increasingly difficult to ignore or explain away.

## *The Slow End of Stability*

Long periods of weak growth rarely begin with collapse. More often, they begin with relief. A crisis passes, markets recover, and policymakers declare success. Growth returns, but in smaller increments. Each year appears better than the panic that preceded it. Confidence stabilizes and the immediate sense of danger fades. The worst seems to be over, yet something fundamental does not return to its former strength.

Investment resumes, but cautiously. Productivity improves, but modestly. Wages rise, but slowly. Living standards advance, though without the momentum that once defined expansion. The economy continues to function, yet it does so without force. What was initially interpreted as a temporary setback gradually begins to resemble a new baseline.

This is how stagnation takes hold. It does not arrive through visible failure, but through diminished ambition. The economy shifts from expanding its productive capacity to preserving existing structures. Over time, this shift becomes embedded. Output continues to grow, but at a slower pace. Credit expands, yet the expansion produces weaker gains in income. Asset prices recover more quickly than wages. Financial markets regain confidence long before households regain financial security. The surface stabilizes while the underlying foundations continue to weaken. The signs accumulated over time.

Since the early 2000s, and particularly following the global financial crisis of 2008, this pattern has become increasingly visible across advanced economies. Global debt has risen to more than three times global output, significantly higher than before the 2008 crisis.[1] Major central bank balance sheets expanded severalfold between 2008 and the mid-2010s and have remained structurally elevated since then. At the same time, productivity growth across many advanced economies since 2008 has averaged roughly half the pace observed between 1980 and 2007.[2] Asset values, meanwhile, have climbed far faster than median incomes.

The system has not collapsed. It has drifted. Over time, that drift ceases to appear temporary and instead becomes structural. Because crises are avoided, the economy appears resilient. Because markets remain orderly, the system appears stable. Because unemployment declines following downturns, policymakers claim recovery. Yet stagnation is not defined by inactivity. It is defined by the gradual loss of renewal.

A healthy economy absorbs shocks and then regains momentum. A stagnant one absorbs shocks and settles onto a lower growth path. It survives, but it does not regenerate. Debt accumulates, intervention expands, and risk tolerance gradually shrinks. As this process continues, the effort required to maintain stability increases. What began as stabilization gradually becomes dependence on continued support.

History suggests that such conditions do not persist indefinitely. Prolonged periods of weak growth in the past, from the debt overhangs of the 1930s to Japan's slow growth following the asset bubble collapse of the early 1990s, eventually encountered limits. Systems that rely on ever-greater intervention to preserve calm gradually become more fragile, not more resilient. Over time, the mechanisms designed to maintain stability begin to curb growth itself and reduce economic dynamism. The reason lies in simple arithmetic.

These limits are not moral. They are mathematical. Debt claims compound over time, while growth does not accelerate at the same pace. At first, this imbalance can be managed. Later, it can only be delayed. Eventually, it must be resolved.

## *Growth Without Renewal*

Prolonged stagnation is not a prolonged recession, nor is it simply a temporary shortfall in demand. It is a condition in which an economy continues to operate, yet gradually loses its capacity to renew itself. Output grows, companies earn profits, governments spend, and credit flows. Markets function and institutions remain intact. Yet the mechanisms that once transformed savings into productive investment begin to weaken, and over time the system shifts from expansion toward preservation. The difference begins with the purpose of credit.

In a healthy system, credit expands because new opportunities exist. Businesses borrow to build factories, develop technologies, and expand into new markets. Rising investment lifts productivity, which supports higher wages and sustains consumption without requiring ever larger debt. This process reinforces itself, creating a virtuous cycle in which growth generates further growth.

In stagnation, this chain weakens. Credit continues to expand, but an increasing share flows into existing assets rather than new productive capacity. Corporations borrow heavily, yet a growing portion of that borrowing finances share buybacks, mergers, and financial restructuring rather than expansion. Asset prices rise and financial wealth increases, but the connection between borrowing and broad income growth weakens.

The decade following the global financial crisis of 2008 illustrates this shift. Between 2009 and 2019, large corporations in the United States issued trillions of dollars in new debt while simultaneously repurchasing significant amounts of their own shares.[3] Equity markets reached repeated record highs during this period, yet business investment as a share of output grew more slowly than in earlier expansion cycles, particularly compared with the expansions of the 1980s and 1990s. Productivity growth remained subdued, and wage gains were uneven. Borrowing supported asset prices, but it did not restore broad-based economic dynamism on a sustained basis.

What distinguishes prolonged stagnation from ordinary downturns is therefore not the absence of growth, but the preservation of existing structures at the expense of future expansion. Inefficient firms remain viable because financing remains available. Losses are rolled over rather than realized. Asset prices are supported to prevent instability. Weak institutions are stabilized rather than restructured. Each intervention helps preserve stability in the short term, but it also postpones the renewal that stronger growth eventually requires.

Over time, this produces a form of economic congestion. Capital becomes tied up in preserving existing claims. Labour mobility slows, risk-taking declines, and investment becomes increasingly defensive. The priority shifts from building new capacity to defending existing valuations. As leverage accumulates, the economy becomes more sensitive to disruption. Even modest increases in interest rates begin to expose vulnerabilities that built up during years of support.

Between 2013 and 2023, several episodes demonstrated how narrow the margin for error had become. In 2013, the Federal Reserve signalled that it might begin reducing asset purchases following years of quantitative easing.[4] Although policy had not yet tightened materially, global bond yields rose sharply, capital flowed out of emerging markets, and financial conditions tightened abruptly. The episode, later described as the taper tantrum, revealed how sensitive markets had become to even the suggestion of reduced support. The dependence on continued monetary support had become increasingly difficult to reverse. The longer support remained in place, the harder it became to withdraw without destabilising markets.

A similar pattern emerged in 2018. The Federal Reserve gradually raised interest rates and began reducing its balance sheet. By the fourth quarter of 2018, equity markets declined sharply, credit spreads widened, and global growth expectations weakened.[5] Financial conditions tightened rapidly, and by early 2019 policymakers reversed course and halted further tightening. What would historically have been considered routine normalization instead triggered instability.

The tightening cycle that began in 2022 provided an even clearer illustration. Rising interest rates led to large losses in bond portfolios held by banks and financial institutions. In the United Kingdom, increases in government bond yields destabilized liability-driven investment strategies used by pension funds, forcing emergency intervention by the Bank of England in September 2022. In the United States, rising rates contributed to stress within regional banks holding long-duration assets, culminating in bank failures in early 2023 that required policy responses to stabilize the system.[6]

These episodes shared a common feature. None involved historically extreme tightening. In each case, relatively modest adjustments exposed vulnerabilities that had accumulated during years of low interest rates and expanding leverage. Stability, which had appeared durable during the period from 2009 to 2021, proved dependent on continued support.

This is why stagnation can coexist with technological progress and financial sophistication. Innovation continues and new companies emerge, yet the broader system struggles to translate innovation into rising productivity across the economy. Gains become concentrated, diffusion slows, and growth becomes increasingly uneven. Productivity growth in many advanced economies since 2008 has remained below the pace observed between 1980 and 2007. Median real wages have grown unevenly, while asset prices have recovered quickly after each downturn, often reaching new highs.

The appearance of prosperity survives, even as the foundations of dynamism weaken. Stagnation, in this sense, is not collapse but imbalance maintained through support. The economy continues to function, though within narrowing limits, and those limits are increasingly defined by debt. That is why debt eventually moves from being a symptom of stagnation to becoming one of its defining constraints.

## *When Debt Becomes the Limit*

At the centre of prolonged stagnation lies excessive debt. This is not a moral judgment but an arithmetic reality. Debt represents a claim on future income. When those claims grow faster than the income available to meet them, the system must eventually adjust.

Adjustment can occur through growth, inflation, or default. Alternatively, it can be postponed through refinancing and intervention. For a time, postponement appears effective. Low interest rates reduce the visible burden of large liabilities. Refinancing extends maturities. Asset prices rise, making household finances, company finances, and government finances appear stronger. Governments borrow to support demand, while central banks expand their balance sheets to prevent disorder and maintain confidence in financial markets.

These measures buy time, but they do not remove the obligations that created the problem. Over time, the burden grows heavier rather than lighter. What appears manageable under low interest rates often becomes more difficult once borrowing costs begin to rise across the economy.

Since the early 2000s, global debt has risen steadily across advanced and emerging economies. Following the global financial crisis of 2008, public borrowing accelerated as governments sought to stabilize growth. Central banks lowered interest rates to historically low levels and, in many cases, expanded their balance sheets through asset purchases between

2008 and the mid-2010s. These policies helped contain immediate instability but also contributed to a structural increase in leverage.

By the early 2020s, global debt exceeded three times global output.[7] Public debt in several major advanced economies rose to levels not seen since the aftermath of the Second World War.[8] Corporate liabilities also expanded significantly during the period from 2010 to 2021, particularly in sectors benefiting from low borrowing costs. Household debt, especially in housing markets, remained sensitive to interest rate movements.

High debt changes behaviour. When liabilities are moderate, economies can tolerate higher interest rates. Investment decisions respond primarily to opportunity. Firms expand because expected returns justify the cost of capital. When liabilities are large relative to income, tolerance shrinks. Even modest increases in borrowing costs can destabilize household finances, company finances, and government finances. Governments face rising interest burdens, corporations confront refinancing risk, and households become more cautious. Policymakers hesitate to return conditions to normal for fear of triggering instability.

The tightening cycles of 2018 and 2022–2023 demonstrated this sensitivity. In both periods, policy adjustments that were modest relative to historical standards produced disproportionate effects in financial markets and segments of the real economy. Housing markets slowed rapidly, bond markets experienced volatility, and financial institutions came under pressure. These developments reflected the cumulative effects of leverage built up during the period of low interest rates that followed 2008.

Debt therefore does more than weigh on growth. It narrows the range of safe policy choices and increases the risk that even modest adjustments trigger instability.

History offers repeated examples. The leverage accumulated during the 1920s constrained policy responses during the Great Depression of the 1930s. Japan's asset bubble collapse in the early 1990s led to decades of public borrowing and suppressed interest rates. Between the early 1990s and the 2010s, Japan's public debt rose to well over twice national output, while growth remained subdued. The post-2008 global response followed a similar trajectory, though on a broader scale across multiple advanced economies at the same time.

In each case, debt did not immediately destroy the system. It constrained it. As debt rises, preserving stability becomes the overriding priority. Interest rates remain low, asset prices are defended, and losses are deferred. The system increasingly protects existing claims rather than reallocating resources toward new opportunities and productive investment.

Growth becomes necessary to sustain debt, even as debt suppresses the growth required to sustain it. The trap develops gradually. In its early stages, it appears manageable. Over time, it becomes self-reinforcing. Policymakers cannot tighten without causing stress. They cannot allow stress without risking contagion. Stability must be maintained, even if maintaining it gradually erodes dynamism and flexibility.

As obligations accumulate, resilience declines. Stability depends less on underlying strength and more on continued support. The system no longer bends easily. It must be held upright. What begins as caution gradually evolves into paralysis.

Debt, in this context, becomes the boundary that defines how long stagnation can continue without rupture. When that boundary is reached, adjustment is no longer optional. The question is no longer whether intervention can continue, but whether intervention alone can still prevent change.

## *Why Management Fails*

A defining feature of prolonged stagnation is the belief that it can be managed. Since the 1980s, and particularly following the global financial crisis of 2008, policymakers have increasingly relied on intervention to stabilize economic cycles. When growth weakens, interest rates are lowered. When markets fall, emergency funding is provided. When unemployment rises, fiscal deficits expand. When instability threatens, regulators intervene. Each response is rational and helps prevent immediate damage. Yet each also deepens reliance on intervention and continued support over the longer term.

Management works in the short term because it suppresses volatility and prevents forced liquidation. The system survives another cycle. But survival is not renewal. Once an economy becomes dependent on intervention to avoid contraction, policy gradually shifts from correcting imbalances to preserving them.

Losses are postponed rather than realized. Fragile structures are preserved rather than reorganized. Asset prices are supported because their decline would expose weaknesses in household finances, company finances, and government finances. Over time, support ceases to be temporary and becomes embedded. Withdrawal then becomes destabilizing.

Attempts to return policy to more normal settings since 2010 have repeatedly demonstrated this dynamic. The taper tantrum of 2013, the tightening cycle of 2018, and the rate increases of 2022–2023 all revealed how sensitive markets had become to changes in policy.[9] Each episode exposed how much stability depended on continued support. Intervention prevented collapse, yet it also enlarged what had to be defended. The perimeter of stability expanded, and shrinking it became increasingly difficult.

Management became circular. Intervention prevented instability but increased dependency. The longer imbalances were preserved, the larger they grew. The larger they grew, the more disruptive their eventual resolution became. Stability gradually became an end in itself, and once that happened, adjustment became politically and socially intolerable.

The problem was not a lack of policy tools. The problem was that the underlying structure no longer generated enough self-sustaining growth to reduce dependence on those tools. This approach ultimately failed not because policymakers lacked tools or intelligence, but because the structure being managed no longer supported self-sustaining growth.

When management shifts from solving problems to postponing them, the question eventually changes. The issue is no longer how stability can be preserved, but what forces adjustment when preservation becomes impossible.

## *What Forces Resolution*

Prolonged stagnations do not end through optimization. They end when preservation becomes impossible.

For years, the system absorbs strain. Debt is refinanced, losses are deferred, and asset prices are supported. Governments extend support while central banks contain volatility. As long as confidence holds, this process can continue.

But preservation depends on credibility. Confidence in government finances, confidence in monetary policy, and public acceptance of existing institutions all play a role. When one weakens, strain increases. When multiple pillars weaken simultaneously, rupture becomes more likely.

History since the twentieth century shows that resolution begins when the cost of maintaining stability exceeds the cost of abandoning it. This threshold is not announced. It is crossed gradually and then suddenly. Inflation may force tightening, as occurred in the 1970s. Funding stress may expose fiscal limits, as seen during sovereign debt crises such as the Eurozone crisis beginning in 2010.[10] Financial instability may force recognition of losses, as occurred during the global financial crisis of 2008. Political realignment may shift policy priorities, as seen in various advanced economies since the 2010s.

What varies is the trigger. What does not vary is the mechanism. Debt that cannot be serviced must eventually be reduced, inflated away, or restructured. Claims must be written down or diluted. Capital must be redirected and institutions must adapt to new economic realities.

Prolonged stagnation persists because losses remain implicit. Resolution begins when losses become explicit. This process redistributes wealth, power, and opportunity. For that reason, it is resisted until resistance itself becomes destabilizing.

When preservation requires ever larger intervention and ever greater borrowing, stability itself begins to undermine confidence. Measures that once reassured markets and the public begin to raise questions about sustainability instead. At that point, adjustment is no longer a policy choice. It is imposed by circumstance rather then choice.

The timing of resolution is difficult to predict, but the pressures that drive it are not. The longer underlying problems are deferred, the more likely it becomes that adjustment arrives through events rather than deliberate policy decisions.

## *Crisis as Accelerator, Not Cure*

Large crises are often remembered as turning points. They are described as resets or moments of renewal. In practice, crises do not create prosperity. They remove the barriers that prevented adjustment from occurring for years or even decades.

In prolonged stagnation, resistance to recognizing losses is strong. Creditors resist restructuring, governments resist austerity, and central banks resist tightening. Voters resist reforms that impose visible costs. The system prefers incremental management to decisive change because the costs of delay are diffuse and gradual and rarely immediate.

Crisis alters that calculus. When financial markets freeze, when inflation destabilizes purchasing power, or when funding pressures threaten sovereign solvency, the range of available choices narrows rapidly. Political leaders can no longer postpone difficult trade-offs. Measures that once appeared politically impossible eventually become unavoidable when options narrow sufficiently over time.

Historical experience illustrates this pattern. The Great Depression of the 1930s forced banking reform, monetary regime changes, and fiscal expansion.[11] The Second World War forced large-scale resource reallocation and financial restructuring. In both cases, crisis accelerated adjustments that had long been resisted or delayed for years.

In the decades following the Second World War, particularly between the late 1940s and the 1960s, high public debt levels were gradually reduced through a combination of growth, controlled interest rates, and moderate inflation.[12] The crisis itself did not create the recovery. It created the conditions under which adjustment could no longer be avoided.

More recent crises follow similar patterns. The global financial crisis of 2008 forced recapitalization of banks, regulatory reform, and extraordinary monetary intervention.[13] The inflation surge of the early 2020s forced tightening after more than a decade of low interest rates. Each episode accelerated recognition of structural imbalances that had developed over many years.

Crisis therefore acts as an accelerator rather than a cure. It removes resistance to change but does not guarantee renewal. In heavily indebted advanced economies, future crises would likely involve adjustments in asset prices, fiscal policy, and financial institutions. Distributional tensions would intensify as losses are allocated across households and institutions.

Stagnation persists because its costs are gradual. Crisis concentrates those costs and makes them visible. What had been postponed becomes unavoidable, and what had remained implicit becomes explicit.

Yet crisis alone does not determine what comes next. Whether adjustment leads to renewal depends on whether economies can generate new sources of productivity, investment, and growth. That is where technology enters the discussion.

History suggests that periods of adjustment often coincide with renewed optimism about innovation. The hope is that new technologies will generate the productivity gains needed to ease existing constraints.

## *Technology and the Debt Trap*

Periods of stagnation often coincide with technological optimism. This pattern has appeared repeatedly, from the spread of electricity in the early twentieth century to the technology boom of the 1990s and the rise of artificial intelligence in the early 2020s. The mechanism is remarkably consistent despite changes in technology and circumstance.

Technology can reshape production, reduce costs, and create new industries. However, it does not eliminate existing financial obligations. In a debt-saturated system, new income is often absorbed by existing claims rather than generating broad-based expansion across the wider economy.

Historical experience illustrates this dynamic. Electricity was widely introduced in the late nineteenth century, yet productivity gains emerged gradually between the 1910s and 1930s as industries reorganized. Computing technology advanced rapidly beginning in the 1970s and 1980s, yet broad productivity acceleration did not appear until the late 1990s. Innovation required structural adaptation before it produced sustained growth.

Since the late 1990s, and particularly after 2008, advanced economies have experienced rapid technological progress. Yet productivity growth has remained subdued compared with the period from 1980 to 2007. Asset valuations in technology sectors have risen sharply, while median wage growth has remained uneven. Innovation has continued, but its benefits have not been shared evenly across the economy.

Technology amplifies the environment in which it operates. In a dynamic system, it accelerates expansion. In a constrained system, it can reinforce concentration. When debt is high and growth is weak, a larger share of the gains created by innovation is often absorbed by existing financial claims rather than supporting broad-based economic renewal. Repairing household finances, company finances, and government finances typically comes before sustained productivity growth can take hold. Innovation can accelerate recovery, but it rarely eliminates the need for economic adjustment first or reduces its cost.

Technology can create new opportunities and strengthen long-term growth. It cannot, by itself, resolve the debt burdens and structural pressures that still require adjustment. As a result, the underlying tensions created by debt, weak growth, and prolonged stagnation eventually find expression not only in economic outcomes but also in politics.

## *Political Realignment*

Prolonged stagnation is not solely an economic condition. It also has a political dimension that becomes more visible over time. When growth slows and opportunities narrow, the distribution of gains becomes more uneven. Asset holders benefit from rising valuations, while wage earners experience slower income growth. This divergence does not immediately produce instability, but over time it weakens trust in institutions and in the economic system itself across large parts of society.

Economic systems depend on public confidence. Inequality is tolerated when upward mobility appears achievable. Adjustment is accepted when it is perceived as temporary. Institutions retain support when they deliver outcomes that are broadly viewed as stable and fair. Prolonged stagnation erodes these conditions.

Since the aftermath of the global financial crisis of 2008, many advanced economies have exhibited these dynamics. Asset prices recovered relatively quickly following the crisis, particularly in equity and housing markets. However, wage growth remained uneven during the 2010s, and in many countries median income growth lagged asset appreciation.[14] As a result, perceptions of inequality and economic insecurity increased even during periods of low unemployment.

These developments contributed to political fragmentation. Electoral volatility increased across advanced economies during the 2010s and early 2020s. Established parties lost support, new movements emerged, and policy debates became more polarized. Fiscal debates grew more contentious even as debt levels rose advanced economies.

At the same time, confidence in institutions came under increasing pressure. Public trust fluctuated following periods of economic stress such as the global financial crisis, the Eurozone crisis beginning in 2010, and the inflation surge of the early 2020s. As economic pressures persisted, many citizens became less confident that existing institutions could deliver rising living standards or address emerging challenges effectively.

This political fragmentation is often interpreted as a purely political phenomenon. In reality, it reflects underlying economic conditions. When growth is strong, compromise is easier because gains can be distributed without imposing visible losses. When growth slows, trade-offs become more explicit. Fiscal discipline competes with social spending. Monetary restraint conflicts with debt sustainability. Open economic structures face growing pressure from domestic concerns.

Political realignment often precedes economic rupture rather than follows it. New coalitions form when existing arrangements can no longer reconcile competing interests. Fiscal consolidation collides with demands for social protection. Monetary tightening collides with financial fragility. Global integration increasingly collides with concerns about living standards, economic security, and domestic stability.

At this stage, political systems face structural choices. They can attempt to preserve the existing framework at rising cost, or they can pursue change that redistributes burdens more directly. Historical experience since the twentieth century suggests that major economic transitions often coincide with shifts in political coalitions and institutional arrangements.

Late-stage political turbulence therefore functions as a signal rather than an anomaly. When fiscal strain, monetary constraint, and political fragmentation converge, stability becomes conditional rather than assumed. Conditional stability rarely persists indefinitely.

This is the political expression of the same pressures discussed throughout the chapter. Debt, weak growth, demographic strain, and declining policy flexibility increasingly shape political outcomes as well as economic ones. Together they create the modern impasse confronting many advanced economies. What often appears as political instability is frequently a reflection of deeper economic constraints that have been building for years. As those constraints become more visible, maintaining consensus becomes increasingly difficult.

## *The Modern Impasse*

Advanced economies now display many of the defining features associated with prolonged stagnation. Debt levels are historically elevated. Since the early 2000s, public debt across major advanced economies has risen significantly, accelerating following the global financial crisis of 2008 and again during the pandemic period of 2020–2021. In several economies, public debt relative to national income has approached levels last seen during or immediately after the Second World War.

Corporate liabilities also expanded significantly between 2010 and 2021, supported by low interest rates and easy financial conditions. Household debt, particularly in housing markets, remained sensitive to interest rate changes. At the global level, total debt rose to more than three times annual output by the early 2020s, leaving economies more exposed.[15]

Growth has continued, but with reduced momentum. Productivity gains since 2008 have remained uneven across advanced economies. Median income growth during the 2010s was inconsistent, and asset valuations in equity and housing markets rose faster than underlying earnings. Financial markets tended to recover quickly following periods of stress, while households often experienced slower recoveries.

Central banks remain central to maintaining stability. Their balance sheets expanded significantly between 2008 and the mid-2010s and again during the pandemic period beginning in 2020. Financial markets have reacted sharply to signals of tightening, particularly during episodes such as the 2013 taper tantrum, the period of policy tightening in 2018 , and the rate increases of 2022–2023. Governments have operated with sustained fiscal deficits, even outside recessionary periods, particularly during the 2010s and early 2020s across much of the advanced world.

This configuration reflects the cumulative effects of policy responses developed over several decades. Since the early 1980s, declining interest rates and expanding credit supported growth and stabilized downturns. Following the 2008 financial crisis, these mechanisms became more central to economic management. Debt expansion, monetary accommodation, and asset price support absorbed shocks that might otherwise have forced structural adjustment and painful correction.

For an extended period, particularly from the mid-1990s through the late 2010s, this approach appeared effective. Inflation remained subdued, financial crises were contained, and expanding global supply chains helped support growth. However, this environment began to shift in the early 2020s. Inflation re-emerged after more than a decade of subdued price growth, forcing central banks to tighten policy. Rising interest rates exposed vulnerabilities in housing markets, sovereign debt markets, and segments of the banking system at the same time.

The pressures discussed throughout this book began to converge. Debt remained high. Growth remained modest. Populations continued to age. Borrowing costs rose after years of unusually low rates. The conditions that had supported stability for decades became less favourable at the same time. The effect left governments less able to absorb future shocks.

Fiscal space narrowed as interest costs increased. Political consensus became more difficult to sustain. Demographic pressures, including ageing populations across much of the advanced world, added to long-term fiscal challenges. Constraints that once appeared distant became visible to policymakers, investors, and households alike.

Maintaining stability increasingly required continued support and borrowing. Restoring dynamism required adjustment and recognition of losses. Pursuing one objective complicated the other. The economy became caught between preservation and renewal. Protecting the existing system increasingly came at the expense of long-term adjustment.

In principle, several paths remained available. Debt could be restructured. Inflation could be tolerated. Fiscal consolidation could be pursued. Financial repression could be expanded. Institutional reforms could be attempted. In practice, each option involved visible costs, and visible costs encountered political resistance almost immediately. Preservation gradually replaced adjustment as the priority.

As a result, the system increasingly relied on preserving existing claims. Mechanisms that once stabilized the system without undermining it began to contribute to fragility. When the limits of the old framework become impossible to ignore, adjustment moves from possibility to necessity, regardless of political preference. History suggests that systems built on rising debt, repeated intervention, and delayed adjustment do not adapt indefinitely. Instead, they eventually give way to new frameworks better suited to changing conditions. The transition is rarely smooth.

The question is not whether change will occur, but how societies respond once preserving the existing system becomes more difficult than adapting to a new one. When the limits of the old framework become impossible to ignore, adjustment moves from possibility to necessity, regardless of political preference.

## *How Stagnations Actually End*

Prolonged stagnations do not end because policymakers discover more effective techniques for managing them. They end because the structure that sustains them can no longer be maintained. Until that point is reached, policymakers often succeed in delaying rather than resolving the underlying pressures. That delay is rarely accidental.

Over long periods, intervention helps preserve stability. Since the 2008 financial crisis, debt has been rolled forward, asset prices supported, and losses deferred. Political compromise has allowed difficult decisions to be postponed. Each cycle has reinforced the perception that the system remains resilient despite growing imbalances and mounting vulnerabilities.

However, resilience based on accumulation has limits. When debt grows faster than income for sustained periods, servicing obligations constrains economic flexibility. When asset valuations depend on continued support, returning conditions to normal becomes destabilizing. When governments operate with persistent deficits, rising interest costs narrow their room to respond. When political systems become more fragmented, consensus weakens.

These pressures build gradually. Eventually, they converge. At a certain point, maintaining stability requires a level of intervention that becomes increasingly difficult to sustain. Confidence erodes not necessarily because collapse is expected, but because preservation loses credibility. The shift usually begins long before institutions themselves begin to change.

What often changes first is not the formal structure of the economy, but the behaviour and expectations within it. Households become more cautious. Businesses shorten their horizons. Younger generations begin to question whether living standards will improve in the way earlier generations assumed. Institutions continue to function, but confidence in their ability to restore broad prosperity gradually weakens.

When this point is reached, adjustment becomes unavoidable. Debt that cannot be sustained under prevailing conditions must be reduced, restructured, or eroded through inflation. Financial claims must be written down or diluted. Capital must be reallocated. Institutional arrangements must evolve.

The process is disruptive because it makes explicit what stagnation kept hidden. Losses that had been deferred become visible. Assumptions that once appeared secure are reassessed. Existing arrangements come under pressure to adapt.

This process redistributes wealth, power, and opportunity. For that reason, it is rarely welcomed and often resisted. Yet the longer adjustment is delayed, the larger the eventual adjustment tends to become and the more disruptive it becomes.

Long periods of stagnation rarely produce immediate collapse. More often, they normalize diminished expectations. Economies continue to function, elections continue to occur, and financial markets may still experience periods of optimism. Yet beneath the appearance of continuity, adaptability weakens. The system becomes less capable of absorbing shocks without increasingly large interventions to restore stability.

Transitions may be managed deliberately or forced by events. Historical experience suggests that forced transitions are more common. In either case, the adjustment is unlikely to be smooth.

The end of prolonged stagnation does not represent a gradual return to a previous growth path. It represents a break from that path. The mechanisms that once sustained stability no longer function in the same way. A new framework emerges only after the limits of the old one have been reached.

This is not a forecast tied to a specific date or crisis. It is a recurring pattern that has appeared repeatedly throughout modern economic history. When stability survives only through rising debt, repeated intervention, and the continual deferral of problems, it becomes increasingly fragile, increasingly conditional, and increasingly dependent on forces that cannot expand indefinitely.

Over time, prolonged stagnation changes societies as much as economies. Political divisions intensify as growth slows and trade-offs become harder to avoid. Trust in institutions weakens when living standards stagnate and younger households struggle to build financial security. Governments become increasingly focused on preserving stability in the short term, even as the long-term foundations of resilience continue to erode. The longer this pattern persists, the more difficult it becomes to reverse.

Eventually, the policies designed to preserve stability begin to undermine it. Debt constrains growth. Intervention directs resources toward preserving existing claims rather than creating new opportunities. Political consensus weakens as economic pressures intensify. The economy continues to function, but its resilience diminishes. What appears stable becomes dependent. What appears durable becomes temporary.

Eventually, the structure that sustained stability can no longer hold. Losses can no longer be deferred. Financial rules are rewritten and governments change course. The era of managed stability gives way to a period of transition.

What follows such periods is rarely linear. Fragility that accumulated slowly beneath the surface can begin moving through financial systems, institutions, and politics with surprising speed. Systems that appeared stable for years can become highly sensitive to shocks once confidence weakens and policy flexibility narrows.

This is how prolonged stagnations end. Not through gradual improvement, but through the breaking of the stability model that defined the advanced world. Stability, once preserved through debt and intervention, gives way to a more uncertain and volatile era. The adjustment may unfold unevenly across countries and institutions, but the broader direction becomes increasingly difficult to avoid.

# 20

## THE SEQUENCE OF SYSTEMIC BREAKDOWN

Economic breakdowns rarely unfold as single events. They develop through a sequence of pressures that gradually weaken the system before disruption becomes visible. Stability gives way to strain, strain gives way to policy constraint, and constraint eventually forces structural change. Understanding this sequence is critical, because by the time instability becomes obvious, the process is already well underway. The stages that follow describe how late-stage stability evolves into systemic adjustment. The transition rarely announces itself.

Systemic breakdowns do not begin with spectacle. They emerge quietly, within economic and financial systems that have grown accustomed to long periods of stability. For much of the period from the mid-1980s through the early 2020s, advanced economies operated on the assumption that shocks could be absorbed, that governments and central banks could stabilize markets, and downturns managed without threatening the broader structure. That assumption is now under strain.

The stability of this period was not accidental. It was financed. Governments borrowed to cushion recessions. Central banks lowered interest rates and expanded their balance sheets to steady markets. Asset prices recovered quickly after each disruption. Growth slowed at times, but collapse was avoided. From the global financial crisis to the pandemic shock, policymakers repeatedly intervened to restore stability. Each intervention reinforced the belief that policymakers could step in and prevent deeper crises, strengthening confidence in the durability of the system.

Yet resilience and dependence are not the same thing. When stability relies on sustained borrowing, low funding costs, and repeated policy support, it becomes conditional. Debt levels across advanced economies are higher than they were before the global financial crisis.[1] Interest rates, which remained unusually low for more than a decade following the 2008 crisis, can no longer remain suppressed without consequence. Inflation has returned as a constraint. Political cohesion has weakened. The margin for error has narrowed considerably in recent years.

In such an environment, breakdown does not arrive as an isolated event. It emerges as a sequence. What appears sudden is usually cumulative. The structure weakens before it fails, and confidence adjusts before collapse becomes visible. By the time instability is widely recognized, the process has often been underway for years.

The advanced world is no longer waiting for disruption to begin. Since the inflationary pressures that followed the pandemic, economies have been operating within a tighter corridor where policy responses are more constrained and vulnerabilities more exposed. The question is no longer whether pressure will build, but how the sequence unfolds as confidence in permanent stabilization begins to erode.

## *Late-Stage Stability*

In the final phase before disruption, an economy can appear outwardly functional. Growth is modest but positive. Employment remains firm. Markets show no signs of panic. Volatility is subdued. The absence of visible stress reinforces the belief that prior dangers have been overcome, creating the impression that stability has returned. This pattern has appeared repeatedly in advanced economies, where periods of calm have often preceded deeper financial strain. Late-stage stability often looks ordinary, even reassuring, making it misleading.

Japan in the late 1980s offered a clear example.[2] Asset prices rose sharply, credit expanded rapidly, and property values detached from incomes. Confidence became widespread. The appearance of strength concealed an economy increasingly dependent on rising valuations and continued borrowing. Stability, in that context, signalled excess rather than balance.

Advanced economies today exhibit similar characteristics, although the structure is broader and more entrenched. Public debt levels are materially higher than they were before the 2008 crisis. Corporate leverage has grown across many sectors. Household balance sheets in several countries remain heavily tied to property values inflated during years of unusually low interest rates. Central bank balance sheets, expanded dramatically during successive crises, particularly after the global financial crisis and the pandemic, have not returned to their pre-crisis scale.[3]

At the same time, the environment has shifted. Inflation, subdued for years, has re-emerged as a constraint following the surge in prices after the pandemic. Interest rates, once near zero for more than a decade, have risen. Funding costs are no longer negligible. Political divisions have deepened across the United States and Europe, complicating fiscal adjustment. Demographic trends in many advanced economies are turning less favourable, as populations age and labour force growth slows, reducing the margin for organic expansion.

None of this has yet produced systemic panic. Markets continue to function. Governments continue to borrow. Institutions continue to operate. That is the nature of late-stage stability. The structure still stands, even as strain builds beneath the surface. The apparent strength of the system increasingly depends on those relationships continuing to function smoothly.

The risk lies in how dependent each part of the system has become on the others. Governments rely on manageable borrowing costs. Financial institutions rely on stable collateral values. Households rely on asset appreciation to sustain balance sheets. When these assumptions hold, the system appears resilient. When they are tested simultaneously, the response becomes less predictable and more fragile.

At this stage, the system does not look broken. It looks settled. Yet when policymakers and markets alike begin to assume that stability will continue through intervention and refinancing, adjustment becomes harder to initiate and harder to absorb. What once could have been corrected gradually now requires either renewed intervention or painful repricing.

## *The Trigger: When Stability Comes Under Strain*

Breakdown rarely begins with underlying weakness alone. It begins when hidden vulnerabilities become visible and assumptions that once felt secure begin to be questioned.

The initiating event is often small relative to the system it unsettles. A shift in interest rate expectations, refinancing difficulty in a leveraged sector, a sovereign funding concern, or a policy error that unsettles bond markets can each appear manageable in isolation. In a debt-heavy system, however, they do not remain isolated from one another.

The early 1930s provide a clear historical example.[4] Individual bank failures in the United States did not initially signal national collapse. Yet once depositors began withdrawing funds in waves, confidence eroded across institutions that had appeared stable. The problem was not a single balance sheet but the realization that fragility was widespread.

In highly leveraged environments, even small changes in funding costs or asset prices place multiple sectors under strain. Governments face higher interest expenses. Corporations struggle to refinance short-term obligations. Households encounter tighter credit conditions. Financial institutions reassess collateral values. What begins as adjustment in one corner spreads through interconnected balance sheets. Experience confirms this dynamic.

Recent episodes illustrate how quickly this process can unfold. During the global financial crisis, short-term funding markets tightened before large institutions formally failed.[5] In the United Kingdom, a rapid rise in government bond yields forced pension funds using leveraged strategies to meet sudden collateral demands. The underlying assets remained, but liquidity pressures required immediate central bank intervention.[6] The trigger was not catastrophic in scale, yet leverage magnified its impact. The same dynamics remain at work, but under far more demanding conditions.

Advanced economies today sit in a similar configuration of sensitivity. Debt burdens are high. Funding structures are layered. Asset valuations remain central to household and institutional balance sheets. When refinancing costs rise or asset prices fall, the impact is no longer confined to a single market. It migrates quickly.

The trigger is rarely the true cause of breakdown. It is the moment when accumulated dependence becomes visible. Investors stop assuming stability and begin actively questioning it. Once that shift begins, stability becomes harder to defend. Collapse is not inevitable in that instant, but the margin for policy error narrows significantly as pressures converge.

In earlier crises, central banks could respond aggressively without facing inflationary constraints. Today, that flexibility is more limited. Intervention remains possible, but it carries visible trade-offs. The system continues to function, yet it is more reactive and more exposed.

Breakdown begins not with panic, but with recognition. Recognition that the structure is more fragile than it appeared. Recognition that continued stabilization requires increasingly forceful support. Recognition that the tools available are less costless than before. Once that recognition spreads, the turning point has been reached. What follows is rarely a dramatic collapse. More often, the first signs appear in the financial system itself. Markets grow more cautious, funding tightens, and confidence erodes before the economy reflects the change.

## *Liquidity Strain and Funding Pressures*

As confidence begins to shift, stress rarely appears first as bankruptcy. It emerges as a funding problem, as borrowers discover that access to cash becomes more difficult even when underlying assets remain intact.

Markets that once functioned smoothly begin to thin. Borrowers who assumed they could refinance maturing debt discover that new loans come at higher cost or not at all. Institutions that relied on short-term borrowing find lenders less willing to roll it over. What had felt routine becomes uncertain.

This stage is often misunderstood. Underlying businesses may still be operating. Governments may still be collecting taxes. Households may remain employed. The issue is not immediate insolvency but difficulty accessing liquidity, meaning the cash required to meet short-term obligations.

During the global financial crisis, the first visible cracks did not come from mass corporate failure. They emerged from the freezing of short-term funding markets.[7] Banks and financial firms dependent on overnight borrowing suddenly faced reluctance from counterparties. Even sound institutions became vulnerable when liquidity evaporated across markets.

A similar dynamic appeared in the United Kingdom when government bond yields rose sharply and pension funds using leveraged strategies faced urgent demands for additional collateral.[8] The bonds themselves did not disappear, but falling prices triggered margin calls requiring immediate cash. The speed of adjustment forced central bank intervention to prevent forced selling from cascading through the market.

In systems where borrowing is widespread and refinancing constant, liquidity strain travels quickly. Governments roll over large volumes of debt each year. Companies refinance bonds and loans on fixed schedules. Households renew mortgages or rely on revolving credit. When interest rates rise or lenders grow cautious, pressure builds simultaneously across sectors. The cumulative strain becomes more visible.

At this point, behaviour begins to change. Companies postpone investment. Banks tighten lending standards. Households become more defensive. Market participants sell what they can rather than what they should. Prices begin to move not because fundamentals have collapsed, but because funding dries up

Markets begin to realize that stability depends on continued access to credit and refinancing. The structure still stands, but it requires continuous support. If authorities intervene quickly and decisively, strain may ease. If intervention is delayed or constrained, liquidity pressure deepens into solvency risk.

In earlier crises, rapid central bank action often restored calm before widespread defaults occurred. Today, the response is more complicated. Inflation has reintroduced limits. Political tolerance for repeated rescues has narrowed. The assumption that liquidity will always be provided is no longer unquestioned.

Liquidity strain marks the point where abstraction ends and mechanics dominate. Borrowing, refinancing, and collateral values begin to shape the narrative. Recognition turns into pressure, and what seemed manageable begins to feel fragile.

## *Revaluation and the Erosion of Confidence*

When funding becomes uncertain, investors begin to reassess risk more broadly. What had been treated as safe is reconsidered. What had been priced generously is discounted. The change is gradual at first, then cumulative, as markets adjust to the possibility that borrowing costs may remain higher for longer.

Government bond yields rise as lenders demand higher compensation for inflation and fiscal risk. Corporate borrowing costs follow. Share prices adjust as expected profits are discounted at higher interest rates. Property markets slow as mortgage costs increase and buyers retreat. The shift does not happen everywhere at once, but the direction becomes harder to ignore. Historical experience confirms this pattern.

The Eurozone sovereign debt crisis provides a clear illustration of how quickly this process can accelerate once confidence in a framework weakens.[9] Borrowing costs for several member states rose sharply not because their economies collapsed overnight, but because investors began to question whether the monetary union would hold. The issue was credibility. Once doubt entered the equation, lenders demanded higher returns, and those higher returns strained public finances further. The feedback loop had begun.

In highly indebted systems, this dynamic feeds on itself. As borrowing costs rise, governments devote a larger share of revenue to interest payments. Companies allocate more cash to servicing debt rather than investing. Households facing higher mortgage rates cut consumption. Slower growth reinforces concerns about sustainability. The adjustment spreads from markets into the real economy, shaping investment, hiring, and consumer spending in increasingly visible ways.

Confidence rarely disappears all at once. Investors typically reassess risk in stages. They first question specific sectors. Then they question the policy environment. Eventually they question the broader arrangement that had kept borrowing inexpensive and markets calm through repeated intervention.

For more than a decade after the global financial crisis, central banks were able to halt these cycles quickly. Lower rates and asset purchases reassured markets that support would be sustained. Today that reassurance carries greater cost. Inflation has reduced the space for aggressive easing. Political scrutiny of central banks has intensified. Fiscal positions are more stretched. Each intervention is more controversial than the last as its costs become clearer.

As a result, the assumption of effortless stabilization weakens. Markets adjust not only to economic data, but also to the possibility that policy responses may be slower, smaller, or constrained. When that possibility takes hold, the entire pricing structure shifts. Borrowing becomes structurally more expensive. Valuations reset to reflect greater uncertainty.

This stage does not yet constitute collapse. It represents something more subtle and more consequential: the gradual loss of the belief that policymakers can always prevent major financial disruptions. Once that confidence erodes, restoring the previous equilibrium becomes far more difficult.

## *Policy Dilemma: Limited Room to Stabilize*

When market stress spreads and borrowing costs rise, policymakers face a narrowing set of choices. The trade-offs are no longer theoretical. They begin to affect inflation, employment, borrowing costs, and government finances directly.

In earlier crises, central banks could cut interest rates aggressively and expand their balance sheets with limited fear of inflation. Governments could borrow heavily to cushion downturns while funding costs remained low. The response followed a familiar pattern. Stabilize first. Deal with long-term consequences later. This approach helped contain disruptions and restore confidence before deeper damage occurred. That framework, however, is now constrained.

Inflation has returned as a political and economic force. Sustained price increases have already eroded purchasing power and strained household budgets. Cutting rates too quickly or resuming large-scale asset purchases risks reigniting those pressures. Doing nothing, however, risks a tightening of financial conditions that exposes overextended balance sheets across governments, companies, and households.

The choice is no longer between growth and recession. It is increasingly a choice between tolerating higher inflation, accepting financial instability, or imposing economic slowdown. Each option preserves one objective only by placing greater strain on another.

If authorities move aggressively to suppress borrowing costs and support markets, they risk weakening credibility and fuelling further price instability. If they maintain tighter policy to defend currency stability and contain inflation, higher interest expenses strain public finances and corporate balance sheets. Defaults rise. Unemployment increases. The social consequences intensify, becoming increasingly difficult to contain.

Fiscal policy offers limited relief. Public debt burdens in many advanced economies are already elevated following years of borrowing. Ageing populations increase long-term spending pressures. Political divisions make sustained consolidation difficult. Raising taxes or cutting spending carries electoral risk. Continuing to borrow shifts the burden forward and leaves the system more exposed to higher rates.

Japan's experience following its asset bubble collapse illustrates one path.[10] Sustained monetary easing and repeated fiscal stimulus prevented immediate collapse but resulted in prolonged weak growth and rising public debt. The Eurozone sovereign debt crisis demonstrated another approach.[11] Efforts to restore fiscal discipline under market pressure led to severe contractions and political upheaval before stability returned.

Today's environment combines elements of both constraints. Debt levels are high. Growth is modest. Demographic trends are less supportive. Political consensus is weaker. Central banks have already expanded their role far beyond traditional boundaries. Each additional intervention carries greater scrutiny and diminishing marginal effect.

This is the core problem of a debt-heavy system approaching its limits. There is no painless option. Each path redistributes cost across time and across society. Inflation erodes savings. Insolvency destroys capital. Austerity fuels political anger. Continued borrowing increases vulnerability to the next shock.

For decades, advanced economies relied on the assumption that policy could absorb disruption without forcing hard choices. That assumption is now under pressure. The capacity to smooth cycles without destabilizing the system is no longer assured.

When a system reaches this point, stability becomes harder to defend, not because policymakers are indifferent, but because the room to manoeuvre has narrowed and every option carries visible economic and political costs. The challenge shifts from preventing instability to managing its consequences as markets test the credibility of policy responses and each intervention is judged by whether confidence can still be sustained.

## *Escalation or Containment of Market Stress*

At this stage, authorities attempt to steady the system. The instinct is familiar, shaped by decades of crisis management. Policymakers seek to prevent disorder, provide emergency support, ensure that banks, pension funds, and governments can continue to borrow, and reassure markets that panic will not be allowed to spread.

In the short term, these actions often succeed. Borrowing markets calm. Share prices recover. Government bond yields stabilize. Access to cash improves. The immediate danger recedes, restoring a sense of temporary equilibrium.

The longer-term consequences, however, are more difficult. When instability is repeatedly met with intervention, behaviour adapts. Investors come to expect support during sharp declines. Governments assume refinancing will remain possible. Financial institutions operate on the belief that systemic stress will trigger assistance. Over time, the expectation of support becomes embedded in market behaviour, and what was once emergency action gradually becomes structural dependence.

Steadying markets in this way does not restore the previous balance. Instead, it reinforces the habits that made the system vulnerable. Public borrowing continues because it must. Central banks remain deeply involved in bond markets. Interest rates are held lower than they would otherwise be to avoid sharper disruption. The visible crisis is postponed, but the exposure increases with each intervention.

If authorities hesitate or refuse to intervene, the adjustment unfolds more abruptly. Higher borrowing costs feed directly into government budgets and corporate balance sheets. Property prices fall more sharply. Companies with thin equity cushions face bankruptcy. Households cut spending as debt servicing becomes more expensive with rising rates.

The choice is not between stability and instability. It is between gradual weakening and sharper rupture. Either markets adjust slowly through continued intervention, or they adjust abruptly through forced repricing with greater disruption.

In earlier decades, repeated intervention was sustainable because public debt burdens were lighter, demographics were more supportive, and inflation was subdued. Today those buffers are thinner. Each round of support begins from a more fragile fiscal position and a more divided political landscape. Public tolerance for rescues has narrowed. Central bank credibility has already been tested under repeated intervention.

Over time, steadying the system in this way changes it. Borrowing grows as a share of national income. Market prices rely more heavily on policy signals. Access to short-term funding becomes more critical. Stability becomes something that must be actively maintained rather than assumed.

Stability now depends increasingly on continued intervention rather than underlying economic strength. The structure remains standing, but it becomes more dependent and more exposed. Each episode leaves it weaker, increasing the likelihood that future interventions restore calm only temporarily rather than permanently as confidence erodes.

Eventually, the strain reaches beyond markets. The same pressures that weaken economic resilience begin to reshape politics, institutions, and public expectations.

## *Political Shift and Growing Institutional Strain*

Economic stress rarely remains confined to markets. It moves into politics, as rising borrowing costs, inflation, and slower growth begin to affect households directly and shape public debate. Government finances come under growing strain.

As borrowing costs rise, public spending becomes harder to sustain without higher taxes or larger deficits. When inflation erodes wages, households demand relief. When unemployment increases, pressure on governments intensifies. What begins as financial strain becomes a dispute over who absorbs the cost.

In the United States, debates over debt ceilings, deficit spending, and central bank independence have grown more polarized.[12] Fiscal negotiations have become more confrontational. Trust in institutions has declined across political lines. Economic policy is no longer treated as technocratic management. It has become a battleground over distribution and fairness. Recent experience makes this clear.

The United Kingdom demonstrated how quickly confidence can turn when fiscal plans appear detached from economic constraints.[13] Government bond yields rose sharply. The central bank intervened to stabilize markets. Political leadership changed within weeks. Financial credibility and political authority became inseparable. The implications extended well beyond a single country, highlighting broader structural weaknesses across advanced economies.

Across Europe, fiscal debates in countries such as Italy and France reveal similar tensions. Public debt remains high and growth is uneven. Efforts to impose budget discipline collide with voter resistance. In Germany, long seen as a model of fiscal restraint, borrowing limits have come under increasing pressure as economic conditions weaken and spending demands rise.

Japan presents another version of the same strain.[14] Public debt has grown for decades following the collapse of its asset bubble. The central bank has intervened heavily in bond markets to prevent yields from rising sharply. While this approach has preserved short-term calm, it has blurred the boundary between fiscal and monetary authority. The longer such arrangements persist, the more difficult it becomes to normalize policy without destabilizing markets or weakening confidence.

In each case, the underlying tension is similar. Economic models built on sustained borrowing and low interest rates require political consent to continue. When inflation rises or growth slows, that consent begins to fray. Voters demand protection from rising costs. Taxpayers resist additional burdens. Younger generations question systems that appear to favour asset holders over wage earners.

Denial often emerges at this stage. Political leaders promise stability while avoiding acknowledgment of structural limits. Fiscal expansion is framed as temporary. Monetary intervention is presented as technical adjustment. Hard choices are deferred even as trade-offs become sharper.

Over time, this refusal to confront limits reshapes politics. Established coalitions weaken. Anti-establishment movements gain ground. Debates shift from managing growth to questioning the framework itself. Public trust in governments and central banks declines when repeated assurances of stability fail to match lived economic experience.

Economic breakdown therefore becomes institutional as well as financial. It alters the relationship between citizens and the state, exposing the gap between promises of perpetual stabilization and the reality of constrained resources. As confidence in economic management erodes, political structures begin to adjust. Policy consensus fractures. Governing coalitions shift. Stability becomes contested rather than assumed.

At this stage, the system is no longer only financially exposed. It becomes politically unsettled, and economic management grows more difficult as political divisions widen. Economic constraints increasingly become political constraints, limiting the scope for effective action.

## *Regime Change and an Uncertain End State*

When economic strain, policy constraint, and political tension converge, the system eventually shifts. The change may not occur in a single dramatic moment. It often unfolds through a series of decisions that gradually alter the structure until the previous arrangement no longer returns intact. What appears gradual at first can, over time, produce a decisive break from the old framework.

History offers clear examples. The abandonment of the gold standard during the Great Depression marked the end of one monetary order.[15] The creation of the Bretton Woods system after the Second World War redefined exchange rates, capital flows, and the role of the dollar.[16] Its later dissolution ushered in the era of floating currencies and financial globalization. Each shift followed a period in which existing rules proved increasingly unsustainable under pressure and mounting debt.

The stability that advanced economies relied upon in recent decades was built on expanding credit, low and predictable inflation, deep capital markets, and repeated policy intervention during stress. That model absorbed shocks that might once have triggered deeper contractions. It also encouraged higher borrowing and greater dependence on steady asset values.

As pressures intensify, instability rarely appears everywhere at once. It usually moves through the system in stages, shifting from one area to another as policymakers attempt to contain stress. Measures that stabilize financial markets can weaken public finances. Policies designed to support growth can intensify inflation pressures. Efforts to restore confidence in one sector often expose vulnerabilities elsewhere. Systems that once absorbed shocks smoothly become increasingly reactive as debt accumulates and room for adjustment narrows.

When that structure reaches its limits, change becomes unavoidable. Debt can be reduced through inflation, default, financial repression, or prolonged stagnation. Monetary frameworks can be tightened or loosened in ways that reshape market expectations. Fiscal systems can be overhauled through reform or crisis. None of these adjustments are neutral, and all redistribute cost across societies and generations.

An orderly transition requires recognition of constraints and willingness to accept trade-offs. It requires political leadership prepared to explain limits rather than postpone them. In the absence of such clarity, adjustment becomes less controlled and more disruptive. Economic realities eventually impose the discipline that politics postpones.

If borrowing costs rise faster than growth, public finances deteriorate. If inflation remains elevated while wages lag, social tension increases. If financial markets lose confidence in the ability of authorities to stabilize without further distortion, capital flows shift abruptly. Under those conditions, fracture is no longer hypothetical but increasingly probable.

What makes these periods dangerous is not simply the presence of strain, but the way pressure spreads through interconnected systems. Banking stress affects sovereign debt markets. Fiscal weakness influences currencies and capital flows. Political instability alters investment behaviour and public confidence. Once trust in the broader framework weakens, instability can move rapidly across institutions and borders.

The end of stability does not mean the end of economic activity. It marks the end of a specific equilibrium in which debt expansion and policy support could smooth disturbances without threatening the broader structure. What replaces it may be a painful but managed recalibration. It may also involve sharper dislocation, institutional strain, and political upheaval.

The outcome depends on choices made under pressure. Yet the pressure itself is becoming harder to avoid. Calm has grown more conditional. Intervention has grown more contested. Trade-offs have become more explicit. Once a system must continually defend its own continuity, it enters a different phase. The objective shifts from improving the system to preserving it.

At that stage, the challenge is no longer limited to restoring growth or stabilizing markets. The challenge becomes maintaining confidence in the institutions, policy frameworks, and financial structures that supported the old order. As stress intensifies, the risk is not only economic deterioration, but a broader weakening of trust in the system's ability to manage disruption without creating further instability.

The advanced world is not approaching a routine downturn. It is approaching the limits of a model that defined a generation. When those limits are reached, the old stability cannot be restored simply through intervention or reassurance. The structure adjusts, and a new equilibrium begins to form, shaped by constraints that had previously been deferred.

What follows such transitions is rarely uniform. Some economies adjust gradually through inflation and stagnation. Others experience sharper financial disruption or political realignment. The path depends on policy choices, institutional resilience, and external conditions.

Yet once systems become highly dependent on continuous intervention, periods of stress become progressively harder to contain. Measures that once prevented localized disruptions lose effectiveness as financial, fiscal, and political strains reinforce one another. Confidence increasingly rests on the belief that policymakers can continue to manage them.

By then, instability no longer remains confined to individual sectors or national economies. It spreads through financial markets, currencies, trade flows, and political systems, making local shocks increasingly difficult to isolate. The stability era does not end with a single event. It gives way, step by step, to a more demanding economic environment in which adjustment can no longer be deferred.

# 21

## THE STABILITY ERA BREAKS

Economic breakdown rarely begins with empty shelves or shuttered banks. It begins when the institutions that once absorbed stress can no longer do so. The warning signs appear gradually, in tighter budgets, rising borrowing costs, and policy decisions that become increasingly constrained. What once seemed manageable begins to reveal limits, and stability that once appeared durable begins to weaken.

The change is often difficult to recognize while it is unfolding. For long periods, the familiar routines of economic life continue. Governments still borrow. Markets still function. Public institutions continue to operate. Yet the capacity that once allowed the system to absorb pressure gradually diminishes, leaving fewer options available when new strains emerge.

For forty years, advanced economies operated under an implicit guarantee. Since the early 1980s, particularly across the United States, Western Europe, and Japan, policymakers increasingly relied on borrowing, financial intervention, and monetary easing to stabilize downturns. When growth slowed, governments borrowed more. When markets fell, central banks lowered rates or purchased financial instruments to push prices back up. When debt burdens rose, refinancing extended the timeline. Each disturbance was met with expansion rather than correction. Success strengthened confidence in the model, reinforcing expectations that future crises were manageable.

These responses were often successful in the short term. Recessions were softened. Financial crises were contained. Asset prices recovered. Over time, however, repeated intervention also encouraged a broader assumption that serious disruptions could always be managed and that adjustment could always be postponed without lasting consequences.

Stability was not accidental. It was engineered, through a framework built on declining interest rates, expanding public borrowing, and repeated institutional intervention, and that engineering now faces hard limits. Those limits are beginning to appear across public finances, asset markets, and policy decisions, revealing the point at which stability stops working.

This chapter examines that turning point. It explores what happens when the mechanisms that once preserved stability begin to lose effectiveness, when borrowing creates new pressures rather than easing old ones, and when the tools used to defer adjustment become increasingly difficult to use. The issue is not whether the old framework suddenly disappears. It is whether it can continue performing the role that defined it for more than four decades.

## *The Moment Stability Stops Working*

Public obligations in several advanced nations now exceed the total annual output of their economies. Government debt in the United States now stands near 120 percent of GDP, while Japan's exceeds 250 percent, levels historically associated with wartime mobilization or major economic crises.[1] In some cases, they approach levels last seen when entire societies were mobilized for existential conflict. The difference today is that the borrowing did not finance reconstruction after destruction. It financed consumption, asset appreciation, and the deferral of adjustment.

For many years, these debt burdens appeared manageable because borrowing costs remained unusually low. Governments could refinance obligations at favourable rates, and financial markets remained willing to absorb expanding debt issuance. As long as those conditions persisted, the underlying pressures remained largely hidden.

Interest costs are rising as rates move higher. In the United States, interest payments on federal debt are projected to approach or exceed one trillion dollars annually within the coming decade, making them one of the fastest growing components of government spending.[2] In some countries, servicing government debt now absorbs a larger share of tax revenue than defense or infrastructure. Pension systems still assume steady returns even as demographic ageing reduces the workforce supporting them. Property values in major cities remain far above what median earnings alone can justify.

Taken individually, none of these pressures necessarily signals crisis. Together, however, they reveal a common problem. The assumptions that supported public finances, retirement systems, and asset markets were built during a period of lower borrowing costs, stronger demographics, and more favourable growth conditions than those now emerging.

Governments face increasingly visible trade offs. In the United States, net interest payments on federal debt have recently climbed to levels not seen in decades, consuming a rapidly growing share of tax revenue. Similar pressures are emerging across parts of Europe, including Italy and France, where elevated debt levels and rising borrowing costs are beginning to narrow fiscal flexibility.[3] Money that once flowed toward public services or long term investment is increasingly directed toward servicing past borrowing, forcing governments to delay infrastructure investment, reconsider social spending, and confront difficult fiscal choices.

This shift does not announce itself as crisis, but as constraint, gradually narrowing policy options and exposing the limits of fiscal flexibility. The change is subtle at first. Roads are repaired later. Infrastructure projects are postponed. Public services face growing pressure. Governments continue to function, but they do so with less capacity to respond to future shocks. Constraint becomes evident not through collapse, but through a steady reduction in choice.

Central banks face limits of their own. Lowering rates aggressively risks reigniting inflation. Keeping rates elevated strains governments, businesses, and households that accumulated large debts under cheaper conditions, particularly during the near-zero interest rate era that followed the 2008 global financial crisis and extended into the early 2020s. There is no painless setting, and the policy choices that once stabilized markets now increasingly expose difficult economic and political trade-offs. The underlying tensions soon became visible across many advanced economies.

The years following the pandemic provided a clear example of this dilemma. Central banks raised rates to contain inflation, but higher borrowing costs also exposed how dependent many parts of the economy had become on cheap money. Measures designed to solve one problem revealed another.

Stability worked because institutions could absorb shocks without exposing those trade-offs. For decades, central banks and governments intervened repeatedly to cushion downturns, reinforcing the perception that volatility could always be contained and that policy support would remain available. That capacity is eroding as debt burdens rise, interest costs increase, and political consensus weakens across advanced economies.

The breaking point is not theatrical. It emerges when policymakers can no longer satisfy competing promises at the same time, when governments must choose between higher taxes, reduced spending, or increased borrowing costs, and when denial begins to yield to arithmetic.

This is the moment stability stops working. Not because institutions suddenly fail, but because the tools that once absorbed pressure become less effective. The system continues to operate, yet it does so under increasingly visible constraints. What had once appeared sustainable begins to reveal its limits.

## *Forces Driving the Break*

Denial does not collapse because leaders suddenly embrace realism. It collapses because circumstances remove alternatives.

For years, advanced economies relied on three shock absorbers. Borrowing expanded when growth weakened. Central banks reduced rates or purchased financial instruments when markets faltered. Political leaders postponed difficult reforms because financing remained available. These tools worked because they did not immediately threaten confidence, and they functioned particularly well during the long decades of declining interest rates between the early 1980s and the late 2010s, when borrowing became progressively cheaper and financial markets absorbed expanding debt issuance with relatively little disruption.

The common feature linking these responses was time. Borrowing created time. Lower interest rates created time. Delayed reform created time. As long as economic conditions remained supportive, policymakers could extend adjustment into the future without immediately confronting the underlying pressures. Those favourable conditions have steadily eroded.

They now collide with structural limits. Governments can no longer borrow as easily without raising concerns about debt sustainability. Central banks cannot lower interest rates as aggressively without risking renewed inflation.

Political leaders also find it harder to postpone difficult decisions when rising interest costs and slower growth begin to narrow their options. These constraints do not emerge all at once, but they gradually reduce the room for manoeuvre that policymakers relied on for decades, transforming temporary pressures into structural ones.

The result is not a single breaking point but a gradual tightening of conditions. Choices that once appeared straightforward become more difficult. Trade-offs that were once hidden become increasingly visible. The flexibility that defined the stability era begins to diminish.

First, debt has grown faster than income for too long. Across many developed economies, total debt, including government, household, and corporate borrowing, has expanded significantly faster than economic output since the 1990s.[4] When obligations rise more quickly than the economy that must support them, the gap does not disappear. It compounds, gradually increasing vulnerability even during periods of growth.

Governments can refinance maturing bonds, but they cannot refinance arithmetic. As interest rates rise, even modestly, the cost of carrying past borrowing increases, and each percentage point matters more when the base is already large. What once appeared manageable under low borrowing costs becomes more difficult when financing conditions tighten, turning accumulated debt into an active constraint on policy.

Debt becomes especially problematic when it stops supporting future growth and begins financing past commitments. At that point, borrowing no longer expands flexibility. It reduces it. More resources are devoted to servicing existing obligations, leaving fewer available for future priorities. Debt is no longer merely a legacy of earlier decisions. It becomes a force that shapes current choices, influencing budgets, investment, and the capacity to respond to new challenges.

Second, central banks no longer operate in a low inflation environment. Inflation returned across advanced economies following the COVID-19 pandemic, first driven by supply chain disruptions in 2020 to 2021 and then reinforced by the energy and food shocks that followed the Russian invasion of Ukraine in 2022.[5] After decades in which inflation appeared contained, price pressures once again became a central constraint on economic policy. Their effects extend well beyond prices.

Inflation weakens purchasing power and erodes public trust, while also constraining monetary authorities. Reducing interest rates too quickly risks reigniting price instability. Keeping them elevated, however, exposes the strain embedded in government, corporate, and household balance sheets built during years of cheaper money and easy credit across advanced economies.

The result is a narrower range of policy choices. The room to manoeuvre is smaller than it was in 2009, when debt levels were lower, inflation remained subdued, and central banks had greater flexibility to ease policy without triggering renewed price pressures. The margin for policy error has narrowed accordingly.

What makes this challenge particularly difficult is that neither path is costless. Lower rates risk renewed inflation. Higher rates expose financial strain. Policymakers are therefore managing a tension that cannot be fully resolved, only managed.

There is precedent for this constraint. In the late 1970s and early 1980s, policymakers confronted inflation that could not be suppressed without painful tightening. The result was recession, rising unemployment, and a sharp repricing of debt. The difference today is scale. Debt burdens are larger, populations are older, and political consensus is thinner, making adjustment more difficult and potentially more disruptive.

The constraints facing policymakers are therefore not entirely new. What is new is the combination of debt, demographics, and political division that now accompanies them.

Third, demographics are no longer supportive, as ageing populations mean fewer workers supporting more retirees. In many advanced economies, the ratio of working age individuals to retirees has declined steadily since the 1990s and is projected to continue falling over the coming decades.[6] This shift reduces the growth of tax revenues while increasing demands on pension and healthcare systems.

Pension systems depend on returns that are difficult to achieve in a slower growth environment, while healthcare commitments expand as populations age. These pressures gradually tighten fiscal constraints and reduce flexibility.

Unlike financial crises, demographic pressures do not emerge suddenly. They build year after year, often attracting less attention precisely because they develop so gradually. Yet their effects can be just as significant because they influence growth, public finances, labour markets, and social spending simultaneously. The constraints do not end there.

Fourth, politics itself has shifted, with public tolerance for austerity limited and trust in institutions weakened. Redistribution decisions that might once have been absorbed through compromise now trigger political division, and the willingness to accept losses is lower precisely when losses must be recognized.

At the same time, political fragmentation makes coordinated responses more difficult. Fiscal reforms become harder to implement. Long term adjustments are postponed. Policies that once would have been negotiated across political lines increasingly become sources of conflict, further narrowing the options available to policymakers during periods of stress.

Politics does not create these economic pressures, but it influences how societies respond to them. When trust weakens and compromise becomes more difficult, even necessary adjustments become harder to implement. Economic constraints and political constraints begin reinforcing one another.

When these forces converge, adjustment ceases to be optional. The break may take different forms in different countries. In one, it may appear as a bond market demanding sharply higher yields before financing additional deficits. In another, it may surface as a currency that weakens abruptly when investors doubt fiscal discipline. In more extreme cases, governments may discover that rolling over debt is no longer automatic and that market access, long assumed, has become conditional.

Advanced economies have not faced this reality for decades. Since the early 1990s, most developed economies have benefited from relatively stable financing conditions and declining interest rates, reinforcing the assumption that borrowing could continue without consequence. The presumption of continuous financing became part of the stability story itself, shaping expectations across markets, governments, and households.

Stability fails when the tools designed to preserve it amplify the problem they were meant to contain. Borrowing more increases interest burdens. Suppressing rates for too long distorts investment decisions. Postponing reform deepens eventual correction. What once cushioned shocks begins to transmit them. Markets adjust first, politics follows, and households feel the consequences last.

The break therefore does not result from a single policy mistake or isolated event. It emerges when the forces that supported stability for decades begin operating in reverse. The mechanisms that once postponed adjustment become the channels through which adjustment eventually occurs.

## *Who Absorbs the Loss*

When a long period of borrowing reaches its limits, the central question is no longer whether losses exist. It is who absorbs them when adjustment finally arrives.

In a debt heavy system, claims accumulate over decades. Governments promise pensions and healthcare. Corporations promise returns to shareholders. Financial institutions promise stability to depositors and investors. Households plan retirement around projected asset growth. These promises were made under assumptions of steady expansion, low borrowing costs, and rising valuations. Much of this period, particularly from the 1990s through the 2010s, was characterized by declining interest rates and rising asset prices that reinforced these expectations. When growth slows and borrowing becomes more expensive, those assumptions fail, and adjustment becomes unavoidable.

For many years, these promises appeared compatible because growth, borrowing, and rising asset values moved in the same direction. Governments could expand commitments. Households could assume that property and financial assets would continue appreciating. Investors could expect returns that seemed consistent with past experience. When those conditions weaken, the tension between promises and resources becomes increasingly difficult to ignore. Eventually, that tension demands resolution as economic constraints tighten.

One path is inflation, where prices rise faster than wages and savings lose purchasing power. The loss is spread broadly, often without formal acknowledgment. Another path is explicit restructuring, where pension benefits are reduced, retirement ages rise, taxes increase, or public services are trimmed. In each case, the burden shifts from abstract balance sheets to households, translating financial strain into real world consequences. The burden ultimately falls on the real economy.

The mechanism may differ, but the outcome is similar. Costs that were previously hidden within financial systems gradually become visible in everyday life. Households face higher living costs, reduced benefits, delayed retirement, or slower wealth accumulation. What once appeared to be a financial problem becomes a social one.

Generational tension becomes increasingly difficult to avoid. Older cohorts often hold a larger share of financial wealth and property accumulated during decades of rising valuations, while younger cohorts face higher housing costs, heavier student debt burdens in some countries, and the prospect of financing pension systems from which they may receive less. When pension systems require higher contributions or lower payouts to remain solvent, the arithmetic becomes visible, forcing societies to confront trade-offs that were previously deferred.

This tension extends beyond economics. It shapes perceptions of fairness and opportunity. Younger workers may question whether the system offers the same prospects available to previous generations, while older retirees may fear the erosion of benefits they were promised after decades of contribution. The debate becomes not only about money, but about expectations, trust, and intergenerational fairness.

Many public pension systems in advanced economies already face substantial funding shortfalls. In the United States, several major public pension systems have funding gaps measured in trillions of dollars when calculated using conservative return assumptions.[7] Assumed annual returns often exceed what slower growth, higher rate environments can reliably deliver. When these assumptions are revised downward, required contributions rise or benefits fall, transforming abstract fiscal pressures into concrete economic decisions.

The politics are difficult. Reducing benefits angers retirees who organized their lives around promised payments. Raising taxes strains younger workers whose real incomes have already struggled to keep pace with housing and living costs. Continuing to borrow postpones the adjustment but increases the eventual correction. The costs cannot be avoided, only redistributed across society.

Every available option creates opposition because every available option imposes a cost on someone. The challenge is not identifying the existence of the loss. The challenge is determining how it is distributed and who bears it.

This is where the breaking of the advanced world becomes tangible. The social contract in many high income countries was built on the expectation that each generation would be better off than the last. Throughout much of the post war period, particularly between 1950 and 2000, productivity growth supported this expectation. When growth weakens and debt levels are already elevated, the margin for honouring all promises narrows, and scarcity rather than expansion begins to define economic outcomes.

The significance of this shift extends beyond budgets and financial markets. Expectations formed over decades begin to change. Assumptions that once appeared secure become uncertain. Economic adjustment becomes intertwined with questions about opportunity, mobility, and the future direction of society itself.

Adjustment forces societies to decide which commitments are sustainable and which must change. These decisions are rarely made in calm conditions. They are made under pressure, often after markets or fiscal realities remove easier options, and once losses become unavoidable, they reshape politics as much as economics. Debates over who bears the burden increasingly dominate public and political life.

This is why periods of adjustment often prove politically contentious. The discussion is no longer about how to distribute gains. It becomes a debate about how to distribute losses. That transition marks a profound change in the way societies experience economic reality. The assumptions that shaped financial decisions begin to change as well.

## *The Repricing of Reality*

For decades, rising property values and steadily advancing stock markets reinforced the belief that wealth accumulation was a normal feature of modern life. From the early 1990s through the post 2008 recovery period, households in many advanced economies experienced repeated cycles of asset appreciation that strengthened the perception that financial markets and property values would continue to rise over time.

Many households came to rely on this pattern. Retirement projections assumed continued growth in equity portfolios. Homeowners expected that property values would outpace inflation over time. Governments benefited from tax revenues linked to these gains.

As the pattern persisted, it increasingly came to be viewed as normal. Rising asset prices were no longer seen as a favourable outcome of specific economic conditions. They became embedded in expectations about retirement, household wealth, and future living standards for millions of people.

When stability weakens, prices adjust, and the assumptions that supported rising valuations begin to unravel. If borrowing costs remain higher than during the era of near zero rates, particularly the period between 2009 and 2021 when policy rates in many advanced economies hovered near historic lows, the mathematics of valuation change.

A home financed at three percent can command a higher price than one financed at seven percent, even if incomes are unchanged. When financing becomes more expensive, buyers qualify for smaller loans, demand softens, and prices begin to adjust downward or stagnate across housing markets.

The effect is straightforward. Households do not purchase homes based only on price. They purchase them based on monthly affordability. When mortgage payments rise sharply, the amount buyers can borrow falls, and that reduction places pressure on property values even if demand remains strong.

This is not theoretical. Following the sharp rise in interest rates beginning in 2022, mortgage costs in several advanced economies roughly doubled within a short period, significantly reducing affordability and slowing housing activity.[8] In several advanced economies, housing affordability has already reached levels that require either sustained wage growth or price correction to restore balance. If wages cannot accelerate meaningfully, valuations must adapt, and that adjustment may unfold gradually in some regions while appearing more abrupt in others. The same logic extends beyond housing.

Equity markets are subject to similar arithmetic. When investors demand higher returns to compensate for uncertainty and inflation risk, the price they are willing to pay for each unit of expected earnings declines. Valuations that were justified when rates were exceptionally low become difficult to sustain when rates are structurally higher, and even profitable companies can see their market prices fall if the assumptions embedded in those prices change. Housing illustrates the same dynamic in a different setting.

When money is cheap and confidence is high, investors are willing to pay more for future profits. When borrowing costs rise and uncertainty increases, those future profits are valued more cautiously. Prices adjust despite profitable businesses.

Asset resets feel destabilizing because they reverse a long pattern of appreciation, yet they reflect a shift back toward income and productivity as anchors of value. For households, the impact is immediate. Falling property prices reduce perceived wealth and limit refinancing options. Lower equity valuations weaken retirement accounts. Reduced paper wealth influences spending decisions, which in turn affects economic activity and reinforces the slowdown. The effects become visible beyond financial markets. The effects become visible beyond financial markets, extending into household finances, public services, and everyday economic decisions.

For many households, this is the point at which economic adjustment becomes tangible. A retirement portfolio that once appeared comfortably funded becomes less secure. Homeowners who expected rising property values encounter stagnation or decline. Financial plans built on assumptions of continual appreciation require revision.

For governments, the consequences are indirect but real. Slower capital gains reduce tax receipts. Housing market weakness can strain banking systems that extended large volumes of mortgage lending. Fiscal pressures intensify at the same time social demands increase, creating a feedback loop between financial markets and public finances that becomes increasingly difficult to manage.

What begins as a change in valuations therefore spreads beyond investors. It affects government revenues, household spending, business confidence, and ultimately economic growth itself. Financial repricing becomes an economy-wide adjustment rather than a market event.

Fiscal constraint gradually spreads through the economy. It moves from public finances to asset prices and then to household confidence. Confidence that once rested on rising valuations gives way to caution. Spending slows. Investment becomes more selective. The illusion that wealth naturally compounds gives way to the recognition that prices depend on economic conditions that can change. Expectations themselves become part of the adjustment process.

Repricing, in this context, is not punishment. It is correction, and correction after a long period of expansion is experienced not as normalization but as loss. That perception matters because societies become accustomed to prevailing conditions. When decades of rising asset values shape expectations, a return to more restrained valuations feels like decline even when it represents a rebalancing between prices, incomes, and underlying economic realities. Repricing assets does not remove accumulated debt.

## *Debt That Cannot Be Preserved*

For years, the priority in advanced economies was preservation. Troubled loans were extended. Maturities were lengthened. Obligations were refinanced rather than reduced. This approach became particularly common after the 2008 global financial crisis, when policymakers prioritized stability and recovery over rapid deleveraging. The objective was to prevent visible loss and maintain confidence in financial institutions and markets.

The strategy was understandable. Policymakers feared that forcing losses too quickly would deepen recession, destabilize banks, and undermine confidence. Extending obligations and delaying adjustment often appeared less risky than confronting losses directly in the short term.

That strategy depends on growth, low borrowing costs, and confidence. When those conditions weaken, preservation becomes harder to sustain, and debts that once appeared manageable begin to reveal their underlying fragility.

What was previously treated as a temporary solution gradually becomes a long-term dependency. Refinancing can postpone adjustment, but it cannot eliminate obligations. Eventually the question shifts from whether debt can be rolled forward to whether it can realistically be supported.

At the corporate level, this may mean restructuring loans, converting debt into equity, or accepting bankruptcy for firms that expanded under overly generous financing conditions. In commercial real estate markets across parts of the United States and Europe, refinancing at higher interest rates has already exposed projects that were viable only under cheaper financing conditions.[9] As borrowing costs rise, business models built on low interest rates become harder to sustain, and weaker firms face pressure to restructure or exit. What once appeared sustainable faces a more demanding economic environment.

The process can be uncomfortable because it forces a reassessment of assumptions once taken for granted. Projects that appeared profitable under cheap financing may no longer make economic sense. Companies that relied heavily on borrowing must adapt to a different environment.

At the household level, increased defaults may emerge where property prices fall and incomes fail to keep pace with obligations. Households that relied on rising property values or refinancing may find those options narrowing, transforming financial strain into broader economic weakness.

For households, the adjustment is often more personal. Refinancing becomes more difficult. Mortgage payments consume a larger share of income. Property values may stagnate or decline. Financial pressures once seen as manageable begin affecting spending, savings, and long-term security.

At the sovereign level, the assumption of automatic repayment deserves scrutiny. Advanced economies have long benefited from deep capital markets and reserve currencies, allowing investors to treat their bonds as safe stores of value. That confidence reduced borrowing costs and reinforced stability, but no government is immune to arithmetic.

If debt grows persistently faster than the tax base supporting it, and if interest payments absorb an increasing share of public revenue, the question shifts from willingness to pay to capacity to pay. Sovereign restructuring in advanced economies remains politically sensitive, but it is not inconceivable. It may not resemble dramatic default, but instead appear through extended maturities, revised coupon rates, inflation tolerated above target levels, or regulatory frameworks encouraging domestic institutions to hold public debt regardless of yield.

History suggests that governments rarely choose the most visible form of adjustment if less visible alternatives remain available. Obligations may be stretched over longer periods. Inflation may gradually reduce the real value of debt. Financial institutions may be encouraged to absorb a greater share of government borrowing. The form varies, but the objective remains the same: easing pressures that can no longer be ignored. The methods change, but the logic does not.

These approaches have historical precedent, including the decades following World War II when several advanced economies relied on financial repression, controlled interest rates, and moderate inflation to reduce debt burdens over time.[10] The distinction between restructuring and preservation lies in honesty. Preservation assumes growth will resolve the imbalance. Restructuring accepts that some promises were based on projections that no longer hold, and that adjustment must occur through changes in expectations and obligations.

That distinction becomes increasingly important as debt burdens rise. The longer adjustment is postponed, the larger the eventual adjustment often becomes. What appears to be stability may simply be a delay in recognizing losses that already exist.

Debt that cannot realistically be serviced does not disappear. It changes form or forces change elsewhere in the system, marking a turning point in the evolution of the financial structure that supported decades of stability.

The question is therefore not whether adjustment occurs, but how it occurs and who bears the cost. Once preservation becomes more difficult than adaptation, the stability era enters a new phase, one defined less by postponement and more by recognition. No advanced economy adjusts in isolation.

## *The Global Fracture*

The reckoning will not remain confined within national borders. Advanced economies are deeply integrated through trade, finance, and currency systems, and strain in one jurisdiction transmits quickly to others through those connections.

For decades, the international financial order rested on the assumption that government bonds issued by major advanced economies were the safest assets available. The United States dollar served as the primary reserve currency, while the euro functioned as a secondary anchor. Global capital flowed toward these markets in times of uncertainty, reinforcing stability and lowering borrowing costs.

This arrangement provided advantages that were often taken for granted. Governments could borrow at lower cost. Investors had confidence that deep and liquid markets would remain available. Financial shocks in one area could frequently be absorbed without undermining the broader system.

Since the end of the Bretton Woods system in the early 1970s, and particularly after the 1990s, the U.S. dollar has dominated global reserves and international trade settlement.[11] That privilege reduced borrowing costs and reinforced financial and economic stability, allowing advanced economies to finance deficits more easily than most countries.

The strength of the system rested not only on economic size, but on confidence. Investors, central banks, and governments believed that the institutions supporting the international order would remain stable and predictable. That confidence became one of the foundations of the stability era itself.

If fiscal pressures intensify and political gridlock deepens, that confidence can weaken gradually. Reserve currency status rarely disappears overnight. It erodes through diversification. Central banks adjust the composition of their reserves. Bilateral trade agreements expand the use of alternative settlement currencies. Sovereign wealth funds shift allocations incrementally.

While each change may appear modest in isolation, the cumulative effect can become increasingly meaningful over time.

Major shifts in the international system rarely begin with dramatic rupture. They often emerge through a series of small adjustments that attract limited attention individually but become significant collectively. Confidence weakens gradually before the consequences become widely recognized.

A gradual diversification has already begun, with some countries increasing the use of alternative currencies in trade and reserve holdings.[12] A currency under pressure raises borrowing costs, amplifies imported inflation, and complicates monetary policy. For countries accustomed to financing deficits at low cost, even modest erosion of reserve currency dominance changes fiscal dynamics and narrows policy flexibility.

The implications extend beyond governments. Higher borrowing costs affect businesses, households, and financial markets. Economic pressures that begin in currency markets eventually influence investment decisions, living standards, and public finances across advanced economies.

The euro faces its own structural questions. Monetary union without full fiscal union creates tension during downturns.[13] Divergent debt levels among member states strain political and fiscal solidarity when borrowing costs rise, and stability depends not only on confidence in individual governments, but also in shared institutional commitment.

The challenge is not unique to Europe. It reflects a broader reality confronting advanced economies: arrangements that function smoothly during periods of stability become harder to sustain when economic pressures intensify.

As risks rise, financial fragmentation becomes more likely. Trade blocs harden. Capital controls become increasingly common. Governments encourage domestic ownership of public debt to reduce external vulnerability. Financial flows that once moved freely become more conditional, reflecting changing perceptions of risk rather than sudden rupture.

These developments do not necessarily signal the collapse of the international system. They signal a shift toward greater caution. Trust that was once assumed increasingly requires reinforcement. Financial relationships that once operated automatically become more conditional as confidence recedes gradually, marking a shift from a system built on trust to one shaped increasingly by caution.

This is how the global dimension of the stability era begins to weaken. The change is not defined by a single crisis or dramatic event. It emerges as confidence slowly erodes, flexibility narrows, and relationships that once appeared permanent become subject to reassessment. What begins as domestic strain ultimately extends beyond national borders, reshaping the wider system that helped sustain stability for decades.

## *The Stability Era Ends*

The period that began in the early 1980s was shaped by conditions that are increasingly difficult to reproduce. Falling interest rates, expanding globalization, favourable demographics, rising asset values, and growing debt combined to create an environment in which economic disruptions could often be absorbed without fundamentally altering the system.

Those conditions helped sustain growth, support financial markets, and cushion recessions. They also encouraged assumptions that gradually became embedded in policy, investment decisions, and public expectations. Borrowing was expected to remain affordable. Asset values were expected to continue rising over time. Governments were expected to intervene when instability threatened. Future growth was expected to ease the burden of present commitments.

For much of this period, those expectations appeared reasonable because the underlying conditions continued to support them. The system delivered enough stability to reinforce confidence in its durability. Success came to be assumed.

The stability era does not end because a single crisis overwhelms the system. It ends because the conditions that supported it become progressively weaker. Debt levels rise while growth slows. Demographic support fades. Interest costs increase. Political divisions deepen. The tools that once postponed adjustment become less effective.

What changes first is not necessarily the appearance of the system, but its capacity. Governments can still borrow. Central banks can still intervene. Financial markets can still recover from periods of stress. Yet each response increasingly requires greater effort and produces smaller benefits than before.

The transition can be difficult to recognize because many features of the old system remain visible. Markets continue operating. Public institutions continue functioning. Elections are held. Budgets are passed. Economic activity continues. What changes is the amount of pressure required to maintain outcomes that once seemed routine.

The distinction is important. A system does not need to collapse in order to enter a new phase. It only needs to lose the ability to deliver the results that previously defined it.

The shift therefore unfolds gradually. Borrowing that once supported growth increasingly finances existing obligations. Intervention that once restored confidence increasingly preserves confidence temporarily. Political debates that once focused on distributing gains increasingly focus on distributing losses.

The adjustment is not driven by a lack of effort or expertise. It emerges because constraints become more visible and because promises accumulated during one era become harder to sustain in another. The issue is not intention. The issue is capacity.

This transformation affects more than economics. It alters expectations about living standards, retirement, public services, taxation, housing affordability, and social mobility. Assumptions formed over decades encounter conditions that no longer support them. The gap between expectation and reality becomes increasingly difficult to ignore.

For many people, this is the point at which economic change becomes personal. Plans that once appeared secure require revision. Opportunities that seemed automatic become less certain. Future outcomes depend less on continuing past trends and more on adapting to new conditions.

The result is not necessarily decline. Some societies adapt successfully. They recognize constraints early, adjust expectations, reform institutions, and accept difficult trade-offs before crisis forces action. Others delay adjustment until financial, political, or social pressures remove easier options.

History suggests that periods of transition often create opportunities as well as disruption. New industries emerge. Institutions evolve. Economic structures adapt. Yet adaptation requires recognition. It begins with understanding that the conditions which shaped one era may not shape the next.

That recognition marks the true end of the stability era. The challenge is no longer preserving a model built for a different set of circumstances. The challenge becomes navigating a world in which old assumptions carry less weight and future outcomes are shaped by choices made under more visible constraints.

The advanced world is entering that transition now. The process will not unfold uniformly, and it will not affect every country in the same way. But the direction is becoming increasingly difficult to ignore. The era in which debt expansion, declining interest rates, and repeated intervention could preserve stability without significant cost is drawing to a close.

What follows will be determined by how societies respond to that reality. Some will adapt gradually. Others may be forced into adjustment by events. In either case, the defining challenge of the years ahead will not be restoring the conditions of the past, but managing the transition to whatever comes next.

The stability era is ending. The question is no longer whether change is coming, but how successfully societies adapt once the assumptions that sustained the old order no longer hold. The scale of that adaptation extends well beyond economic policy.

The end of the stability era is not simply the conclusion of one economic period. It marks the beginning of another, shaped by higher uncertainty, more persistent constraints, and more difficult choices. Understanding that new environment requires looking beyond the institutions and assumptions of the past to the forces that will define the world after stability.

# 22

## THE WORLD AFTER STABILITY

Periods of stability often appear permanent while they last, yet history suggests that stability is rarely enduring. It is usually the product of favourable conditions that eventually shift before the underlying foundations begin to change. As those foundations evolve, what once appeared stable begins to reveal itself as contingent, dependent on conditions that cannot be assumed to persist indefinitely.

As the era of stability draws to a close, a more fractious and volatile world begins to take shape. For much of the period since the early 1980s, stability defined economic life in the advanced world. Inflation remained subdued, financial crises were contained, and downturns were typically followed by relatively quick recoveries. Governments borrowed at manageable interest rates, financial markets expanded, and central banks developed reputations as capable stewards of economic calm. For many households and businesses, this environment came to feel normal, even inevitable for an entire generation.

Yet this period was not simply the product of sound policy or good fortune. It reflected a unique combination of declining interest rates, expanding globalization, favourable demographics, relatively inexpensive energy, and the growing ability of governments and central banks to intervene during times of stress. Together, these forces created an environment in which many economic pressures could be absorbed without fundamentally altering the broader system.

What made the post-1980 period unusual was not the absence of economic pressures, but the ability of the system to absorb them without fundamentally changing its structure. Successive disruptions were managed, postponed, or contained. Over time, that experience encouraged the belief that stability itself had become a permanent feature of advanced economic life.

The stability that defined the advanced world after the early 1980s therefore reflected an unusual alignment of forces, one that shaped expectations but could not be assumed to persist indefinitely. Each of these conditions reinforced the others. Low borrowing costs encouraged rising debt, globalization helped contain inflation, favourable demographics supported economic growth, and repeated policy intervention reduced the immediate consequences of financial instability.

The result was an economic environment unlike most previous periods of modern history. The pressures that had constrained earlier generations appeared less significant, while governments and central banks acquired increasing confidence in their ability to manage instability through monetary and fiscal policy. That confidence gradually reshaped expectations.

The environment that emerged from these conditions shaped more than economic outcomes. It also shaped expectations. Policymakers assumed that future disruptions could be managed much as past ones had been. Investors became accustomed to repeated recoveries. Households planned around rising asset values and improving living standards.

Over time, this pattern shaped expectations. Stability came to be viewed not as a favourable set of circumstances but as a permanent feature of modern economic life. Institutions appeared capable of managing shocks, financial markets adapted to the expectation that liquidity would be available, and governments operated on the understanding that borrowing costs would remain manageable.

What emerged, however, was not stability as a permanent condition, but stability as an outcome that required increasing effort to sustain. Policies that once addressed temporary disruptions began to play a more continuous role in maintaining economic equilibrium. Stability came to depend less on underlying economic strength and more on ongoing intervention and favourable financial conditions.

The appearance of resilience remained, but preserving that resilience became progressively more demanding. The foundations supporting the system grew increasingly dependent on conditions that were already beginning to weaken. The world after stability begins where those conditions begin to change. Recognizing that shift is essential for what comes next.

## *The Model Beneath the Stability*

The stability of the post-1980 era did not sustain itself. It came to depend on expanding debt, persistent policy intervention, and the confidence that governments and central banks would continue to prevent serious disruptions. These measures proved effective for long periods, but they also altered the structure of the economic system in fundamental ways.

Each period of intervention solved an immediate problem while creating conditions that made future intervention more likely. Lower interest rates encouraged additional borrowing. Expanding debt increased the economy's sensitivity to borrowing costs. Financial markets became more reliant on central bank support during periods of uncertainty. Governments found it easier to postpone difficult fiscal decisions when borrowing remained inexpensive. Over time, these responses became less exceptional and more routine.

Debt accumulated across governments, corporations, and households. Financial markets became more sensitive to interest rates and central bank policy. Asset prices increasingly reflected expectations of continued monetary support, while economic growth became more dependent on borrowing and financial conditions than in earlier decades.

For a time, these developments appeared manageable because the broader environment remained supportive. Low borrowing costs reduced the pressure created by rising debt. Strong asset markets reinforced confidence. Growth, though often slower than in earlier decades, remained sufficient to postpone more difficult adjustments. Only much later did the underlying vulnerabilities become fully apparent as economic conditions became less favourable.

What once appeared to be stability now reveals itself as something more fragile. The system required continual support to maintain equilibrium, and the margin for error narrowed as imbalances accumulated. The foundations remained standing, but they became more dependent on conditions that could no longer be taken for granted.

This evolution was not the result of a single policy decision or one economic crisis. It developed through successive responses to changing circumstances, each of which appeared reasonable in isolation. Collectively, however, they created an economy increasingly reliant on favourable financial conditions.

Viewed in that light, the end of stability becomes easier to understand. Debt expanded. Demographic support weakened. Political consensus became harder to sustain. Financial markets grew more dependent on continued policy support. Taken together, these developments point toward a common conclusion: the conditions that made the stability era possible are giving way to a more demanding economic environment.

This does not mean that economic activity will cease or that prosperity will disappear. It does not imply the collapse of capitalism or the end of growth. Rather, the change underway is fundamental. The transition reflects the end of a particular economic regime rather than the end of capitalism, growth, or society itself. Everything that follows depends upon recognizing that distinction and acting upon it.

The stability era did not end because one crisis became too large to contain. It is ending because the conditions that sustained it are becoming progressively more difficult to maintain. That distinction is essential because it shifts attention away from individual events and towards the broader forces that are reshaping the economic landscape. Those forces are already changing the choices available to governments, businesses, and households in fundamental ways.

## *The End of Easy Choices*

The economic environment that supported decades of relatively predictable growth, declining interest rates, and expanding financial markets is giving way to a more demanding and less predictable world. Public debt has reached historically high levels, leaving governments with less freedom to respond to future crises. Central banks face the difficult task of controlling inflation while preserving financial stability. Demographic changes are slowing labour force growth across much of the advanced world, while geopolitical rivalry and supply chain disruption are reshaping trade and investment. Each of these pressures can be managed individually. What has changed is that they increasingly reinforce one another in powerful ways.

None of these developments is entirely new. Governments have always faced fiscal pressures. Economies have always been influenced by demographics, resource availability, technological change, and political uncertainty. What made the stability era exceptional was that favourable conditions made difficult economic choices easier to postpone. Borrowing remained inexpensive, growth continued, and financial markets generally recovered from periods of instability without requiring fundamental adjustment.

That environment is now changing. Higher debt makes rising interest rates more costly. Slower growth reduces the scope for expanding public expenditure. Ageing populations place increasing pressure on pensions, healthcare, and public finances. Geopolitical fragmentation raises costs while reducing some of the efficiencies created by globalization. None of these developments, on its own, determines the future. Together, however, they reduce the room for policy error and increase the consequences of poor economic decisions for years afterwards.

Economic policy therefore becomes more demanding. Governments must balance competing priorities with fewer financial resources and less flexibility than during much of the stability era. Central banks must weigh the risks of inflation against the risks of financial instability. Businesses face a more uncertain investment environment, while financial markets have become increasingly sensitive to changes in interest rates, public borrowing, and geopolitical events.

What is emerging is not a sudden break with the past, but the end of an environment in which governments, businesses, and financial markets repeatedly benefited from unusually favourable conditions. Borrowing becomes more expensive. Sustaining growth becomes more difficult. Demographic support weakens. Policy decisions carry greater consequences. The easy choices that characterized much of the stability era begin to disappear.

This does not mean that prosperity becomes unattainable or that economic progress comes to an end. It means that prosperity once again depends more heavily on productivity, innovation, sound institutions, disciplined public finances, and effective economic decision-making because favourable conditions no longer hide underlying weaknesses or make difficult decisions easier to postpone. The challenge is no longer simply to achieve prosperity, but to sustain it under more demanding conditions.

The end of easy choices is one of the defining characteristics of the world after stability. The question is no longer how unusually favourable conditions can be extended indefinitely. The question is how successfully governments, institutions, and markets respond as those conditions begin to fade. That is the economic environment now emerging. Its consequences are already becoming visible across the advanced economies.

## *A More Volatile Economic Landscape*

Every economic system operates within economic and political realities that cannot be ignored indefinitely. Fiscal conditions influence how much governments can borrow. Demographic trends shape the size and productivity of the workforce. Political institutions determine how societies respond to difficult trade-offs, while energy and resource availability influence production, investment, and long-term growth. Stability depends not on the absence of these pressures, but on the ability of economies to manage them successfully without creating larger problems.

For a time, unusually favourable conditions allowed many of these pressures to remain in the background. Declining interest rates reduced the cost of borrowing, expanding global trade lowered prices, and demographic expansion supported labour force growth and consumption. As these conditions changed, governments and institutions increasingly found themselves confronting realities that had long appeared distant.

The result is a more volatile economic environment. Volatility does not arise because one problem suddenly becomes overwhelming. It emerges because several long-term pressures begin operating simultaneously. Slower growth reduces government revenues. Higher debt limits fiscal flexibility. Demographic ageing increases public expenditure. Geopolitical rivalry disrupts trade and investment. Together, these developments leave governments and central banks with less room for error in responding to future crises.

The challenge for advanced economies is therefore no longer simply managing the next recession or responding to the next financial disruption. It is preserving long-term economic resilience in an environment where favourable conditions can no longer be assumed. Decisions that once produced limited consequences now carry greater significance because governments, businesses, and financial markets have less room for error. The room for policy error has narrowed.

This changing environment affects governments, businesses, and financial markets alike. Governments face increasing pressure to balance competing priorities with fewer financial resources and less policy flexibility. Businesses must make long-term investment decisions despite greater uncertainty about costs, supply chains, and global demand. Financial markets now respond more quickly to inflation, interest rates, government borrowing, and geopolitical events around the world.

Economic policy therefore becomes less about responding to short-term fluctuations and more about dealing with long-term structural pressures. Fiscal decisions carry greater long-term consequences, while monetary policy becomes more difficult as central banks balance the need to control inflation against the need to preserve financial stability. Governments, in turn, find themselves balancing competing priorities rather than pursuing objectives that once appeared mutually compatible.

Periods of stability are therefore likely to become shorter and recoveries more uneven than during the decades following the early 1980s. Economic expansions may prove less durable, while periods of adjustment become more frequent. These changes do not imply continuous crisis. They reflect an environment in which favourable conditions no longer offset underlying weaknesses as consistently as they once did.

Volatility, in this context, does not necessarily mean crisis. It means greater variation in economic outcomes. Financial markets may fluctuate more sharply. Government finances become more sensitive to changes in borrowing costs. Businesses face greater uncertainty when making long-term investment decisions. Policymakers operate in an environment where the consequences of decisions become less predictable and more difficult to reverse. Economic pressures rarely remain confined to the economy itself.

Political debate also changes. As economic choices become more constrained, disagreement over priorities becomes more pronounced. Questions that were once largely technical increasingly become political because they involve competing claims on limited public resources. Fiscal policy, taxation, pensions, healthcare, defence, industrial policy, and energy strategy all become subjects of more intense public debate.

The result is not necessarily a poorer society, but a society operating within a more demanding economic environment. Success depends less upon unusually favourable external conditions and more upon productivity, institutional strength, sound public finances, and the quality of economic decision-making. Stability becomes something that must be earned repeatedly rather than assumed or taken for granted.

This environment may feel unfamiliar because it differs from the exceptional conditions that shaped the stability era.. From a longer historical perspective, however, it represents a return to circumstances that earlier generations would have recognised more readily. Understanding that change is essential to understanding the world after stability.

## *Adapting to a Post-Stability World*

The transition to a post-stability world will not follow a single predictable path. History shows that prolonged periods of economic imbalance resolve themselves in different ways.

Inflation can reduce the real burden of accumulated debt. Governments may rely more heavily on financial repression, keeping interest rates below inflation for prolonged periods so that debt becomes easier to manage while savers lose purchasing power. Extended periods of weak growth can reduce existing imbalances, while in some cases restructuring or default becomes unavoidable. The path differs, but adjustment cannot be postponed indefinitely increasing the eventual cost.

History provides many examples of societies adapting to changing economic conditions. Some adjustments have been achieved through policy reform, institutional change, and improved productivity. Others have followed periods of financial or political strain. The route differs from one country to another, but the need to adapt remains constant.

The historical record also suggests that adjustment is rarely immediate. Britain emerged from the Napoleonic Wars carrying public debt exceeding 250 percent of national income, yet restored long-term stability over several decades through sustained economic growth, fiscal discipline, and institutional reform. Following the Second World War, many advanced economies reduced high debt burdens through a combination of growth, moderate inflation, and financial regulation. More recently, Japan has demonstrated that prolonged economic adjustment can extend over decades rather than years.

The precise course of adjustment depends upon political choices, institutional strength, and the broader international environment. What is already clear, however, is that preserving economic stability has become more demanding and requires more difficult decisions than at any time since the early 1980s. Those decisions will increasingly shape far more than economic outcomes. They will influence society more broadly.

The adjustment extends beyond economic policy because changing economic conditions eventually reshape political priorities, institutional behaviour, and the way governments allocate increasingly limited public resources. Fiscal policy, industrial strategy, energy security, defence spending, healthcare, pensions, and taxation become more closely interconnected as economic choices become more demanding.

The end of stability does not mark the end of innovation, economic progress, or rising living standards. It marks the beginning of an environment in which each depends more heavily upon productivity growth, institutional quality, fiscal discipline, technological progress, and sound economic decision-making than upon unusually favourable economic conditions.

Periods of adjustment have occurred repeatedly throughout economic history. Although the circumstances differ, the underlying pattern remains remarkably consistent. Economic systems eventually adapt to changing conditions because governments, institutions, and markets adjust to realities that can no longer be postponed.

In that sense, the transition now underway is neither unprecedented nor exceptional. What makes it significant is that it challenges the belief that advanced economies can indefinitely postpone the difficult adjustments that periodically accompany major economic change.

Recognizing this reality requires perspective rather than pessimism. Economic history is neither a story of uninterrupted progress nor one of inevitable decline. It is a record of societies adapting to changing circumstances through reform, innovation, institutional development, and economic renewal.

The long era of stability that shaped the modern advanced economy was genuine, but it was also exceptional. It depended upon a combination of favourable conditions that cannot be assumed to persist indefinitely. As those conditions weaken, the character of economic life changes with them.

The central question is therefore no longer whether advanced economies will change. They already are. The more important question is how effectively governments, institutions, and markets adapt to a more demanding economic environment. The answer will shape the world after stability.

No government can recreate the unusually favourable conditions that shaped the stability era. The challenge now is to respond successfully to a world where economic resilience depends less on favourable circumstances and more on the quality of decisions, institutions, and the capacity to adapt. That is the setting in which the world after stability will take shape.

## *The World After Stability*

The world after stability should not be understood as a prediction of one inevitable outcome. History includes periods of prolonged adjustment as well as episodes of severe economic disruption, most notably the Great Depression of the 1930s. Whether the coming decades resemble one experience more than another will depend upon decisions yet to be made and events that cannot be predicted with certainty. What can be stated with much greater confidence is that the economic environment itself has fundamentally changed.

That change is already visible. Growth has slowed across much of the advanced world. Public debt has reached historically high levels. Demographic support has weakened. Geopolitical rivalry is reshaping trade, investment, and national priorities. Governments face more difficult fiscal choices, while central banks operate with less freedom than they enjoyed during much of the stability era. None of these developments, viewed in isolation, determines the future. Taken together, however, they alter the conditions under which future prosperity will be achieved.

Different countries will respond to this environment in different ways. Those with strong institutions, sound public finances, adaptable economies, and effective leadership are likely to navigate the adjustment more successfully than those that continue relying on assumptions formed during more favourable times. Some economies will experience prolonged stagnation. Others will endure repeated financial or political crises before a new balance is established. A few may adapt more successfully than current expectations suggest. The outcomes will differ, but the environment in which they unfold has already changed.

This is why the end of stability matters. For more than four decades, unusually favourable conditions often made difficult economic choices easier to postpone. Declining interest rates reduced the cost of rising debt. Expanding globalization lowered costs and supported growth. Demographic trends strengthened labour markets and public finances. Repeated policy intervention helped contain successive crises before they threatened the broader system. As those conditions weaken, governments, businesses, financial markets, and institutions must operate without the same margin for error that existed during the stability era.

The world after stability is not defined by a single crisis, nor by uninterrupted decline. It is defined by the disappearance of the unusually favourable conditions that shaped the advanced economies throughout the stability era. Economic success increasingly depends upon productivity, innovation, sound institutions, disciplined public finances, and the quality of economic decision-making rather than favourable economic conditions alone.

The economic environment has changed. The adjustment has already begun. Understanding the implications of that adjustment is the final step in understanding the end of stability.

# 23

# THE COMING ECONOMIC RECKONING

The long era of stability is now drawing to a close. The economic reckoning is already taking shape. It is unfolding not because a single crisis suddenly changed the world, but because the exceptional combination of economic conditions that sustained that era no longer defines the advanced economies.

Beginning in the early 1980s, declining interest rates, expanding globalization, favourable demographic trends, relatively inexpensive energy, and repeated intervention by governments and central banks created an unusually supportive economic environment. Together, these conditions sustained economic growth, contained inflation, supported rising asset prices, encouraged expanding debt, and reinforced the belief that serious economic instability could usually be managed without fundamental change.

That period has now ended. Borrowing costs have risen from the exceptionally low levels that prevailed during much of the stability era. Public debt has reached historically high levels across many advanced economies. Population ageing is slowing labour force growth while placing increasing pressure on already strained public finances.

Globalization has given way to growing geopolitical rivalry, more fragmented supply chains, and renewed concern over economic and national security. Governments and central banks now operate under far more demanding conditions than those that prevailed during the stability era.

The conditions that shaped the stability era no longer define the advanced economies. They have given way to a less forgiving economic environment, one in which governments, businesses, and households face more difficult choices and policymakers have far less room for error.

History offers no single blueprint for what happens next. It includes prolonged periods of adjustment as well as episodes of severe economic disruption, most notably the Great Depression of the 1930s. Whether the coming decades resemble one experience more than another will depend upon the quality of institutions, political choices, technological progress, geopolitical developments, and events that cannot be predicted with certainty. What can be stated with confidence is that the environment in which future economic decisions will be made has fundamentally changed. That change is the economic reckoning already under way.

The reckoning is not one dramatic event waiting somewhere in the future. Nor is it a prediction that every advanced economy will follow the same path. It is the adjustment that follows when an exceptional economic era comes to an end. Some countries will adapt more successfully than others. Some may experience years of weak growth and recurring financial pressures. Others may face a much deeper economic crisis before a new economic balance is established. The outcomes will differ, but every advanced economy now confronts a more demanding environment than the one that shaped the stability era.

The question is therefore no longer whether the advanced economies are entering a different era. That transition has already begun. The more important question is how governments, businesses, and households respond to the challenges and opportunities presented by the more demanding world now taking shape in the years ahead.

The consequences of that adjustment extend well beyond governments and financial markets. They shape the everyday economic decisions of millions of people.

## *Living Through the Reckoning*

The economic reckoning is often described in terms of public debt, inflation, productivity, or financial markets. These measures help explain what is happening within the economy, but they do not explain how people experience it. The consequences of economic change are ultimately felt in everyday decisions: whether younger generations can afford to buy a home, whether families feel financially secure, whether businesses invest with confidence, and whether retirement appears more certain or more precarious than it once did. Those expectations did not develop by accident.

For much of the stability era, these decisions were made against a backdrop of unusually favourable economic conditions. Borrowing costs generally declined. Inflation remained relatively subdued. Globalization lowered the cost of many goods and services. Rising asset prices supported household wealth, while repeated policy intervention reinforced confidence that periods of economic disruption would prove temporary. These conditions shaped expectations because they shaped the economic environment in which those expectations were formed.

The economic reckoning changes those expectations because it changes the environment in which they were formed. Housing affordability has deteriorated across much of the advanced world. Saving for retirement has become more demanding. Younger generations often enter adulthood carrying higher housing costs, heavier debt burdens, and less confidence that they will enjoy the same economic opportunities as their parents. Many households already sense that something fundamental has changed, even if they cannot always identify its cause.

This is one reason why the reckoning has already begun. It is visible not only in government finances or central bank decisions, but in the growing gap between what many people expected economic life to provide and what it now delivers. Living standards no longer improve as consistently as they once did. Financial security often feels harder to achieve. Planning for the future requires greater caution because the assumptions that shaped the stability era have become less dependable.

Businesses experience the same change from a different perspective. During the stability era, efficiency, global integration, and minimizing costs often defined competitive success. The world now emerging places greater value on resilience alongside efficiency. Supply chains become more diversified. Energy security assumes greater importance. Financial strength, adaptability, and the capacity to withstand disruption increasingly become competitive advantages rather than desirable attributes.

Governments also face a different reality. Public expectations formed during the stability era increasingly collide with tighter fiscal conditions. Demands for better healthcare, pensions, defence, infrastructure, and public services continue to grow, yet the financial capacity to satisfy all of them simultaneously has become more limited. Choices that could once be postponed through borrowing increasingly require difficult political decisions affecting entire societies

The reckoning therefore extends well beyond economics. It challenges assumptions that became deeply embedded during the stability era. Expectations formed under exceptional conditions cannot guide decisions indefinitely once those conditions begin to unravel. Recognizing that reality is not pessimism. It is the beginning of successful adaptation.

This distinction is central to understanding the period now unfolding. Economic history shows that societies repeatedly adjust to changing conditions. The challenge is rarely whether adjustment occurs. It is whether it is recognized early enough for governments, businesses, and households to respond successfully. The economic reckoning has already begun. Understanding its implications is the first step toward adapting to the world that follows. The challenge lies not only in recognizing the change, but in responding to it successfully.

Every period of profound economic change ultimately becomes a test of judgment, leadership, and resilience. The coming economic reckoning will be no different.

## *The Choices Ahead*

The economic reckoning does not remove choice. It changes the nature of the choices available. During the stability era, favourable economic conditions often allowed difficult decisions to be postponed. Rising debt remained affordable while borrowing costs stayed low. Slower productivity growth attracted less attention while financial markets continued to expand. Structural weaknesses accumulated without immediately forcing fundamental change. That environment no longer exists.

Governments now face a more demanding set of decisions. Fiscal discipline competes with growing demands for public investment. Ageing populations increase spending on pensions and healthcare while reducing the growth of the workforce. National security, energy resilience, industrial policy, and infrastructure require resources at the same time that debt servicing absorbs an increasing share of public expenditure. Choices that once appeared separate have become increasingly interconnected across the economy.

Central banks confront a similar challenge. For much of the stability era, monetary policy operated in an environment of subdued inflation and declining interest rates. Today, controlling inflation, preserving financial stability, and supporting economic growth can no longer be pursued independently. Actions taken to achieve one objective now affect the others, making policy decisions more difficult and their consequences more significant.

Businesses also operate in a different environment. Efficiency alone is no longer sufficient. Supply chains, energy security, technological capability, and financial resilience have become central considerations alongside cost and profitability. Investment decisions increasingly reflect a world in which geopolitical risk, higher borrowing costs, and greater economic uncertainty are expected rather than exceptional.

The choices facing societies extend beyond economic policy. They involve the balance between present consumption and future investment, between borrowing and fiscal sustainability, between efficiency and resilience, and between short-term political priorities and long-term economic strength. None of these trade-offs is entirely new. What has changed is that they can no longer be deferred as easily as they were during the stability era.

History suggests that periods of major economic transition reward societies that recognize changing realities rather than those that attempt to preserve conditions that no longer exist. Successful adjustment has rarely depended upon avoiding change. It has depended upon adapting institutions, policies, and expectations to a different economic environment.

The coming decades will therefore be defined less by the pursuit of a return to the stability era than by the ability to respond effectively to the world that follows it. The economic reckoning is not a temporary interruption before normal conditions resume. It marks the beginning of a period in which economic success depends increasingly upon the quality of decisions made after the stability era has ended.

## *A Final Thought*

The long era of stability shaped the expectations of governments, businesses, financial markets, and households across much of the advanced world. Beginning in the early 1980s, declining interest rates, expanding globalization, favourable demographic trends, relatively inexpensive energy, and repeated policy intervention created an environment in which economic progress appeared increasingly secure and major disruptions seemed more manageable than they had been for previous generations despite growing imbalances.

The evidence presented throughout this book points to a different conclusion. The conditions that sustained that exceptional period no longer define the advanced economies. Borrowing costs have risen from the exceptionally low levels that prevailed during much of the stability era. Public debt has reached historically high levels, while population ageing has reduced one of the strongest sources of economic growth. Meanwhile, geopolitical rivalry has replaced much of the international cooperation that supported globalization between major economies.

Together, these changes have created a far more demanding environment for governments and central banks than the one they confronted during the stability era. They have also reshaped the conditions under which businesses invest, households plan for the future, and economies generate sustainable growth.

History offers no certainty about how this adjustment will unfold. It includes prolonged periods of adaptation as well as episodes of severe economic disruption, including the Great Depression of the 1930s. Which path individual countries ultimately follow will depend upon the strength of their institutions, the decisions they make, technological progress, and events that cannot be predicted with certainty. What history demonstrates, however, is that no economic era lasts indefinitely. Every period eventually gives way to another shaped by different conditions and different challenges.

The coming decades are therefore unlikely to resemble those that followed the early 1980s. Economic progress, innovation, and prosperity can no longer be assumed. Where they are achieved, they will be achieved under more demanding conditions than those that prevailed during the stability era. Growth will be harder to sustain. Public finances will remain under greater pressure. Governments will face more difficult choices. Financial markets will become less forgiving. Success will depend less upon unusually favourable circumstances and more upon productivity, sound institutions, disciplined public finances, and the quality of economic decision-making.

The outcomes will not be the same for every country. Some advanced economies will adapt successfully and continue to prosper. Others will struggle through years of weak growth, recurring financial pressures, and declining living standards. A few may experience a much deeper economic crisis before a new balance is established. The economic reckoning will be shared, but its consequences will depend largely on how successfully each society responds to a more demanding economic environment.

The end of stability does not mark the end of progress. It marks the end of an exceptional period in which favourable conditions made economic success easier to achieve and difficult choices easier to postpone. The economic reckoning has already begun. Its consequences will unfold over many years rather than through one defining event. The evidence examined throughout this book points towards one clear conclusion.

The future is not predetermined.

But it will be harder than the past.

# NOTES

## Introduction

1. Federal Reserve, Historical Data: Effective Federal Funds Rate. Peak policy rates occurred during the anti-inflation tightening cycle of the early 1980s.
2. World Bank, *World Development Indicators*. Global trade measured as a percentage of world GDP, 1980–2008.
3. Institute of International Finance, *Global Debt Monitor*. Figures include combined government, corporate, and household debt relative to global GDP.
4. Federal Reserve, *Financial Accounts of the United States*. Balance sheet expansion reflects policy responses following the 2008 financial crisis and pandemic-related interventions.
5. World Bank, *World Development Indicators*. Population aged 65 and older as a percentage of total population across advanced economies.

## 1 The Illusion of Prosperity

1. Organisation for Economic Co-operation and Development, *Housing Price Indicators*; World Bank, *World Development Indicators*. Data show house prices rising faster than incomes across major advanced economy cities, 2000–2023.
2. Federal Reserve Bank of St. Louis, FRED Database; U.S. Census Bureau, Income and Housing Data. Long-term trends in median house prices and median household income, 1980–2023.
3. Organisation for Economic Co-operation and Development, *Wealth Distribution Database*; World Inequality Database. Data highlight the concentration of financial asset ownership across advanced economies.
4. Bank for International Settlements, *Credit Statistics*; Institute of International Finance, *Global Debt Monitor*. Long-term debt-to-GDP trends across advanced economies

5. International Monetary Fund, *Global Financial Stability Report*. Analysis of asset price sensitivity to monetary policy and global liquidity conditions.
6. Organisation for Economic Co-operation and Development, *Housing Price Indicators*. Comparative affordability metrics across major metropolitan regions in advanced economies.

## 2 The Market Is Not the Economy

1. Standard & Poor's, *S&P 500 Historical Performance Data*. Total return reflects the increase from the 2009 trough to the 2021 peak.
2. United States Census Bureau, *Real Median Household Income*. Figures are adjusted for inflation.
3. Organisation for Economic Co-operation and Development, *Productivity Statistics*. Growth rates across advanced economies compared with late twentieth-century averages.
4. U.S. Small Business Administration, *Small Business Economic Profile*. Small firms account for approximately half of private-sector employment.
5. Federal Reserve, *Financial Accounts of the United States*. Balance sheet expansion reflects quantitative easing and crisis-era interventions.
6. S&P Global; Federal Reserve. Data on corporate share buybacks, 2010–2020.
7. Institute of International Finance, *Global Debt Monitor*. Post-pandemic update.

## 3 Stability That Cannot Hold

1. Federal Reserve, *Financial Accounts of the United States*. Balance sheet expansion reflects large-scale asset purchases following the 2008 financial crisis and the COVID-19 pandemic.
2. Organisation for Economic Co-operation and Development, *Housing Affordability Indicators*. Price-to-income ratios compared with long-term averages across advanced economies.
3. International Monetary Fund, *Fiscal Monitor*; *World Economic Outlook*. Public debt figures represent general government gross debt across advanced economies.
4. Organisation for Economic Co-operation and Development; national household finance surveys. Estimates reflect the share of

households lacking sufficient liquid savings to cover unexpected expenses.

5. Organisation for Economic Co-operation and Development, *Productivity Statistics*. Long-term growth comparisons across advanced economies.
6. Congressional Budget Office, *Long-Term Budget Outlook*. Projections based on current policy assumptions for federal interest payments.

## 4 The Age of Easy Money

1. Bank for International Settlements; International Monetary Fund, monetary policy data. Policy rates in advanced economies remained near zero for an extended period following the 2008 financial crisis, longer than in previous tightening cycles.
2. Federal Reserve, Historical Federal Funds Rate. The target rate remained near zero from late 2008 through late 2015.
3. Federal Reserve, *Financial Accounts of the United States*. The Federal Reserve's balance sheet expanded from approximately $900 billion in 2007 to over $4 trillion by 2014, reflecting quantitative easing.
4. World Trade Organization; World Bank, global trade data. Global trade contracted sharply during the 2008–2009 financial crisis.
5. World Trade Organization, *Merchandise Trade Volume Statistics*. World merchandise trade fell by roughly 12 percent in 2009.
6. Organisation for Economic Co-operation and Development; Bank for International Settlements, household debt and income data. Household debt levels rose relative to income across advanced economies following the financial crisis.
7. International Monetary Fund; World Bank, real interest rate data. Inflation exceeded deposit rates across many advanced economies during the 2010s, resulting in negative real returns.
8. S&P Global; MSCI, equity index data. Major indices, including the S&P 500, more than doubled between 2009 and 2019.
9. Organisation for Economic Co-operation and Development; Bank for International Settlements, housing market data. Price-to-income ratios and housing affordability pressures increased across major advanced economy cities.
10. Institute of International Finance, *Global Debt Monitor*. Global debt exceeded 350 percent of GDP in the early 2020s.

11. International Monetary Fund, sovereign debt data. Government debt levels in several advanced economies reached or exceeded post–World War II peaks.

## 5 Where the Money Actually Goes

1. International Monetary Fund, *World Economic Outlook Database*; World Bank, *World Development Indicators*. Data reflect broad real GDP growth trends across advanced and high-income economies in recent decades.
2. Institute of International Finance, *Global Debt Monitor*. Estimates place global debt at approximately $348 trillion by the end of 2025.
3. Institute of International Finance, *Global Debt Monitor*. Debt-to-GDP figures refer to the combined total of government, corporate, and household debt relative to global output.
4. Federal Reserve; European Central Bank; Bank of Japan; Bank of England. Combined balance sheets expanded significantly following successive rounds of quantitative easing after the global financial crisis and the COVID-19 pandemic.
5. Federal Reserve, *Financial Accounts of the United States*; Federal Reserve Bank of St. Louis, FRED Database (WALCL series). Data track total Federal Reserve assets over time.
6. Federal Reserve; European Central Bank; Bank of England; Bank of Japan, policy rate data. Data reflect the prolonged near-zero interest rate environment following the global financial crisis.
7. Bloomberg. The global stock of negative-yielding debt exceeded $15 trillion in 2019.
8. S&P Dow Jones Indices. Historical total return data for major equity benchmarks show substantial gains following the 2009 market trough.
9. Organisation for Economic Co-operation and Development, *Housing Affordability and Price-to-Income Indicators*; International Monetary Fund, *Finance & Development*, *"Housing Costs Mount."* Data show house prices rising significantly relative to incomes across many advanced economies.
10. S&P Dow Jones Indices; Federal Reserve, corporate financial accounts. Data support the sustained rise in corporate share buybacks following the global financial crisis.

## 6 Living on Borrowed Time

1. Bank for International Settlements, *Credit to the Non-Financial Sector.* Data track total credit to governments, households, and non-financial corporations across advanced economies.
2. Organisation for Economic Co-operation and Development, *Productivity and Income Indicators.* Data show weak productivity growth and subdued real income gains across several advanced economies following the early 2000s and the 2008 financial crisis.
3. Federal Reserve Bank of St. Louis, *Federal Debt: Total Public Debt as Percent of GDP.* U.S. federal debt stood near 30 percent of GDP around 1980 and rose significantly in subsequent decades.
4. Eurostat, *Government Finance Statistics.* Euro area government debt increased materially after the global financial crisis and remained elevated in later years.
5. International Monetary Fund, *Productivity Developments in Advanced Economies.* Research documents a sustained slowdown in productivity growth following the global financial crisis.
6. Organisation for Economic Co-operation and Development, *Global Debt Report 2025.* The report highlights the expansion of corporate borrowing and debt-market activity, including increased issuance in advanced economies.
7. Organisation for Economic Co-operation and Development, *Ageing Populations: Fiscal Implications and Policy Responses.* Analysis projects rising fiscal pressures associated with demographic ageing.
8. Organisation for Economic Co-operation and Development, *Household Debt Indicator.* Data show household debt exceeding 100 percent of disposable income in several advanced economies.
9. Federal Reserve, *Monetary Policy Reports and Historical Data.* Post-crisis policy reflects a significant expansion in central bank intervention and balance-sheet measures.
10. Federal Reserve, *Financial Accounts of the United States.* The Federal Reserve's balance sheet expanded from roughly $900 billion before the global financial crisis to approximately $9 trillion by 2022.
11. International Monetary Fund; Organisation for Economic Co-operation and Development, productivity and growth studies. Both institutions document weaker trend growth and slower productivity performance across advanced economies in the post-crisis period.

12. International Monetary Fund; Organisation for Economic Co-operation and Development, debt sustainability analyses. These studies show that borrowing can stabilize downturns while increasing vulnerability when debt burdens persist and refinancing conditions tighten.

## 7 The Hidden Cost of Stability

1. Organisation for Economic Co-operation and Development; World Bank, inflation, real wages, and housing indicators. Data covering advanced economies, 2020–2023.
2. Office for National Statistics, *Consumer Price Inflation and Real Wage Data*. United Kingdom, 2020–2023.
3. Office for National Statistics, *House Price Index and Median Earnings*. Long-run housing affordability trends in the United Kingdom.
4. Bank for International Settlements, real yield trends in advanced economies. Post–global financial crisis developments.
5. International Monetary Fund, *Global Financial Stability Report*. Sovereign bond yields relative to inflation.
6. Bank for International Settlements, negative-yielding debt estimates. Global totals during the low-rate period, including 2020.
7. Federal Reserve, *Treasury Inflation-Protected Securities (TIPS) Yield Data*. Real yield trends, 2011–2021.
8. Institute of International Finance, *Global Debt Monitor*. Total debt-to-GDP across government, corporate, and household sectors.
9. Federal Reserve; European Central Bank, policy rate data. Monetary policy trends following the 2008 financial crisis.
10. Federal Reserve, *Financial Accounts of the United States*. Central bank balance sheet expansion.
11. Institute of International Finance, *Global Debt Monitor*. Global debt trends, 2008–2023.
12. Federal Reserve, *Distributional Financial Accounts*. Equity ownership concentration across households.
13. Organisation for Economic Co-operation and Development, *Housing Affordability Indicators*. Comparative data across major global cities.
14. Organisation for Economic Co-operation and Development; Bank for International Settlements, pension fund asset allocation trends. Advanced economies.

15. Congressional Budget Office, interest cost sensitivity analysis. U.S. federal debt and interest rate changes.
16. Organisation for Economic Co-operation and Development, *Productivity Growth Data*. Trends across advanced economies.
17. International Monetary Fund; Bank for International Settlements, global monetary tightening cycle. Developments from 2021–2023.

## 8 Profits Without Production

1. Bureau of Economic Analysis; Federal Reserve Economic Data. U.S. corporate profits as a share of GDP, postwar to present.
2. Federal Reserve Economic Data; Penn World Table. Labour share of national income in the United States.
3. Bureau of Labor Statistics; Economic Policy Institute. Trends in productivity growth and median real wages.
4. S&P Dow Jones Indices, *S&P 500 Buybacks Report*. Aggregate share repurchases, 2010–2022.
5. Federal Reserve, *Financial Accounts of the United States (Z.1)*. Non-financial corporate debt as a share of GDP.
6. Bureau of Economic Analysis. Recovery in U.S. non-residential fixed investment following the 2008 financial crisis.
7. S&P Dow Jones Indices, *S&P 500 Buybacks Report*. Total share repurchases exceeding $6 trillion between 2010 and 2022.
8. Organisation for Economic Co-operation and Development; International Monetary Fund. Decline in labour's share of income alongside rising corporate margins across advanced economies.
9. Federal Reserve, *Survey of Consumer Finances*. Distribution of equity ownership by wealth percentile in the United States.
10. Organisation for Economic Co-operation and Development; Bank for International Settlements. Household debt as a share of disposable income across advanced economies.

## 9 When Saving No Longer Works

1. Organisation for Economic Co-operation and Development, *Historical Interest Rate Statistics*; World Bank, *World Development Indicators*. Real interest rates across advanced economies were generally positive during the postwar period through the early 1980s.

2. Federal Reserve, Historical Data: Federal Funds Rate. Policy rates were reduced to near zero following the 2008 financial crisis and remained exceptionally low for an extended period.
3. Bank for International Settlements, *Long-Term Interest Rate Statistics*. Ten-year government bond yields in advanced economies remained within a low range between 2009 and 2021.
4. Organisation for Economic Co-operation and Development, *Economic Outlook*. Inflation in advanced economies frequently exceeded returns on deposits and short-term government securities during the post-crisis low-rate period.
5. Bank for International Settlements, *Global Debt Statistics*; International Monetary Fund, *Global Debt Database*. Both datasets document the sustained rise in public and private debt across advanced economies since the 1980s.
6. Organisation for Economic Co-operation and Development, *Pensions at a Glance*. Long-term return assumptions for pension funds in advanced economies historically ranged between 6 and 8 percent.
7. Bank for International Settlements, *Long-Term Interest Rate Statistics*. Government bond yields in advanced economies declined significantly following the global financial crisis, with several jurisdictions experiencing near-zero or negative yields.

## 10 The Housing Divide

1. Organisation for Economic Co-operation and Development; Federal Reserve, *Survey of Consumer Finances*. Housing consistently represents the largest component of household wealth across advanced economies.
2. Bank for International Settlements; Organisation for Economic Co-operation and Development. Long-run housing valuation data show that house price-to-income ratios in advanced economies typically ranged between three and four times income during the postwar decades.
3. Federal Reserve, Historical Mortgage Rate Data; Bank for International Settlements, *Long-Term Interest Rate Statistics*. Mortgage rates in advanced economies declined from double-digit levels in the early 1980s to low single digits following the global financial crisis.

4. Organisation for Economic Co-operation and Development, *Housing Price Indicators*; Bank for International Settlements, *Property Price Statistics*. House price-to-income ratios increased significantly across advanced economies from the 1990s onward, with many countries experiencing a doubling of valuations.
5. Bank for International Settlements; International Monetary Fund. Cross-country housing market studies show that global housing price cycles display strong synchronicity not fully explained by local supply or demographic factors.
6. Bank for International Settlements, *Global Debt Statistics*; Organisation for Economic Co-operation and Development, *Household Debt Indicators*. Mortgage debt as a share of GDP rose substantially across advanced economies from the 1990s onward.
7. Organisation for Economic Co-operation and Development, *Housing Affordability Indicators*; Office for National Statistics. Deposit requirements and house prices increased faster than household savings and incomes in many advanced economies.
8. Organisation for Economic Co-operation and Development, *Housing Cost Overburden Rate*; Eurostat. Housing costs frequently exceed 30 percent of disposable income for renters in major urban areas across advanced economies.
9. Bank for International Settlements, *Credit Statistics*; European Central Bank. Residential mortgage lending represents the largest share of household and bank lending exposure in most advanced economies.
10. Organisation for Economic Co-operation and Development; International Monetary Fund. Household wealth and financial stability data show that housing remains a dominant asset in household balance sheets and a critical component of financial system collateral structures.

## 11 The Great Expansion of Inequality

1. Federal Reserve, *Distributional Financial Accounts* (2023). The top 10 percent of U.S. households hold approximately 85 to 90 percent of equities, while the bottom 50 percent hold only a minimal share.
2. World Bank; Organisation for Economic Co-operation and Development. Data show that since 2008, equity markets in

advanced economies have significantly outpaced median real wage growth.

3. Bank for International Settlements, *Unconventional Monetary Policy Tools* (2019). Quantitative easing became a central policy tool after the global financial crisis.
4. International Monetary Fund, *Global Financial Stability Report*. Lower interest rates increase the discounted value of future cash flows, supporting higher asset valuations.
5. Federal Reserve, *Survey of Consumer Finances* (2022). Equity ownership remains highly concentrated among higher-income households.
6. World Bank; International Monetary Fund. Post-2008 recovery patterns show strong asset price growth relative to income growth across advanced economies.
7. Organisation for Economic Co-operation and Development, *Housing Affordability Indicators* (2023). House price-to-income ratios in many advanced economies exceed pre-2008 levels.
8. International Monetary Fund, *World Economic Outlook* (2023). Public debt levels exceed 100 percent of GDP in several advanced economies.
9. Bank for International Settlements, *Annual Economic Report* (2022). Prolonged low interest rates and asset purchases have increased financial market sensitivity to policy changes.
10. International Monetary Fund; World Bank. Data indicate that advanced economy stabilization since the 1980s has relied on fiscal expansion, monetary intervention, and institutional credibility.

## 12 The Productivity Paradox

1. Bureau of Labor Statistics, Labor Productivity and Costs; Economic Policy Institute, *The Productivity–Pay Gap*.
2. Federal Reserve, *Financial Accounts of the United States*; World Bank, *Global Debt Database*.
3. Bank of England, *Household Debt Statistics*; Office for National Statistics, *UK Sector Financial Accounts*.
4. Organisation for Economic Co-operation and Development, *Productivity Statistics*; Deutsche Bundesbank, *Wage Developments in Germany*.

5. Office for National Statistics, *Labour Productivity and Earnings Data*; Organisation for Economic Co-operation and Development, *Real Wage Growth Statistics*.
6. General Motors, historical employment data; U.S. Bureau of Economic Analysis, industrial employment records.
7. Apple; Microsoft; Alphabet, annual reports and employment filings (latest available data).
8. Federal Reserve; European Central Bank; Bank of England, monetary policy and quantitative easing programmes, 2008–2021.
9. Federal Reserve, *Balance Sheet* (H.4.1 Release).
10. S&P Dow Jones Indices; U.S. Census Bureau, *Real Median Household Income*.
11. International Monetary Fund, *World Economic Outlook*; World Bank, *Global Debt Database*.
12. International Monetary Fund, *Fiscal Monitor*; Organisation for Economic Co-operation and Development, *General Government Debt Statistics*.
13. Organisation for Economic Co-operation and Development, *Housing Price Database*; Bank for International Settlements, *Property Price Statistics*.

## 13 The Demographic Breaking Point

1. United Nations, *World Population Prospects 2022*. Dependency ratios, United Nations Department of Economic and Social Affairs (2022).
2. Organisation for Economic Co-operation and Development, *Fertility Rates (Total Fertility Rate per Woman)*; World Bank, *Fertility Rate, Total (Births per Woman)*, 2023–2024.
3. National Bureau of Statistics of China, *Population Decline Report* (2023); United Nations, *World Population Prospects 2022*.
4. Statistics Bureau of Japan, *Population Estimates and Labour Force Data* (2023); Organisation for Economic Co-operation and Development, *Old-Age Dependency Ratios* (2023).
5. Organisation for Economic Co-operation and Development, *Labour Force Growth and Economic Output Trends* (2022).
6. Statistics Bureau of Japan, *Labour Force Survey and Population Data* (2023).

7. International Monetary Fund, *Japan: Article IV Consultation Report* (2023); Bank of Japan, monetary policy and government bond data (2023).
8. Bank for International Settlements, *Quarterly Review*. Global long-term interest rate trends (2022).
9. International Monetary Fund, *Global Financial Stability Report* (2019); Bank for International Settlements, real interest rate developments (2021).
10. Bank for International Settlements, *Property Price Statistics*; Organisation for Economic Co-operation and Development, *Housing Prices to Income Indicators* (2023).
11. Organisation for Economic Co-operation and Development, *International Migration Outlook* (2023); Government of Canada, Immigration Levels Plan; Australian Bureau of Statistics, migration and population growth data (2023).

## 14 Democracy Meets Arithmetic

1. Organisation for Economic Co-operation and Development, *Economic Outlook* (2023); World Bank, *World Development Indicators*. Long-term GDP growth trends across advanced economies show a decline from approximately 3 percent (1970s–1990s) to around 1 to 2 percent in recent years.
2. United Nations, *World Population Prospects 2022*. Projections show populations aged 65 and older rising from approximately 20 percent to around 25 percent in many advanced economies by 2040.
3. International Monetary Fund, *Fiscal Monitor* (2021–2023). Advanced economy debt rose sharply following both the global financial crisis and the COVID-19 pandemic.
4. North Atlantic Treaty Organization, *Defence Expenditure Reports* (2023–2024). Multiple European members committed to spending at or above 2 percent of GDP.
5. International Monetary Fund, *World Economic Outlook Database* (2023); Bank for International Settlements. Debt-to-GDP levels in advanced economies are at or near post–World War II highs.
6. European Commission, *Economic Adjustment Programmes*; International Monetary Fund, country reports (Greece, Spain, Italy). Austerity measures were associated with electoral turnover and political instability.

7. International Monetary Fund, *Fiscal Monitor: Database of Country Fiscal Measures in Response to COVID-19*. Several advanced economies deployed fiscal support exceeding 10 percent of GDP.
8. International Monetary Fund, *World Economic Outlook Database* (2023); World Bank. U.S. and several European economies exceed 100 percent debt-to-GDP, while Japan exceeds 250 percent.
9. Congressional Budget Office, *Budget and Economic Outlook* (2024). Net interest outlays are projected to become one of the largest federal spending categories.
10. Organisation for Economic Co-operation and Development, *Pensions at a Glance* (2023). Old-age dependency ratios are rising across advanced economies due to ageing populations.
11. International Monetary Fund, *World Economic Outlook* (2022–2023); Organisation for Economic Co-operation and Development. Inflation reached multi-decade highs across advanced economies following the pandemic.
12. Bank for International Settlements, *Annual Economic Report* (2023). Rising yields increase sovereign refinancing costs and fiscal vulnerability.
13. World Bank, *Global Economic Prospects* (2024); International Monetary Fund. Structural slowdown, demographic pressures, deglobalisation trends, and rising debt burdens are widely documented across advanced economies.

## 15 When Energy Becomes the Limit

1. World Bank, *World Development Indicators*. Global GDP (current USD) shows output rising from approximately $23 trillion in 1990 to over $87 trillion by 2019, more than doubling in both real and nominal terms.
2. Eurostat; European Central Bank, inflation decomposition data (2022). Data show that energy contributed over 50 percent of headline inflation in several euro area economies during peak price shocks.
3. Ofgem; Office for National Statistics. United Kingdom household energy price data show typical annual bills rising from approximately £1,100 before 2021 to over £2,500 to £3,000 in 2022–2023.
4. BASF, corporate announcements and investor briefings (2022–2023). Data indicate that structurally high European energy costs

contributed to reduced domestic operations and increased investment in lower-cost regions, including China.

5. International Monetary Fund; Organisation for Economic Co-operation and Development. Historical inflation and growth data show that the oil shocks of the 1970s triggered simultaneous increases in inflation and unemployment across advanced economies.
6. U.S. Energy Information Administration; Federal Reserve Bank of St. Louis. Historical gasoline price data and recession timelines show repeated slowdowns associated with sustained gasoline prices above $4 per gallon, including inflation-adjusted comparisons.
7. International Energy Agency, *Gas Market Report* (2022–2023). Global LNG prices surged sharply as European demand increased following reduced Russian pipeline supply.
8. World Bank; International Energy Agency. Reports on energy access disruptions (2022–2023) document fuel shortages and electricity outages in emerging economies due to LNG market tightening.
9. Bank for International Settlements; International Monetary Fund. Long-term data show declining interest rates and rising debt levels across advanced economies from the 1980s to the 2020s.
10. International Energy Agency, *World Energy Outlook 2023*. Identifies tightening supply conditions, geopolitical fragmentation, and investment constraints as structural features of modern energy markets.
11. International Monetary Fund, *Fiscal Monitor* (2023–2024). Rising interest rates significantly increase debt servicing burdens for high-debt advanced economies.

## 16 When Stability Becomes Fragility

1. Bank for International Settlements; International Monetary Fund. Long-term data on total debt across advanced economies show combined public and private debt rising from roughly 120 to 140 percent of GDP in the early 1980s to over 250 percent by the early 2020s.
2. Chicago Board Options Exchange, *VIX Index Historical Data*. Sustained low volatility between 2004 and 2007 relative to long-term averages.

3. Federal Reserve Bank of St. Louis, *Household Debt Data*. U.S. household debt rose from approximately 80 percent of GDP in the late 1990s to near 100 percent by 2007.
4. Institute of International Finance; International Monetary Fund, *Global Debt Database*. Global debt reached levels above 320 percent of global GDP by 2019.
5. International Monetary Fund, *Fiscal Monitor*. Public debt in many advanced economies exceeded 100 percent of GDP outside wartime periods by the late 2010s.
6. S&P Dow Jones Indices; Federal Reserve Bank of St. Louis. Global equity markets fell by more than 30 percent in early 2020 during the onset of the COVID-19 pandemic.
7. Federal Reserve, *Balance Sheet Data*. Central bank assets expanded from under 20 percent of GDP before 2020 to over 35 percent within one year following pandemic interventions.
8. Historical market data on the U.S. equity market collapse during the Wall Street Crash of 1929. Equity markets declined by approximately 89 percent from peak to trough between 1929 and 1932.
9. International Monetary Fund. Fiscal arithmetic based on debt servicing dynamics shows that a 2 percentage point increase in borrowing costs on debt levels of 120 percent of GDP results in approximately 2.4 percent of GDP in additional annual interest burden.
10. International Monetary Fund; Organisation for Economic Co-operation and Development. Public debt levels in advanced economies commonly exceeded 100 percent of GDP by the early 2020s.
11. World Bank; Organisation for Economic Co-operation and Development. Demographic data show ageing populations across advanced economies increasing dependency ratios and fiscal pressure on pensions and healthcare systems.

## 17 When Trust Breaks, Stability Fractures

1. Bank for International Settlements; International Monetary Fund. Long-term data on total public and private debt across advanced economies show levels rising to historically elevated levels relative to output by the early 2020s.

2. Congressional Budget Office; Federal Reserve Bank of St. Louis. U.S. federal debt held by the public rose from approximately 35 percent of GDP in 2007 to around 100 percent in the early 2020s.
3. Office for National Statistics; Nationwide Building Society. United Kingdom housing affordability data show house prices rising from roughly 3 to 4 times earnings in the 1980s to around 8 times earnings in recent years.
4. Organisation for Economic Co-operation and Development; International Monetary Fund. Housing price data across major advanced economies show prices rising faster than incomes following the 2008 financial crisis and again after the 2020 pandemic.
5. Federal Reserve, *Balance Sheet Data*. Central bank assets expanded from under $1 trillion before 2008 to over $8 trillion following pandemic-era interventions.
6. Bank of England. Market reports and policy actions during the 2022 United Kingdom gilt crisis document sharp increases in government bond yields and central bank intervention to stabilize pension fund exposures.
7. Organisation for Economic Co-operation and Development; Pew Research Center. Data show increased support for populist and anti-establishment movements in advanced economies following the 2008 crisis and during periods of weak income growth.
8. Federal Reserve; Federal Deposit Insurance Corporation. Reports on the 2023 U.S. regional banking stress document rapid intervention to stabilize deposits and liquidity conditions.
9. International Monetary Fund; World Bank. Public debt data show advanced economy debt levels reaching historical highs relative to peacetime norms.
10. European Central Bank; International Monetary Fund. Analysis of the Eurozone sovereign debt crisis (2010–2012) documents rising borrowing costs and central bank intervention to stabilize markets.
11. World Bank; Organisation for Economic Co-operation and Development. Demographic data show ageing populations increasing pension and healthcare obligations across advanced economies.

## 18 The Breaking of the Old Model

1. Bank for International Settlements; International Monetary Fund. Long-term data show total debt across advanced economies rising to historically high levels relative to GDP by the early 2020s, while policy interest rates approached lower bounds after decades of decline.
2. International Monetary Fund; Organisation for Economic Co-operation and Development. Historical policy rate data show rates in double digits in the early 1980s declining to near zero or negative levels in advanced economies by the 2010s.
3. International Monetary Fund. Inflation data for the period commonly referred to as the Great Moderation show stabilization around 2 percent in many advanced economies.
4. Federal Reserve; European Central Bank. Policy responses after 2008 included near-zero interest rates and large-scale asset purchase programmes to stabilize financial systems.
5. International Monetary Fund. Fiscal data confirm that public debt exceeded 100 percent of GDP in several advanced economies by the early 2020s.
6. World Bank; Organisation for Economic Co-operation and Development. Demographic data show fertility rates below replacement levels across most advanced economies.
7. Organisation for Economic Co-operation and Development. Ageing population data show rising pension and healthcare expenditure obligations in advanced economies.
8. International Monetary Fund. Post-2008 inflation data show persistently subdued inflation despite accommodative monetary policy.
9. Bank for International Settlements. Long-term analysis shows falling interest rates offsetting rising debt burdens across advanced economies for several decades.
10. International Monetary Fund; World Bank. Data confirm high debt levels across public and private sectors in advanced economies by the early 2020s.
11. International Monetary Fund. Historical analysis of debt cycles shows turning points when rising debt and constrained policy flexibility limit stabilization options.

## 19 When Long Stagnations End

1. Institute of International Finance; International Monetary Fund. Global debt data show total debt rising to more than three times global output by the early 2020s.
2. Organisation for Economic Co-operation and Development; World Bank. Productivity data show growth in advanced economies since 2008 averaging significantly below the pace observed between 1980 and 2007.
3. Federal Reserve; S&P Dow Jones Indices. Corporate finance data show large-scale debt issuance alongside substantial share buybacks by U.S. corporations between 2009 and 2019.
4. Federal Reserve; International Monetary Fund. The 2013 taper tantrum saw sharp increases in bond yields and capital outflows following signals of reduced asset purchases.
5. Federal Reserve; Bank for International Settlements. The 2018 tightening cycle coincided with equity market declines and widening credit spreads.
6. Federal Reserve; Federal Deposit Insurance Corporation. The 2022–2023 tightening cycle exposed vulnerabilities in banking systems, including failures among U.S. regional banks.
7. Institute of International Finance. Global debt levels exceeded three times global output by the early 2020s.
8. International Monetary Fund; World Bank. Public debt in advanced economies reached levels comparable to those observed after the Second World War.
9. Federal Reserve; International Monetary Fund. Episodes of policy tightening in 2013, 2018, and 2022–2023 triggered significant financial market reactions.
10. European Central Bank; International Monetary Fund. Analysis of the Eurozone debt crisis beginning in 2010 documents rising sovereign borrowing costs and intervention to stabilize markets.
11. The Great Depression. The economic collapse of the 1930s led to major banking reforms and changes in monetary and fiscal policy frameworks.
12. International Monetary Fund. Post-war data show public debt reduction through a combination of growth, moderate inflation, and controlled interest rates between the late 1940s and 1960s.

13. The Global Financial Crisis. The crisis led to bank recapitalization, regulatory reform, and large-scale monetary intervention across advanced economies.
14. Organisation for Economic Co-operation and Development; Pew Research Center. Data show uneven wage growth and rising perceptions of inequality across advanced economies during the 2010s.
15. Institute of International Finance; World Bank. Global data confirm total debt exceeding three times annual output by the early 2020s.

## 20 The Sequence of Systemic Breakdown

1. International Monetary Fund; World Bank. Data show advanced economy debt levels significantly higher in the early 2020s than prior to the Global Financial Crisis.
2. Bank of Japan; International Monetary Fund. Japan's late 1980s asset bubble was characterized by rapid credit expansion and elevated property and equity valuations relative to fundamentals.
3. Federal Reserve; European Central Bank. Central bank balance sheets expanded significantly after 2008 and again during the COVID-19 pandemic and have remained structurally elevated.
4. Bank runs during the Great Depression. Banking crises in the early 1930s involved widespread depositor withdrawals that destabilized financial institutions.
5. The Global Financial Crisis. Early stress during the crisis included tightening in short-term funding markets before major institutional failures.
6. Bank of England. The 2022 United Kingdom gilt crisis involved sharp yield increases and forced intervention to stabilize pension funds using leveraged strategies.
7. Federal Reserve; Bank for International Settlements. Data show the freezing of interbank and short-term funding markets during the 2008 financial crisis.
8. Bank of England. Pension fund liquidity stress in the United Kingdom in 2022 required central bank intervention to prevent forced asset sales.
9. European Central Bank; International Monetary Fund. The Eurozone sovereign debt crisis beginning in 2010 involved rising sovereign borrowing costs driven by declining confidence.

10. Bank of Japan. Japan's post-1990 economic period featured prolonged low growth, low interest rates, and rising public debt.
11. European Central Bank. Fiscal tightening and rising borrowing costs during the Eurozone crisis led to economic contraction in several member states.
12. Pew Research Center; Organisation for Economic Co-operation and Development. Data show increasing political polarization and declining institutional trust in advanced economies, particularly after 2008.
13. Bank of England. Market reactions to fiscal announcements in the United Kingdom in 2022 triggered sharp increases in bond yields and policy intervention.
14. Bank of Japan. Long-term policy in Japan reflects sustained monetary intervention and rising public debt following the collapse of its asset bubble.
15. Abandonment of the gold standard during the Great Depression. Countries left the gold standard to regain monetary flexibility.
16. The Bretton Woods Conference. The post-war monetary system established fixed exchange rates and shaped global financial architecture until its collapse in the 1970s.

## 21 The Stability Era Breaks

1. U.S. Congressional Budget Office; Federal Reserve Economic Data. Gross federal debt in the United States is near 120 percent of GDP in recent years, while Japan's public debt exceeds 250 percent of GDP according to International Monetary Fund; World Bank data.
2. U.S. Congressional Budget Office, *Budget and Economic Outlook* (2024). Federal net interest payments are projected to approach or exceed $1 trillion annually within the coming decade.
3. International Monetary Fund, *Fiscal Monitor* (2023–2024). Rising borrowing costs are increasing debt servicing pressures in high-debt European economies, including Italy and France.
4. Bank for International Settlements; Institute of International Finance. Long-term data show total debt across advanced economies rising faster than GDP since the 1990s.
5. International Monetary Fund; Organisation for Economic Co-operation and Development. Inflation surged across advanced economies following pandemic-related disruptions and was

amplified by energy and food shocks after the Russian invasion of Ukraine in 2022.

6. United Nations; Organisation for Economic Co-operation and Development. Demographic data show dependency ratios in advanced economies rising steadily since the 1990s as populations age and fertility rates decline.
7. Pew Charitable Trusts; U.S. Federal Reserve. Estimates indicate multi-trillion-dollar funding gaps across major U.S. public pension systems under conservative return assumptions.
8. Bank of England; European Central Bank; Federal Reserve. Mortgage rates in advanced economies increased sharply following policy tightening beginning in 2022, significantly reducing affordability.
9. Bank for International Settlements; national central bank reports. Higher refinancing costs have exposed vulnerabilities in commercial real estate markets in the United States and Europe.
10. World Bank; International Monetary Fund. Post-war data show that debt reduction in advanced economies relied on financial repression, controlled interest rates, and moderate inflation following the Second World War.
11. International Monetary Fund, *Currency Composition of Official Foreign Exchange Reserves*. The U.S. dollar has remained the dominant global reserve currency since the end of the Bretton Woods system.
12. International Monetary Fund; World Bank. Recent data indicate gradual diversification of reserve holdings and increased use of alternative currencies in trade settlement.
13. European Central Bank; academic literature on the Eurozone. Monetary union without full fiscal integration creates structural tensions during periods of financial stress.
14. Organisation for Economic Co-operation and Development; national statistical agencies. Housing prices in many advanced economies have risen faster than wages over recent decades, reducing affordability for younger households.

# SELECTED BIBLIOGRAPHY

Bank for International Settlements (BIS). *Annual Economic Report.* Various years.

Bernanke, Ben S. *The Courage to Act: A Memoir of a Crisis and Its Aftermath.* New York: W. W. Norton & Company, 2015.

Bremmer, Ian. Us vs. Them: The Failure of Globalism. New York: Portfolio, 2018.

Congressional Budget Office (CBO). *Budget and Economic Outlook.* Various years.

Dalio, Ray. *Principles for Navigating Big Debt Crises.* Westport, CT: Bridgewater Associates, 2018.

Eichengreen, Barry. *Globalizing Capital: A History of the International Monetary System.* 3rd ed. Princeton: Princeton University Press, 2019.

European Central Bank (ECB). *Financial Stability Review.* Various years.

Federal Reserve. *Financial Accounts of the United States.* Various years.

Federal Reserve Bank of St. Louis. *FRED Economic Database.*

Ferguson, Niall. *The Ascent of Money: A Financial History of the World.* New York: Penguin Press, 2008.

Galbraith, John Kenneth. *The Great Crash 1929.* Boston: Houghton Mifflin, 1955.

Geithner, Timothy F. *Stress Test: Reflections on Financial Crises.* New York: Crown Publishers, 2014.

Goodhart, Charles, and Manoj Pradhan. *The Great Demographic Reversal: Ageing Societies, Waning Inequality, and an Inflation Revival.* London: Palgrave Macmillan, 2020.

Gordon, Robert J. *The Rise and Fall of American Growth: The U.S. Standard of Living Since the Civil War.* Princeton: Princeton University Press, 2016.

Institute of International Finance (IIF). *Global Debt Monitor.* Various years.

International Energy Agency (IEA). *World Energy Outlook.* Various years.

International Monetary Fund (IMF). *Fiscal Monitor.* Various years.

International Monetary Fund (IMF). *Global Financial Stability Report*. Various years.

International Monetary Fund (IMF). *World Economic Outlook*. Various years.

Kindleberger, Charles P., and Robert Aliber. *Manias, Panics, and Crashes: A History of Financial Crises*. 7th ed. London: Palgrave Macmillan, 2015.

Minsky, Hyman P. *Stabilizing an Unstable Economy*. New York: McGraw-Hill, 2008.

Organisation for Economic Co-operation and Development (OECD). *Economic Outlook*. Various years.

Organisation for Economic Co-operation and Development (OECD). *Housing Price Indicators*. Various years.

Organisation for Economic Co-operation and Development (OECD). *Pensions at a Glance*. Various years.

Organisation for Economic Co-operation and Development (OECD). *Productivity Statistics*. Various years.

Piketty, Thomas. *Capital in the Twenty-First Century*. Cambridge, MA: Harvard University Press, 2014.

Rajan, Raghuram G. *Fault Lines: How Hidden Fractures Still Threaten the World Economy*. Princeton: Princeton University Press, 2010.

Reinhart, Carmen M., and Kenneth S. Rogoff. *This Time Is Different: Eight Centuries of Financial Folly*. Princeton: Princeton University Press, 2009.

Summers, Lawrence H. "Reflections on the 'New Secular Stagnation Hypothesis.'" In *Secular Stagnation: Facts, Causes and Cures*, edited by Coen Teulings and Richard Baldwin. London: CEPR Press, 2014.

Tooze, Adam. *Crashed: How a Decade of Financial Crises Changed the World*. New York: Viking, 2018.

United Nations. *World Population Prospects*. Various years.

Volcker, Paul A., and Toyoo Gyohten. *Changing Fortunes: The World's Money and the Threat to American Leadership*. New York: Times Books, 1992.

Wolf, Martin. *The Shifts and the Shocks: What We've Learned — and Have Still to Learn — from the Financial Crisis*. New York: Penguin Press, 2014.

World Bank. *Global Economic Prospects*. Various years.

World Bank. *World Development Indicators*. Various years..

# About the Author

Ranga Chand is an international economist and author whose work examines the structural forces reshaping the global economy, including debt, monetary systems, financial instability, geopolitical change, and the shifting balance of economic power. His writing focuses on how long periods of economic stability are constructed, how they begin to weaken under pressure, and how major transitions reshape societies, institutions, and everyday life. Known for his global perspective and long-term analytical approach, he writes about the economic and political tensions emerging as the post-1980 order begins to fragment under rising debt burdens, demographic pressures, slowing growth, and geopolitical fragmentation.

Over the course of his career, he has worked across government, financial markets, economic research, and international policy analysis. His experience spans public policy, investment strategy, and global market analysis, giving him a perspective shaped by both policymaking and financial markets. He represented Canada at major international forums including the OECD in Paris, the United Nations, and the Kiel Institute for the World Economy in Germany. At the invitation of Nobel Laureate Robert Mundell, he taught economics at the University of Waterloo during the early 1970s.

In addition to his work in economics and finance, he became known through his writing, investment research, and media commentary, including the television program *Talking Mutual Funds with Ranga Chand,* which aired nationally on ROBTV, now BNN Bloomberg. He is the author of *The Fall of the Dollar Empire*, *Holding Ground,* and *Essays on the Global Economy & World Financial Markets*, and also writes *The New Global Order,* a newsletter examining the long-term structural forces reshaping the global economy and the changing international order.

www.ingramcontent.com/pod-product-compliance
Lightning Source LLC
LaVergne TN
LVHW100724061126
851857LV00011B/379
* 9 7 8 1 0 6 6 8 2 1 8 0 8 *